Reason and Freedom in Sociological Thought

Reason and Freedom in Sociological Thought

FRANK HEARN

Department of Sociology/Anthropology, State University of New York at Cortland

Boston
ALLEN & UNWIN
London   Sydney

Allen & Unwin, Inc.,
Fifty Cross Street, Winchester, Mass 01890, USA

George Allen & Unwin (Publishers) Ltd,
40 Museum Street, London WC1A 1LU, UK

George Allen & Unwin (Publishers) Ltd,
Park Lane, Hemel Hempstead, Herts HP2 4TE, UK

George Allen & Unwin Australia Pty Ltd,
8 Napier Street, North Sydney, NSW 2060, Australia

First published in 1985

Library of Congress Cataloging in Publication Data

Hearn, Frank.
  Reason and freedom in sociological thought.
Bibliography: p.
Includes index.
1. Sociology——Philosophy. 2. Reason. 3. Liberty.
I. Title.
HM26.H43 1985   301'.01   85—6071
ISBN 0—04—301194—2 (alk. paper)
ISBN 0—04—301195—0 (pbk. : alk. paper)

British Library Cataloguing in Publication Data

Hearn, Frank
  Reason and freedom in sociological thought.
1. Social sciences
I. Title
300'.1   H91
ISBN 0—04—301194—2
ISBN 0—04—301195—0 (Pbk)

_48, 321_

Set in 10 on 11½ point Goudy by V & M Graphics Ltd, Aylesbury, Bucks
and printed in Great Britain by Billing and Sons Ltd, London and Worcester

Contents

Acknowledgements

My understanding of many of the issues, ideas, and themes examined in this book has been immeasurably enriched in the course of teaching sociological theory and modern Western thought to undergraduates at the State University of New York at Cortland over the past five years. In their insistence that I speak to them and to their concerns, these students have encouraged me to give my presentation a degree of clarity it otherwise would have lacked.

Four colleagues also deserve my thanks — Gerry Surette, Dev Kennedy, Judy Best and Henry Steck. Working with them to prepare and teach an interdisciplinary undergraduate course on modern Western thought has been a valuable learning experience for me. No doubt, they will not entirely agree with many of my claims and interpretations, but they should know my discussion would be worse than it is had I not the benefit of their knowledge.

Mary Anne Mead, never hesitant to note where she found my argument wrongheaded or ineptly stated, typed the manuscript with exemplary skill and kindness. I thank her and, as well, the editors of three journals who gave me their permission to rework brief passages from some of my previously published work: 'The dialectical uses of ideal types', *Theory and Society*, vol. 2, no. 4, 1975; 'Rationality and bureaucracy', *The Sociological Quarterly*, vol. 19, Winter, 1978; and 'Adaptive narcissism and the crisis of legitimacy', *Contemporary Crises*, vol. 4, no. 2, 1980.

My greatest debt is to Priscilla and our two children, Michael and Caitlin. For all they do to keep my spirits high, my optimism strong, and my love of life robust, I dedicate this book to them.

Introduction

In his influential and controversial *The Sociological Imagination*, C. Wright Mills eloquently argued that the moral and intellectual responsibility of sociology is to defend, sustain, and cultivate the development of reason and freedom. Writing at the end of the 1950s, Mills insisted that prevailing circumstances make more urgent the need for sociologists, and social theorists in particular, to recognize and to commit themselves to this responsibility. Today, the values of reason and freedom are in jeopardy. With the development of modern society, reason has been reduced to a 'rationality without reason', and in this form promotes the deterioration of mind and culture and erodes the very foundations of freedom. The Enlightenment promise that the alliance of reason and freedom would bring a more just, decent, and human society, one governed by reflective, autonomous individuals, is betrayed in modern society.

A primary objective of this book is to update and enrich Mills's argument. I do this in large part by interpreting his concern with the development of 'rationality without reason' and the attack on freedom it sponsors in terms of the critique of instrumental reason formulated in the critical theory of Herbert Marcuse and Jürgen Habermas. A second aim is to use the theme of reason and freedom which Mills established to examine the key concerns of classical sociological theory, most especially the analyses and the arguments put forth by Karl Marx, Emile Durkheim, and Max Weber. A third purpose is to analyze the recent revitalization of interest in the relation of reason and freedom found in the increasingly significant segment of social thought and criticism represented by Daniel Bell, Harry Braverman, Christopher Lasch and Richard Sennett, among others. Through their work we are able to arrive at a clearer understanding of how freedom is threatened by the eclipse of the individual, the collapse of the public sphere, the bureaucratization of work, the corporatization of politics, and the commodification of social relations that result from the spread of rationality without reason. Against this background, Mills's call for a renewed and strengthened commitment to the values of reason and freedom takes on a more immediate importance. In light of this call, an additional objective of this book is to suggest the bases of a social theory capable of making and maintaining a commitment to the values of reason and freedom in the midst of rationalizing forces that move toward the impoverishment of thought.

My treatment of these issues is divided into three parts. Part 1 places Mills's argument in historical and theoretical context by examining the thematization of reason and freedom in classical sociological thought. Throughout the three chapters which comprise this part of the book, the transformation of reason from an ally to an enemy of freedom is viewed largely as a theoretical project. Part 2 is designed to show the contemporary relevance of this theoretical project by demonstrating how the thematic – an increase in rationalization does not make for an increase in freedom – is realized concretely in society. The effort here is to display the present-day importance of the classical concern with reason and freedom, and to emphasize in effect that the tendency to regard discussions of such issues as reason and freedom as mere intellectual exercises carried out by academic philosophers unconcerned with real and pressing questions of the day is itself a sign of the impoverishment of thought brought by rationality without reason.

The effort to secure more firmly our commitment to the values of reason and freedom forces us into confrontation with the key social, economic, and political questions of the day. The nature of this confrontation and the very practical and concrete implications it offers are examined in Part 3. The purpose of this final part of the book is to consider what should be done to rectify the separation of rationality and reason and, in turn, to restore reason as an ally of freedom. As a theoretical project, this task requires inquiry into the bases, character, commitments, and responsibilities of a critical social theory. As a project of political education, it involves a search for the conditions of a vibrant public life, the social ground of reason and freedom.

PART 1

Chapter 1 examines Mills's discussion of reason and freedom – what he means by the two values, how he defines the relation between them, why he regards commitment to them as the basis of the promise of sociology, and why he sees these values in serious peril in contemporary society. The concern with reason and freedom found in Enlightenment thought is examined next along with a consideration of how Mills's treatment both derives and diverges from that of the Enlightenment thinkers. The last part of Chapter 1 discusses the critique of instrumental reason formulated within critical theory in order to clarify and expand Mills's position.

The purpose of Chapter 2 is to analyze the origin of sociological thought in the context of the conservative reaction to the Enlightenment and the new society of industrial capitalism it helped spawn. Formulated on the basis of a synthesis by Saint-Simon and Comte of conservative and Enlightenment thought, early sociology embodied instrumental reason, most clearly in its positivism, and as a result its proposals for societal reconstruction implied a diminution of human freedom. Durkheim perfected positive sociology, and in his work as well reason is reduced to scientific rationality and freedom is defined as submission to social constraints. In this tradition, we find the roots of the rationality without reason which Mills regards as characteristic of much contemporary sociology.

Chapter 3 examines the view Marx and Weber had of the relation of reason and freedom, through an assessment of their discussions of the rational and rationalizing features of industrial capitalist society. Marx grounded reason and freedom in the material world, regarding the former as an aspect of the objectification involved in human labor activity and the latter as a result of reductions in socially necessary labor time. History, for Marx, involves the movement toward greater reason and freedom, a movement which will culminate in socialism and, later, communism. The rationalization of the productive forces, Marx claimed, leads to the rationalization of human consciousness, the creation of reasonable people able to safeguard their freedom against the repressive aspects of instrumental reason. Weber rejected this view, arguing, first that the rational administration of things eventuates in the rational administration of people and, secondly, that socialism would simply represent an extension and completion of the rationalizing tendencies found in industrial capitalism. The Marx–Weber dispute is usefully clarified by considering Lenin's misreading of the Marxian view of reason and freedom and Habermas's recent effort to rectify this misunderstanding. Such consideration occupies the concluding sections of this chapter.

In summary, Part 1 has two primary objectives. The first is to present Mills's theoretical project as an effort to reverse those developments which destroy reason and freedom. By highlighting the affinity Mills's project has with the Enlightenment thought that preceded it and with the critical theory that follows it, we are able to formulate more clearly its tasks and implications. The second objective is to introduce the classical tradition in sociology as represented by Marx, Durkheim, and Weber in order to show that the rationality without reason which Mills takes to be the main enemy of reason and freedom today is already developed in the founding statements of sociological thought.

1

On Reason and Freedom

Since its publication in 1959, C. Wright Mills's *The Sociological Imagination* has become a part of the early education of many, if not most, sociologists. Countless introductory textbooks and anthologies make extended reference to or carry excerpts from *The Sociological Imagination*, and with good reason, for Mills presents a morally compelling image of sociology – a sociology both compassionate and strong, committed to a decent society and unrelentingly antagonistic to the indifferent, the apathetic, and the pedestrian. 'What we represent – although this is not always apparent,' Mills claims, 'is man become aware of mankind. It is on the level of human awareness that virtually all solutions to the great problems must lie' (Mills, 1959, p. 193). Through Mills, we celebrate as we introduce sociology to the beginning student.

Too often, however, the celebration is insincere and short-lived, followed quickly by the practice of sociology as usual. Mills makes very clear that he is discussing the promise, not the reality, of sociology and that the realization of this promise requires a deep commitment to the values of reason and freedom. The practice of sociology as usual – research technicians wallowing in discrete bits of information on the one hand, grand theorists mapping out elaborate conceptual universes on the other – both denies and insults this commitment. The sociological imagination, a quality of mind which enables its possessors to locate themselves in history and in society and thus understand themselves better, is to be acquired in spite of and against the conventions of everday sociology; the promise of sociology requires for its achievement that we cherish the ideals of reason and freedom – safeguard them in their moment of peril, understand and oppose what threatens them, consider how they are to be strengthened, and anticipate a future society in their terms.

The project Mills formulates in *The Sociological Imagination*, with its unabashed and unqualified allegiance to reason and freedom, is an Enlightenment project. Throughout the eighteenth century, Enlightenment thinkers railed against the injustice, ignorance, and prejudice of the old order in the name of reason and freedom. In Enlightenment thought, reason and freedom became allies in the struggle against the chains of the *ancien régime* and in the journey toward a more humane set of social arrangements. Eventually, of course, the Enlightenment, particularly through its contributions to the French and Industrial Revolutions, won this struggle. But in the new society which emerged in the wake of this victory – industrial capitalist society – reason and freedom became enemies.

The story of this development is best told within the tradition of critical theory. Critical theory rests on a synthesis of Max Weber's despairing view that the penetration of calculative, instrumental reason to all areas of social life is the fate of modern society with Karl Marx's optimistic claim that the rationalization of the productive forces narrows the realm of necessity and expands the realm of freedom. Thus, critical theory is sensitive to the contradictions that have come to mark the relation of reason and freedom and it gives context to the present dangers to this relation. In important respects, critical theory expands and enriches Mills's concern with reason and freedom.

In this chapter, I try to make sense of Mills's discussion of reason and freedom. After examining this discussion in its own terms, I move backward to trace its roots to Enlightenment thought, then forward to broaden, clarify, and update it with the assistance of critical theory.

C. Wright Mills: Rationality Without Reason

For Mills the moral, political, and intellectual promise of sociology resides in its ability to sustain reason and freedom as cherished values and in its willingness consistently to formulate problems and carry out projects around these values. To the extent that reason and freedom are threatened, the fundamental problems of the day remain unclarified and unanswered. Freedom, for Mills, involves much more than doing what is found pleasing or selecting between established alternatives. Initially, it entails the chance to formulate, debate, and choose from among the available choices. Freedom, in this sense, requires the active presence of reason in the conduct of human affairs, for 'the social task of reason is . . . to enlarge the scope of human decisions in the making of history' (Mills, 1959, p. 174). Reason and freedom are thus prerequisites for one another. We are able to exercise our distinctively human faculty of reason to discover or create the ends, purposes, and objectives of human life that guide our efforts to make history, only when we are free from the constraints of nature, toil, ignorance and political bondage. Similarly, our use of reason to learn the laws of nature and to discover what is possible enhances both the material basis of freedom and the wish to be free. With the growth of reason aspects of social life previously regarded as natural, inescapable, and outside the reach of human influence become transformed into ends or objects of human decision-making and choice. As a consequence, we are freer to choose how we want to live, how we shall make history. We are freer, that is, to be reasonable in the conduct of human affairs. Reason and freedom, then, apply not simply to the means we adopt in pursuit of goals. More importantly, they are concerned with the formulation of the goals themselves – the ends, purposes, and objectives of human life.

Those sociologists who have accepted the values of reason and freedom assume as their primary task the development of a theory of history which identifies both the limits of freedom and the limits of the role of reason in the making of history, and what must be accomplished for the greater realization of reason and freedom. To the extent they take seriously the values of reason and freedom, Mills (ibid., pp. 184–5) argues,

> one of [their] themes for study has to do with the objective chances available for given types of men within given types of social structure to become free and rational as individuals. Another of [their] themes has to do with what changes, if any, men in different positions in different types of society have, first, by their reason and experience, to transcend their everyday milieux, and second, by virtue of their power, to act with consequence for the structure of their society and their periods. These are the problems of the role of reason in history.

In pursuing these themes, sociologists committed to reason and freedom engage in political education. For their task is to educate people, to assist them in regaining awareness of themselves as the active yet limited makers of history, and to politicize people, to have them act upon this awareness to acquire the capacity – as well as the right and the power – to determine the ends and purposes of their actions. The future will be reasonable and free only to the extent that it has been constructed willfully and consciously on the basis of reason and freedom.

This project of political education presently takes on a particular urgency. While modern society makes possible a major expansion of reason and freedom, at the same time it possesses powerful tendencies, to date unchecked, which severely jeopardize the values of reason and freedom. In modern society, Mills argues, reason is reduced to an instrumental rationality. No longer used in the formulation and discovery of the ends of life, reason as rationality is a means, an instrument, employed in the efficient pursuit of pre-established goals. In the form of science, bureaucracy, and rational management and administration, instrumental rationality is placed in the service of manipulation and domination and develops as an enemy of individual freedom. The rationalization of social life – the pervasive penetration of the logic of calculation and administration to spheres such as leisure and the family – takes from people their capacities to act freely and reasonably and assigns the task of formulating goals and objectives to impersonal, centralized organization. As a consequence, the deterioration of mind and culture has accompanied the economic abundance wrought by unparalleled advances in material and social technology. Instrumental rationality remains the central force behind material and technological progress but it has retarded the growth of the mind, the locus of human reason, and weakened culture as the general expression of actively created values, ideals, and purposes.

Mills puts well the wide-ranging implications these developments have for human freedom. 'The increasing rationalization of society', Mills (ibid., pp. 159–60) writes,

> the contradiction between such rationality and reason, the collapse of the assumed coincidence of reason and freedom – these developments lie back of the rise into view of the man who is 'with' rationality but without reason, who is increasingly self-rationalised and also increasingly uneasy ... It is not too much to say that in the extreme development the chance to reason of most men is destroyed, as rationality increases and its focus, its control, is moved from the individual to the big-scale organization. There is then rationality without reason. Such rationality is not commensurate with freedom but the destroyer of it.

The man with rationality but without reason, he who receives the benefits of technological advancement but at a heavy cost to his mind and culture, represents the very 'antithesis of the Western image of the free man'. In the forms of the 'Cheerful Robot' and, with specific reference to sociology, the 'abstracted empiricist', this type of person flourishes in modern society.

The 'Cheerful Robot' and the 'abstracted empiricist' are ideal constructs formulated by Mills with some measure of exaggeration to highlight what it is that characterizes the person with rationality but without reason. The rise to prominence of the cheerful robot contradicts the assumption that all naturally wish to be free and are willing and able to acquire the reason that makes for freedom. The cheerful robot is eminently capable of acting rationally, of deciding on the basis of impersonal calculation which of the available means is most appropriate for the acquisition of a given end and, in turn, efficiently implementing this means. But the cheerful robot is unable to reflect upon, to comprehend meaningfully, the purposes for which his action is undertaken; he is incapable of participating in the formulation of the ends of his rational pursuit. Prevented from active involvement in the articulation of purpose and objective, that is, without reason, the cheerful robot acts rationally; his action is a calculated means to a pre-established, imposed end. He lacks the freedom to discuss, debate, dispute, and decide on the basis of reason the end in question. The cheerful robot knows what to do but not why it is to be done. The goals provide no meaning and subsequently offer no basis for reflecting upon what is done. How you do it, not what it is done for, becomes the primary standard of assessment in the world of the cheerful robot, where reason is reduced to rationality and means, not ends, rise to the center of attention.

In the student, the factory worker, the corporate executive, the government administrator, the soldier, and the bureaucratic functionary who are well familiar with and ably carry out the rational means for the attainment of goals set for them without their active involvement and participation, we find signs of the cheerful robot. In the practice of abstracted empiricism, these signs also appear today in sociology.

Classical social theorists took as significant problems those which bore directly upon the future course of history and society, and they brought to their understanding of these problems wisdom, patience, insight, attentive care, and compassion. To be sure, they brought as well a coherent methodology, but the methodology remained subordinate to qualities of mind and character, and history much more than methodology influenced the classical analysts in deciding what was worthy of study. The concern with ends, the search for the limits of freedom and reason in modern society, expressed by the classical theorists was not circumscribed by the means or methodology they employed. The classical theorist stands in direct contrast to a relatively new breed of sociologists described by Mills as abstracted empiricists.

Abstracted empiricists practice their sociology in strict compliance with the standard formulae and procedures of the scientific method. The problems they address are shaped if not determined by their methodology. Those matters that do not readily lend themselves to investigation by the scientific method, those questions that defy operationalization and quantification (for instance, questions having to do with the relation of reason and freedom) are precluded from analysis. Prevented by their method from being historical, comparative, perceptive, and working with anything but the trivial and unimportant, abstracted empiricists lack firm connections with and deep convictions and passionate curiosity about the problems they encounter.

Abstracted empiricists succumb to what Abraham Kaplan (1968) calls the 'Myth of Methodology', which states that it does not matter what you do as long as you do it right; ends do not count as much as the means.

Doing it right for the abstracted empiricist means doing it in a way that is procedurally correct, consistent with the canons of the scientific method. Truth, in this context, is no longer defined with reference to ends and purposes. Rather, truth becomes a function of the means, the method, employed. The social theory which results embodies not a comprehensive understanding of the limits of freedom and reason but an arrangement of operational concepts, measurable variables, that permit the quantitative analysis of statistical findings. Where classical theory encouraged us to grapple with the grand issues of the day, provoked us into active confrontation with them, abstracted empiricism displays little interest in the major social problems and great human issues of our time (Mills, 1959, p. 73). Like the cheerful robot, the abstracted empiricist is with rationality – the rationality of the scientific method, but without reason – incapable of passionate struggle with questions of substance and consequence. Abstracted empiricists do what they do well. But it has little bearing on their lives, society, and history.

Mills's argument, in sum, has two general parts. The first develops a moral and intellectual justification for a commitment to the values of reason and freedom. The second claims that in modern society reason is reduced to a calculative rationality which destroys human freedom. In this setting, the need to commit ourselves to reason and freedom becomes ever more urgent. To arrive at a fuller appreciation of Mills's argument it is necessary, first, to locate it within the Enlightenment tradition from which it is largely drawn and, secondly, to develop more clearly the theory of history implicit in the argument. This will be accomplished with reference to the approach formulated by the critical theorists, Max Horkheimer, Theodor Adorno, Herbert Marcuse, and Jürgen Habermas, an approach which has a strong affinity with Mills's general position.

The Enlightenment Project: Reason and Progress

The Enlightenment, the Age of Reason, is roughly coextensive with the eighteenth century. The base metaphor of Enlightenment, of course, is light, and it refers to the lightness of intellectual understanding which is forcefully contrasted to the darkness of ignorance and emotional confusion associated with the old order. While Enlightenment thinkers disagreed, in places quite substantially, on a number of specific points, they generally concurred with the view that their task was one of political education. The Enlightenment project sought to eliminate custom, superstition, backwardness and the social practices and institutions that nurtured them. The aim was to emancipate people from the heavy restraints and deep-seated prejudices of tradition and medieval Christianity. With the removal of these age-old blinders, it was claimed, reason as self-control guided by self-reflection will flourish and the movement toward a better, more decent society surely will ensue.

The Enlightenment emphasizes, as Morse Peckham (1962, p. 69) notes, 'the power of the individual mind to create, on its own, a vision of order, to discover by itself a true ground for the sense of value, its own source of identity'. Ignorance, not sin, is the cause of our discomfort in the world, and once this ignorance is overcome, once individual reason assumes its proper position of prominence, the world will become a better place in which to live. 'Enlightenment', Immanuel Kant (1959, p. 85) exclaimed, 'is man's emergence from immaturity. The motto of Enlightenment is: Dare to know! Have the courage to use your own understanding.' And, indeed, during Kant's time one had to be courageously daring to use his own understanding in the face of repressive custom, virulent prejudice, and the arbitrary, unaccountable exercise of power. The implications of Kant's exhortation are clear. Access to the true and the good is not a privilege limited to particular institutions and certain people. Such access is available to all of us as a result of the uniquely human capacity of reason.

Enlightenment thought is negative thought. It critically evaluated and, in turn, negated or rejected the existing arrangements in terms of future possibilities. The established order was judged and its injustices magnified in light of the social order made possible by the free development of human reason. Enlightenment thinkers painstakingly repudiated the then prevailing view that the established order was natural or God-given, an immutable Great Chain of Being within which each eventually found his proper station in life. Existing ways of life, they insisted, were subject to change. Under the guidance of enlightened thought, change would produce a better society. The possibility of a more reasonable and freer society would be realized.

The master themes of Enlightenment thought center around and give forceful expression to the view that reason and freedom are allies in the struggle to demolish the old order standing in the way of the better society. In examining the Enlightenment in terms of its master themes – reason, individual liberty, equality, and progress – a word of caution is in order. It would be extraordinarily easy to identify a number of Enlightenment figures whose work deviated from or even opposed one or more of these themes. It is possible, however, to regard the Enlightenment as a school of thought with a distinctive, coherent, and consistent point of view. This is done below in an effort to present a general picture of the defining aspects of Enlightenment thought.

Most firmly emphasized in Enlightenment thought is the capacity of reason, a universal human faculty, to understand the universe and through this understanding to shape the universe in light of what is required to satisfy human needs. Knowledge of the universe, of nature and society, allows not simply a fuller appreciation of the major forces at work. Beyond this, such knowledge also permits us to influence significantly the direction these forces take and the consequences they have. Through reason we acquire the knowledge that is the foundation of both power and happiness.

The preoccupation with the attainment of universal happiness which characterizes much of Enlightenment thought rests squarely on the identification of reason with freedom. Reason and freedom are portrayed as partners in the progressive struggle against the superstitions of tradition and the arbitrary harshness of nature and political bondage. Freedom appears as the essence of reason, the primary, if not only, form in which reason can be. The Enlightenment project, Kant (1959, pp. 86-7) insisted, 'requires nothing but *freedom* – and the most innocent of all that may be called "freedom": freedom to make public use of one's reason in all matters'. Similarly, for Hegel, 'the concept of reason contains the concept of freedom ... For such examination and judgment [of everything given by the means of the power of knowledge] would be meaningless if man were not free to act in accordance with his insight and to bring what confronts him into accordance with reason' (Marcuse, 1968, p. 136). In their mutual interpretation of one another, reason and freedom will contribute to the erosion of established constraints and sustain the journey to a more decent society. For this to happen it is imperative that the more speculative, imaginative, and fantastic exercises of reason be curbed. Reason must be disciplined by the empirical world.

The Enlightenment thinkers were attracted to the natural scientific method, and not surprisingly, given its proven and celebrated success in assisting man to understand and better control the physical universe. In terms of this method, they sought to construct a science of humanity through which reason (the use of mind) would be supplemented by experience (the use of the senses, especially observation). In an important reversal, the empirical world, that part of reality subject to sense-certainty, came to be regarded as rational and a chief source of knowledge. Reason, in this view, is not separate from experience. Indeed, it is informed by experience, and in the framework of the scientific method experience is disciplined. Disciplined in this way, reason will acquire the knowledge that will direct future advances and improvements. Based on this linkage of reason and science, there emerged for the first time a widely accepted conception of a future built with the aid of scientific knowledge.

The Enlightenment's attraction to the scientific method underlay what was its most fundamental dilemma. Science, the methodical application of the human senses to the empirical world, provides knowledge only of what is. We experience only that which already exists. The scientific method appears to run counter to the negativism of Enlightenment thought, its preoccupation with future possibilities, what should be as distinct from what is. For the Enlightenment thinkers, through science we are able to discover not simply the present dynamics and features of the factual order but its inherent possibilities as well. We scientifically examine the existing arrangements in an effort to go beyond them by realizing their possibilities. 'It was self-evident to the philosophers that inalienable rights existed in regard to such things as liberty, prosperity, and happiness', Daniel Rossides (1978, pp. 55–6) writes, 'and that rights not only would be realized through science but were also based on science. However the dilemma remains: *On what basis are these rights established when they have never been part of human experience?*'

This dilemma is never resolved satisfactorily within Enlightenment thought. On the one hand, reason is associated with the use of the human senses, the experience of the empirical world. On the other, it involves the use of the mind to discover the ends and purposes of life, that which is possible but does not yet exist, that not subject to sense-certainty. Reason in the latter capacity is to be employed in the determination of where we should go; reason as science is to be used as a means to answer the question of how we are to get there. The important point in all this is that the Enlightenment thinkers argued only that reason must be disciplined by – never did they claim that it should be subordinated to – the empirical world. Despite their commitment to a science of humanity, they continued to value reason as a faculty indispensable to the determination of human objectives. The most important among these objectives were individual liberty, equality, and progress.

In crucial respects, the Enlightenment stands as an affirmation of the sanctity of the individual. All are capable of reason, and reason is a faculty of the individual. In this view, notes Robert Nisbet (1966, p. 43), 'not the group but the *individual* was the heir of historical development; not the guild but the *entrepreneur*; not class or estate but the *citizen*; not corporate or liturgical tradition but *individual reason*'. The Enlightenment's celebration of the individual appears in its demand for the freedoms of speech and thought, freedoms necessary for the exercise and growth of the reason that makes us human. We find it as well in its defense of private property, especially that most essential of all private property, one's self. The individual is human only when free and free only when the sole proprietor of his person and capacities. Accordingly, freedom requires that the individual be under no obligations except those incurred in relationships entered into voluntarily. We own ourselves, and in this ownership resides the right of individual liberty.

As part of its defense of individual liberty, Enlightenment thought called for a redefinition of sovereignty. Sovereign or supreme power belonged not to the king but to the people, and it should be placed in a state accountable and responsive to the people. From compliant subjects of a monarchy, people should be encouraged to become active citizens standing as individuals in direct relation to the state. As a citizenry the people will hold the ultimate power of the land. In the eyes of the state, all individuals, from the nobleman to the peasant, are to be treated the same – as citizens. The demand for equal treatment accompanied the defense of individual liberty.

Prior to the Enlightenment, the prevailing view held that men are by nature unequal and there exists a natural rank order among them. Social inequalities simply mirror the natural inequalities found among men, and to the extent they do so, they are just. The Enlightenment successfully challenged this assumption and replaced it with another: all men are created equal. It follows, of course, that if men are by nature equal, existing social inequalities are not established on the basis of nature or ordained by God. They are subject, therefore, to change.

As Ralf Dahrendorf (1968, p. 157) observes, the Enlightenment assumption about the basic equality of man raised a fundamental question. 'If men are by nature equal in rank, where do social inequalities come from? If all men are born free and equal in rights, how can we explain that some are rich and others poor, some respected and others ignored, some powerful and others in servitude?' The Enlightenment provided two contending responses to this question, and each was presented in the name of safeguarding individual liberty.

The first response, drawn from the principles of radical egalitarianism, insisted that justice demands the abolition of all social inequalities. Crucial to this response is the view that private property impedes both equality and liberty. Rousseau (1959, p. 348) states the argument most eloquently.

The first man who, having enclosed a piece of ground, bethought himself of saying, *'This is mine'* and found people simple enough to believe him, was the real founder of civil society. From how many crimes, wars and murders, from how many horrors and misfortunes might not anyone have saved mankind, by pulling up the stakes, filling up the ditch, and crying to his fellows, 'Beware that the fruits of the earth belong to us all, and the earth itself to nobody.'

Freedom requires equality – not merely equality before the law but also equality of life conditions – and such equality comes at the expense of the freedom to accumulate private property. The further development of this argument had to wait for Marx.

The second and more popular response, drawn from the premises of liberalism, retained the assumption that individual liberty is made possible by the right to private property. The liberal position regarded as fair those social inequalities that result both from activities freely entered into and from differences in individual talent, ability, and ambition. According to this view, we are born equal in the sense that all of us, by virtue of our sole proprietorship of our persons and capacities, have the same chance to develop our talents and abilities. Equality is thus defined in terms of opportunity, not life conditions. Each has the same opportunity to maximize his self-interest and those who best use this opportunity deserve the greater rewards they achieve. Equality in the sense of equal opportunity is made possible by an individual liberty secured by the institution of private property.

Common to both the Rousseauean and liberal views is the claim that equality is indispensable to the full exercise of reason. In a system of inequality which by custom or law locks people into statuses or estates for the duration of their lives, the capacity to reason withers. The overriding task of the Enlightenment was to revitalize this capacity, to bring into wider recognition the inalienable rights of liberty and equality. The confidence Enlightenment thinkers had in the success of their mission is reflected in their wholehearted commitment to the idea of progress.

The idea of progress, the belief that society has changed and will continue to change in a desirable direction, received its first full expression in Enlightenment thought. The idea of progress was formulated in direct contrast to the cyclical conception of change which had dominated earlier thought and which had viewed history as an endless succession of cycles of growth and decay, development and degeneration. History moves upward then downward, but never forward; the highest point of development represents the beginning of decline. The Enlightenment thinkers rejected the view that growth necessarily eventuates in decay and degeneration. Indeed, they argued, historical change generally has been progressive, a continuous, more or less uninterrupted movement forward, resulting in irreversible improvements and advances. Today is better than yesterday, and tomorrow will be clearly better than today. But better in what sense? 'Better' in the context of Enlightenment thought is defined in terms of reason and freedom. Tomorrow's social order will be constructed on the basis of reason and freedom and in the name of liberty and equality. Progress, in short, involved the movement toward a set of social arrangements conducive to reason and freedom, liberty and equality. In its optimistic quest for a more perfect society, the Enlightenment project highlighted the idea of progress, convinced that, freed from traditional constraints, people would act reasonably and freely to make for themselves and others a more human place to live.

The various strands of Enlightenment thought come together in the assumption that the essential predicate of increased freedom is increased rationality. The liberating demands of the Enlightenment for popular education and political democracy, as well as its main ideal of progress resulting from an enlarged role of reason in the conduct of human affairs, Mills observes, 'rested upon the happy assumption of the inherent relation of reason and freedom. Today, however, it is clear that increased rationality may not be assumed to make for increased freedom.' We have witnessed 'the collapse of the expectations of The Enlightenment, that reason and freedom would come to prevail as paramount forces in human history' (Mills, 1959, pp. 166–7, 183). Mills shares the Enlightenment's firm commitment to the values of reason and freedom and to what these values entail – liberty, equality, and a public sphere where discourse is free from domination, but not its optimism. In modern society, reason is reduced to an instrumental rationality which restricts human freedom. How does this happen? Why do the historical forces unleashed with the assistance of Enlightenment thought culminate in the cheerful robot? To answer these questions, we turn to critical theory.

Critical Theory: the Dialectic of the Enlightenment

With the rise of industrial capitalism, the alliance of reason and freedom dissolves. Reason is instrumentalized, reduced to a rationality which from the start is antagonistic to freedom. Reason as instrumental rationality becomes an enemy of freedom, used not to enlighten but to dominate, to control more efficiently both nature and man. Enlightenment comes to consist 'above all in the calculation of effectiveness and of the techniques of production and distribution', write Horkheimer and Adorno (1977, pp. xiv, xvi). And while the subsequent 'growth of economic productivity furnishes the conditions for a world of greater justice, ... [it also] allows the technical apparatus and the social groups which administer it a disproportionate superiority to the rest of the population'. Horkheimer and Adorno sense in the Enlightenment project a dark side, a tendency to establish a repressive order based on reason, which became apparent with the emergence and expansion of industrial capitalism. The social progress promised by the Enlightenment project required that reason be transformed into an instrument of production. The instrumentalization of reason contributed to considerable advances in material culture, but these advances were accompanied by the suppression of the critical thrust of reason. Reason's capacity both to penetrate and dissolve the appearance of the necessity and unalterability of the actual and to evaluate the given with reference to transcendent ideals was weakened. Industrial capitalist society falsifies the promise of the Enlightenment project in its effort to fulfill it. This is the 'dialectic of enlightenment'.

By the 'dialectic of enlightenment', Horkheimer and Adorno refer to the instrumentalization of reason upon which the growth of industrial capitalism was partially predicated. The Enlightenment conception of reason essentially denoted the capacity to know reflectively and bring to realization a way of life consistent with what should be. It was, then, critical, practical, and comprehensive – critical in the sense that it provided criteria for evaluating the given, practical in that it served as a guide to enlightened practice, and comprehensive to the extent that it offered the basis for understanding and determining the ends of human life. Instrumental reason is based on a renunciation of the view that what should be is knowable. Instrumental reason, Horkheimer observes, 'is essentially concerned with means and ends, with the adequacy of procedures for purposes more or less taken for granted ... It attaches little importance to the question whether the purposes as such are reasonable' (Horkheimer, 1974, p. 3). Primarily concerned with formal calculation and the impersonal, efficient selection of appropriate means for given ends, instrumental reason has surrendered its autonomy from and has become subordinated to the 'givenness' of the established arrangements. Lacking substantive content, instrumental reason is restricted to the assessment of means appropriate to pre-established goals; without any claims toward objective validity, it is a conforming and not a critical reason. 'What appears to be the triumph of subjective rationality', write Horkheimer and Adorno (1977, p. 26), 'is paid for by the obedient subjection of reason to what is directly given.'

The instrumentalization that underlay the dialectic of enlightenment represented, in Disco's (1979, p. 185) words, the 'embourgoisement of reason'. Integrated into the bourgeois mode of production as empirical science and technology, reason was used in the removal of obstacles not to enlightenment and human freedom but to continuous economic growth and industrial expansion (a point to be taken up again and further developed in the following chapters).

In its instrumentalized form, the repressive aspects of reason predominate. Impulse, emotion, and imagination come to be subordinated to the rules and procedures of science, market, and bureaucracy. As instrumental rationality, reason loses its critical thrust, its capacity to go beyond the established order to discover the potentiality it contains yet suppresses. Reason as a rational means utilized by individuals in their pursuit of selfish interests and by societies in their efforts to become technologically advanced is confined to, no longer simply disciplined by, the empirical world, the realm of what already exists. As a consequence, the contrast between the given and the possible is cancelled. In this setting, argues Herbert Marcuse (1964, p. 12), there emerges a pattern of *one-dimensional thought and behavior* in which ideas, aspirations, and objectives that, by their content, transcend the established universe of discourse and action are either repelled or reduced to terms of this universe. They are redefined by the rationality of the given system and of its quantitative extension.

One-dimensional society develops from the suppression of culture and consciousness and of the capacity for critical transcendence which they sustain. By eliminating the transcendent ends of culture, instrumental rationality 'thereby eliminates or reduces those factors and elements which were antagonistic and alien to the given forms of civilization' (Marcuse, 1965, p. 193).

Two-dimensional qualities of thought and behavior recognize and express the historical tension between 'ought' and 'is', potentiality and actuality, freedom and necessity, future and present. They depend on a critical reason which searches for what should be, the potentiality of the established order, a reason that evokes the uncompromised needs and hopes of man and that refuses submission to the facts of that order. The 'historical validity of ideas like Freedom, Equality, Justice, Individual', Marcuse writes,

> was precisely in their unfulfilled content – in that they could not be referred to the established reality, which did not and could not validate them because they were denied by the functioning of the very institutions that were supposed to realize these ideas. They were normative ideas – nonoperational, not by virtue of their metaphysical, unscientific character, but by virtue of the servitude, inequality, injustice, and domination institutionalized in society.

Yet, in contemporary society, Marcuse continues, the tendency is to

> identify the normative concepts with their prevailing social realization, or rather [to] take as norm the way in which society is translating these concepts into reality, at best trying to improve the translation; the untranslated residue is considered obsolete speculation. (Marcuse, 1965, p. 197)

In this way, the second dimension, concerned with that which should be but does not yet exist, is collapsed into the first dimension, the world of that which is. The tension between actuality and potentiality is lost and what ought to be appears as one with what already exists. The negative, negating capacities of reason are severely constrained, and reason is reduced to an instrument of adaptation to the prevailing arrangements. Instrumental rationality 'protects rather than cancels the legitimacy of domination, and the instrumentalist horizon of reason opens on a rationally totalitarian society: ... The liberating force of technology – the instrumentalization of things – turns into a fetter of liberation; the instrumentalization of man' (Marcuse, 1964, p. 159).

Marcuse's discussion of one-dimensional thought closely resembles Mills's analysis of abstracted empiricism. Claiming that 'that which is cannot be true', Marcuse proceeds to critique the empirical conception of reality – the view that only that which can be experienced by the senses is real – which underlies one-dimensional thought. Reality, Marcuse argues, must be defined in terms of its totality to include potentiality as well as actuality, and truth is a function of this totality. By defining reality simply in terms of actuality and, in turn, by insisting that concepts be operationalized – defined exclusively in terms of that which already exists – one-dimensional logic constitutes a repressive reduction of thought in that it precludes from serious consideration, and relegates to the level of obsolete speculation, that which should be. Precisely in this way does one-dimensional thought confine us to the established universe of discourse. One result of the insistence that concepts be operationalized is that 'the criteria for judging a given state of affairs are those offered by the given state of affairs. The analysis is "locked"; the range of judgment is confined within a context of facts which excludes judging the context in which the facts are made, man-made, and in which their meaning, function, and development are determined' (ibid., pp. 115–16). In other words, we are reduced to assessing the established arrangements in their own terms; we lose the ability to examine them with reference to what they should be or are capable of becoming.

Consider how this repressive reduction of thought occurs with the operationalization of the concept of legitimacy. Legitimacy involves conformity to rule or principle. A particular exercise of power, whether by a person or a government, is legitimate or not depending on its conformity with rules or principles of conduct having the consent of those whose actions are influenced by the use of power. Illegitimate exercises of power take the form of force. Compliance is a result of the application or threat of harm. Legitimate uses of power meet with some degree of voluntary submission and asume the form of authority. Here, compliance is forthcoming because people regard the exercise of power as consistent with accepted standards of rightness or legitimacy. For obvious reasons, a social order based largely on force is highly unstable. Sooner or later, all governments and people in positions of power seek the cloak of authority and thus exercise power in accordance with certain standards of legitimacy.

As John Schaar (1974, p. 67) observes, the older definitions of legitimacy

> all revolve around the element of law or right, and rest the force of a claim upon foundations external to and independent of the mere assertion or opinion of the claimant. Thus, a claim to political power is legitimate only when the claimant can invoke some source of authority beyond or above himself ... As [Hannah] Arendt has pointed out, 'In all these cases, legitimacy derives from something outside the range of human deeds; it is either not man-made at all ... or has at least not been made by those who happen to be in power'.

Authority, in this context, rests on a rationale which

> consists of a more or less coherent body of shared memories, images, ideas, and ideals that gives to those who share it an orientation in and toward time and space. It links past, present, and future into a meaningful whole, and ties means and ends into a continuum that transcends a merely pragmatic or expediential calculation. (ibid., p. 74)

Defined in this way, the concept of legitimacy was not a mirror-image of the existing order. It was, rather, a strongly normative concept, and whether it defined the norms to which action should conform for legitimacy to be possible in terms of the laws of nature, or the laws of God, or the rights of man, the important point is that it provided 'some source of authority beyond or above' the particular exercise of power. In other words, the exercise of power was not self-legitimating. People could and did assess it in terms other than those offered by the established arrangements. The existing state of affairs, then, was examined with respect to – and the utilization of power was expected to be in accordance with – higher principles of conduct expressive not of what already is but of what should be.

The older, normative conceptions of legitimacy, Schaar discovers, have been replaced by scientific, operational definitions. Typical and perhaps best known of the newer definitions of legitimacy is the one formulated by Seymour Martin Lipset. 'Legitimacy', according to Lipset (1960, p. 64), 'involves the capacity of the system to engender and maintain the belief that the existing political institutions are the most appropriate ones for the society.' In this view, legitimacy is made to consist almost entirely in belief or public opinion. There are no objective standards to which we can turn to aid in our assessment of the given. Legitimacy is reduced to a function of observable and measurable subjective opinions. Unlike the older definition of legitimacy which demanded conformity to ends which evoked the true, the right, and the possible, the newer definition transforms ends into matters of opinion. Objective, normative standards of truth are replaced by subjective, empirical opinions. What is right is what most people believe to be right at the moment.

In addition, the new definition regards legitimacy as an outcome of the system's capacity to persuade its members that it is appropriate. Thus, writes Schaar (1974, p. 68), it sees 'a polity not as a people with a culture seeking together the forms of order and action that will preserve and enhance that culture but as a mass collective that is made into a unit of control by propaganda'. In other words, a system is legitimate if it can convince its members that it is legitimate. The system, by this analysis, becomes self-legitimating. To remain legitimate it simply has to meet the criteria which it has set for itself. It becomes impossible to rely on trans-systemic principles of assessment; we judge the system in its own terms, the terms set by the established universe of discourse. People attribute legitimacy to exercises of power because of acquiescence to this universe of discourse, not because they recognize their claim to a foundation in some principle or source outside themselves.

The operational concept of legitimacy corresponds well to and accurately reflects the empirical reality of most contemporary forms of rule. Studies focusing on the United States, for instance, demonstrate that legitimacy rests neither on normative acceptance (a voluntary adherence to and agreement with the ultimate values of society) nor on false consciousness (a coerced perception that what is actually bad is either good or unavoidable), but on pragmatic acceptance where compliance with the dictates of the established order is based on the inability to perceive realistic alternatives to that order (Mann, 1970; Sennett and Cobb, 1973; Hearn, 1978). Thus the operational concept of legitimacy does well what it is supposed to do – accurately describe what presently exists. Yet, in its obsession with the facts of the established order, the operational concept transforms legitimacy from a set of ideals and ends denoting proper action to a neutral means for achieving compliance. Like the instrumental reason on which it rests, the operational concept asks us to submit not to what is right but to what is. Legitimacy is defined in terms of what already exists; 'the criteria for judging the given state of affairs are those offered by the given state of affairs'.

We are able to appreciate more fully the eclipse of reason, the rise of one-dimensional thought, the spread of rationality without reason and their consequences for human freedom in light of Jürgen Habermas's (1971) effort to formulate an epistemology, a theory of knowledge, which is at the same time a theory of history. Habermas's initial concern is to clarify the relation between knowledge and human interests, those basic orientations inherent in the activity of the human species which guide the way the species secures its existence and makes and remakes itself. People pursue the satisfaction of these interests not simply in order to survive, but also to become human.

Habermas identifies three fundamental human interests. The first is a technical interest in extending certainty and control. The technical interest is expressed in man's relationship with nature. Man seeks to control, master, manipulate, and dominate nature in an effort to satisfy better his physical and material needs. Labor, productive activity, mediates man's interaction with nature. Through its labor the species subordinates nature to the satisfaction of human needs. In his interaction with other people, man is guided by a second interest, namely, a practical interest in expanding intersubjective understanding. This relation, the relation of people to one another, is mediated by language and communication. We interact with others not to manipulate and dominate them but to increase mutual understanding, to enter into agreements to formulate commonly shared and consensually validated norms and values.

These two interests, according to Habermas, are regulated by a third, an emancipatory interest – an interest in the emancipation of man from the pattern of established natural and socio-historical laws. In other words, we are able to understand why the human species does what it does, why it seeks to achieve greater control over nature and greater mutual understanding, in terms of the interest in emancipation. There is a purpose to human history and that purpose is human emancipation. Human emancipation is made possible by advancements both in productive activity which improve the species' control over nature, and in communicative activity which enhance the capacity of the members of the species to discuss openly and decide freely what kind of life it is they wish to live.

These three human interests make possible three categories of knowledge. They are:

> information that expands our power of technical control; interpretations that make possible the orientation of action within common traditions; and analyses that free consciousness from its dependence on hypostatized powers. (Habermas, 1971, p. 313)

Information, then, is associated with the technical interest and provides us with knowledge upon which we are better able to control phenomena. To know something in this regard means we have the knowledge to control it – to bring about or prevent the occurrence of a state of affairs or, at least, to influence its effects. The interpretations entailed by the practical interest enhance the possibility of communication. The knowledge obtained from interpretations, writes Brian Fay (1975, p. 81), creates the conditions for mutual understanding between different members of the same social order or between members of different social orders, which is to say that it makes possible communication between them where none existed before, or where, if it did exist, such communication was distorted. Moreover, in so far as it opens channels of communication, such knowledge expands the horizons of those who are now able to discourse, because learning how to communicate is learning both new ways of characterizing oneself as well as highlighting one's own presuppositions.

Where the truth of information is a function of our ability to control, the truth of interpretations rests on our capacity to engage in communicative interaction.

When we apprehend reality in terms of the interest in emancipation, we acquire knowledge in the form of critical analyses that highlight human history as a self-constituting process and thereby restore to people a recognition of themselves as the active yet historically limited makers of history. Critical analyses, if true, emancipate human subjects from dependence on seemingly natural and immutable forces. Accordingly, these analyses assume an educative role, which is 'to enlighten the social actors so that, coming to see themselves and their social situation in a new way, they themselves can decide to alter the conditions which they find repressive' (Fay, 1975, p. 103). Knowledge in this form initiates a transformation of both the knower and the known, a transformation that brings people closer to the realization of the interest in human emancipation.

Habermas's three-fold model of epistemology affords the basis for conceptualizing the history of mankind and the development of human societies in terms of the continuing interaction of two action systems: 'purposive rational action that secures the human capacity to satisfy human needs, and symbolic interaction systems which form the institutional framework of society based upon grammatical rules and social norms that enable men to engage in communication and interaction' (Schroyer, 1972, p. 93). The system of purposive rational action develops from the effort to satisfy the technical interest and thus is a series of instrumentalities designed to enlarge our control over nature. This system represents the dimension of work in as much as technical progress is measured quantitatively with respect to scientific and technological improvements in the productive forces and the growing material standard of living they deliver. The system of symbolic interaction emerges from the pursuit of the practical interest in enhanced mutual understanding and represents the dimension of social interaction which gives rise to human culture. Practical or cultural progress is defined qualitatively in terms of the improvements in social relationships made possible by more open, less distorted forms of communication.

Each dimension, Habermas argues, has its own logic of rationalization. Technical (or instrumental) rationalization occurs as the productive forces, the means by which we control nature, come to rely more on science, formality, standardization, calculation, and administration. 'But this process of the development of the productive forces can be a potential for liberation if and only if it does not replace rationalization on another level' (Habermas, 1970, p. 118). Rationalization on the level of culture entails the removal of restrictions on communication. As class, race, sex, and other barriers to open discourse are eliminated, more and more people are able to participate in the formulation of cultural ends, values, and ideals. Cultural or practical rationalization 'does not lead *per se* to the [more efficient] functioning of social systems, but would furnish the members of society with the opportunity for further emancipation and progressive individuation. The growth of productive forces is not the same as the intention of the "good life". It can at best serve it' (ibid., p. 119).

Technical rationalization, by strengthening our ability to manipulate and control nature, frees us from hunger, toil, and the exigencies of nature, but such 'freedom from' is not the same as human emancipation, which also requires 'freedom to' reflect on what we are doing and what we want to do. For critical theory, reason involves 'a notion of freedom that signifies both freedom from the blind necessity of natural causality and freedom to self-consciously determine one's own actions' (Draenos, 1982b, p. 158). Emancipation, then, requires practical as well as technical rationalization, the improvement of mind and culture in addition to advancements in the productive forces. Reason, quite simply, entails self-control guided by self-reflection (Gouldner, 1973, pp. 101–4). The possibility for enhanced self-control is given by progress on the dimension of work, that for improved self-reflection by progress on the dimension of culture. In sum, the reason which develops from the continuing interaction of work and culture, technical and practical rationalization, promotes the 'freedom from' and the 'freedom to' that together define human emancipation. In this view, reason and freedom are indeed allies.

Clearly, this view emphasizes the overriding importance to human freedom of the simultaneous development of both dimensions. When one dimension develops at the direct expense of the other, domination rather than emancipation is the beneficiary. Habermas argues that the history of Western society, particularly since the Industrial Revolution, is understandable precisely in these terms. Progress on the level of work has been partly based on the suppression of the cultural dimension. Technical rationalization has occurred in such a way to prevent practical rationalization. We have as a consequence Mills's (technical) rationality without reason (for reason requires practical rationality as well) and Marcuse's one-dimensional society (where the dimension of culture is absorbed into the dimension of work, the tension between the two lost). As a result of this development, reality comes to be defined in terms of the scientific, instrumental logic of technical rationality, and our capacity to formulate ends, purposes, and objectives and through them to reflect on the established order is thwarted. To the extent that emancipation is pursued exclusively with reliance on the logic of instrumental rationality, the mastery of nature engendered leads to the mastery of people and the result is movement toward total domination, not merely the domination of nature.

In this setting, our interaction with other people is guided by the same principles that regulate our relation to nature. The technical interest reigns supreme, and we seek in our interaction with others not to enhance mutual understanding in order to arrive openly at a shared view of the 'good life'. Rather, just as in our interaction with nature, we aim to manipulate, exploit, and dominate others. Information, knowledge which enables us to do but one thing, control, replaces interpretations and critical analyses in the effort of the human sciences to know man and society. Economists provide information for controlling business cycles. Political scientists gather information for controlling the perceptions and attitudes of the electorate. Psychologists amass information used by advertisers to manipulate consumers. Sociologists offer information which enable managers to control their workers better. Applied to the physical world and the conquest of nature, the logic of technical rationality doubtlessly has been progressive in its consequences. The development of electricity, for instance, has enabled us to do at any time, night or day, winter or summer, what nature once limited us to perform during the day or the summer. Medical science has provided information which allows us to control deadly diseases and other threats to a decent life. When, however, in the form of the human sciences this logic is applied to the social world, to human interactions, the general result is information which allows some to expand their power of technical control over others. Reason as technical rationality serves the interest of domination, not that of human emancipation.

Conclusion

The Enlightenment claim, that reason and freedom come together to define and make possible the 'good life', is shared by Mills and the critical theorists. Yet neither Mills nor the critical theorists sustain the Enlightenment's unbounded optimism. For both, reason in modern society has been reduced to an instrumental, technical rationality which counters the movement toward human freedom by promoting submission to that which already exists. The development of modern industrial capitalist society, in important respects a child of the Enlightenment, has been fuelled by the spread of the logic of instrumental reason – the unremitting extension of the principles of science, technology, and bureaucracy to ever increasing spheres of social life. While this has meant increasing technological sophistication and material abundance, it has also brought about, in Mills's words, the deterioration of mind and culture. Reason as instrumental reationality becomes an enemy of freedom.

Sociological thought, like the instrumentalization of reason, originates in the rise of industrial capitalist society. Not surprisingly, then, from the start sociological thought has been strongly influenced by the logic, dynamics, and consequences of instrumental reason. Karl Marx and Max Weber offered contending assessments of the long-run historical implications of the operation of instrumental reason which they placed at the center of their sociological theories (examined in Chapter 3). Similarly, two contemporary social thinkers, Daniel Bell and Christopher Lasch (discussed in Chapter 4), attribute the key contradictions and crises in modern society to the erosion of culture engendered by technical rationalization. Of more immediate concern, we will see in the next chapter how early sociological thought, most influenced by Henri Saint-Simon and Auguste Comte, gave very forceful expression to instrumental reason and the forces leading to its ascendency.

2

Conservatism and the Rise of Sociology

Enlightenment thought contributed mightily to the intellectual climate which helped spawn the French and the Industrial Revolutions and, in turn, the new society of industrial capitalism. The creation of the new society was neither smooth nor easy. In the midst of the social disorganization and cultural and psychological disorientation that accompanied its development, there emerged a well-developed conservative reaction to the Enlightenment and its consequences. Demanding a restoration of traditional, non-rational values and customs, the conservatives attributed many, if not most, of the prevailing problems to the Enlightenment's celebration of the debunking and speculative aspects of individual reason.

Conservatism strongly influenced the early development of sociological thought. Henri Saint-Simon and Auguste Comte, the two central figures in this development, sought to synthesize conservative and Enlightenment thought in order to formulate a strategy for the successful reorganization of society. As a result of this synthesis, early sociology came to rely on an instrumental conception of reason in the form of positivism. Emile Durkheim carried on this tradition, and by examining his writings as well as those of Saint-Simon and Comte, we will be able to discern how the instrumental reason characteristic of the new society came to be reflected in sociology, the discipline designed to improve our knowledge of and control over the new society.

Enlightenment, Revolution, and the New Society

Sociology and, more importantly, modern society were given distinctive shape in a time of profound crisis and upheaval. The period encompassing the last quarter of the eighteenth century and the first half of the nineteenth century has been characterized by observers as the age of revolution, the age of democracy, and the era of the great transformation. It is unmistakably a period of drastic, fundamental, and often abrupt change that affected the way people perceived, experienced, and acted upon the world. During this period, new intellectual disciplines, particularly economics and sociology, and major political doctrines, especially liberal democracy and socialism, were born; formal, impersonal, efficient organizations in the form of the factory system and the bureaucratic state took the place of community and kinship; contract replaced trust, the market – free, self-regulating, rational, and insensitive to human suffering – became the accepted decision-maker in the economic sphere, and tradition gave way to science, law, and reason.

Important changes in life and thought are eventually reflected in language. During this decisive period, new words were created – for example, 'ideology', 'rationalism', 'scientist', 'humanitarian', 'utilitarian', 'bureaucracy', 'capitalism', 'socialism', 'egalitarian', 'liberalism', and 'unemployment' – and old words were given new meaning – 'progress', 'reform', 'revolutionary', 'industry', 'democracy', and 'class' (Williams, 1958, p. xv). 'To imagine the modern world without these words (i.e., without the things and concepts for which they provide names)', writes the historian E. J. Hobsbawm (1962, p. 1), 'is to measure the profundity of the revolution which broke out between 1789 and 1848, and forms the greatest transformation in human history since the remote times when men invented agriculture and metallurgy, writing, the city and the state.' Propelling this leap into the modern world, undermining the basis of the old order and establishing the conditions for the new, were the French and the Industrial Revolutions.

Stability, not change, characterized Europe for most of the eighteenth century. For the most part, people worked and played, married and worshipped, led and followed, obeyed and resisted in ways that would have been understood and accepted a century earlier. Most people lived their lives and died in the county, if not the village, of their birth, protecting and protected by tradition and custom. Expectations were deeply rooted in tradition, relationships were governed by custom, and on this basis there developed a coherent world-view. Social order was highly valued, so much so, as one observer of the period notes, that its 'preservation ... took precedence over economic progress' (Wilson, 1965, p. 375). Change was acceptable – only so long as it did not threaten to weaken the traditional and the customary.

Eighteenth-century Europe was overwhelmingly rural and agricultural. After mid-century, it is true, industrial production began to expand, particularly in England, but its expansion took the form of the domestic system and thus did not conflict with the established order. In the domestic or household system of manufacture, merchants brought for sale in a larger market the products made by craftsmen or agricultural laborers working in their spare time. This form of production usually involved the entire household and did not require migration to cities or the construction of large factories. With reference to the cotton weaving industry, Neil Smelser (1959, pp. 74–5) describes the domestic system in this way: 'The father wove and apprenticed his sons into weaving. The mother was responsible for preparatory processes; in general she spun, taught the daughters how to spin, and allocated the picking, cleaning, drying, carding, etc., among the children.' This kind of household production, which was consistent with the traditions of an agricultural society, was controlled more by custom than by market considerations. Of more concern to employers than how the work was completed 'was that the finished goods should be delivered at the end of the week or fortnight as prescribed by custom' (Ashton, 1955, p. 6).

Although Enlightenment thought advocating freedom from the shackles of traditional restraints existed at the time, its influence was limited throughout most of the eighteenth century. Bonds of dependence and obligation, similar to those that prevailed in the feudalism of the middle ages, continued to link the rich and the poor, the powerful and the powerless. The 'theory of dependence', observed John Stuart Mill, required that the lot of the lower orders – the poor and the laborers –

> should be regulated for them, not by them. They should not be required or encouraged to think for themselves ... It is the duty of the higher classes to think for them, and to take the responsibility of their lot ... This function the higher classes should prepare themselves to perform conscientiously, and their whole demeanor should impress the poor with a reliance on it, in order that, while yielding passive and active obedience to the rules prescribed for them, they may resign themselves in all other respects to a trustful *insouciance*, and repose under the shadow of their protectors. The relation between rich and poor should be only partially authoritative; it should be amiable, moral, and sentimental; affectionate tutelage on the one side, respectful and grateful deference on the other ... The lower orders, morality and religion should be provided for them by their superiors, who should see them properly taught it, and should do all that is necessary to insure their being, in return for labor and attachment, properly fed, clothed, housed, spiritually edified, and innocently amused. (Mill, 1895, pp. 319–20)

Mill's description provides a vivid, though slightly exaggerated, picture of status relations in eighteenth-century Europe. The higher orders, in particular the landed aristocracy, controlled the major areas of social life. Clearly, their relation to the lower orders was seen more in terms of the relation between father and child rather than master and slave, but the fact remains that the *ancien régime*, no matter how benevolent it may or may not have been, strongly influenced the lives of most of the people. The power and authority of the *ancien régime* around which eighteenth-century social life revolved was seriously and successfully challenged by the French and the Industrial Revolutions.

The Industrial Revolution, beginning in the late eighteenth century and continuing throughout most of the nineteenth century, was an economic revolution and, much more abrupt and dramatic, the French Revolution of 1789 was essentially a political revolution. Yet the fundamental impact of each was the same, for each brought about the separation of the individual from the traditional structures of community, guild and church and from the patriarchal ties of the theory of dependence. Together, the French and Industrial Revolutions undermined the traditional authority and absolutism of the old order, and thus permitted the development of a political system based on equality before the law and an economic system based on private property.

The French Revolution adopted for its aims and enemies those of the Enlightenment project. It vehemently opposed the traditional privileges of monarchy, aristocracy and the church in the name of liberty, equality and brotherhood (in the form of popular sovereignty and the nation-state). In important respects, the French Revolution was a Western revolution. It highlighted, by bringing together in concentrated form, the monumental changes occurring in Western society, particularly those changes generated by the growing conflict between the representatives of the old order and the rising social forces symbolic of the new. The fundamental changes brought about by the French Revolution proved irrevocable, irresistible and indispensable to the making of modern society.

The French Revolution, most historians agree, was a bourgeois revolution. Although the artisans, the laboring poor, and, especially, the peasants provided the shock troops which successfully demolished the old order of nobility and aristocratic privilege, the bourgeoisie – the doctors and lawyers, printers and publishers, merchants, emerging industrialists, and government officials – supplied the leadership, goals, and ideology of the revolution. At the core of the ideology fashioned by the bourgeoisie was the demand that the traditional authority of the king and the aristocracy be replaced by popular sovereignty. The principle of popular sovereignty requires that supreme power be placed by law or constitution in the people of the nation, regardless of their rank, estate, or class. In other words, the law of the nation abolishes traditional distinctions of rank and privilege and treats all people equally. The nobleman and the peasant in the eyes of the law are the same – both are citizens of the nation-state, and the rewards they receive and the influence they acquire should be based on their individual talents and capabilities, not on their status or family background.

The defense of popular sovereignty and nationalism, equality before the law, and liberty and private property received full expression in the Declaration of the Rights of Man and Citizens drafted in 1789. The Declaration of 1789 guided the rationalization of French society (and, later, of many other societies as well). In its name, fundamental changes were made – occupational guilds were abolished; patriarchal power was weakened as women were given several grounds for divorce and children, upon reaching legal age, were freed from paternal control; the responsibility for education was taken from the family and church and transferred to the political bureaucracy; a new currency system, a new calendar, even a new system of weights and measures were introduced (Nisbet, 1966, pp. 36–8). Immense in impact, the French Revolution

changed the very nature and definition of property; it transformed ... the church, the army, the educational system, institutions of public relief, the legal system, the market economy, and the relationship of employers and employees. It introduced new crucial values, new status strivings, new levels of expectation. It changed the essence of the community and of the individual's sense of his membership in it and his relationship to fellow citizens and to fellow men. It even changed the feeling for history, or the idea of what could or ought to happen in history and in the world. (Palmer, 1959, p. 411)

The French Revolution, in short, contributed substantially to the making of modern society.

The Industrial Revolution transformed the struggle for existence. It qualitatively altered productive activity and, by so doing, changed the way people interacted with nature and with one another. Industrialization mechanizes the productive process, shifting the emphasis from animate (human or animal) labor to inanimate (machine) labor. The mechanization of the productive process, which occurred most forcefully in England, brought the factory system into prominence. By relying on machinery and material technology, the new industrial system was better able to exploit and control nature, and, by using the social technology reflected in the organization of the factory system, it was better able to exploit and control man.

Industrialization could only take place after traditional protections and restraints had been eliminated. The land-owning aristocracy who benefited from these protections were often opposed to industrial expansion or, for that matter, any developments which would fundamentally change the social arrangements which made their life very comfortable and secured their power and privilege. In the wake of the French Revolution, however, traditional protections were quickly eliminated and industrialization rapidly ensued. Indeed, industrial expansion was defended by its beneficiaries – the bourgeoisie – in the same terms used to justify the French Revolution. Industrialization would deal the final blow to the shackles of tradition and the oppressiveness of the old order, and would create the social conditions for freedom and equality.

In fact, the Industrial Revolution represents the dark side of the 'great transformation'. In this context, the concern with freedom, equality before the law, and individualism was really a concern with denying social responsibility. Traditional customs exacted many duties from the lower orders, but they also gave the peasant and the laborer certain rights. During periods of poor harvest or unemployment, for instance, the higher orders were responsible for providing a suitable standard of living for their 'inferiors'. This partly accounts for the low rate of immigration since people were protected in bad times and need not move in search of employment. Social responsibility proved to be a major obstacle, for the development of the factory system required a mobile and full-time labor force. 'What was needed', Sidney Pollard (1965, p. 213) observes, 'was regularity and steady intensity in place of irregular spurts of work; accuracy and standardization in place of pride in one's tools.' While these new skills were relatively easy to acquire, the proper attitudes which presuppose the adoption of such skills were absent. By using the carrot of wage increases or the stick of dismissal, fines and physical punishment, the owners of the new factories could effectively instill the needed work ethic. Before doing this, however, they had to get the laborers into the factory – the workers had to be freed from the higher orders, they had to be free to work in the dark, damp, foul-smelling, dangerous factories for fourteen hours a day, or starve. First in England and, later, throughout Western Europe, poor-relief systems were changed to reflect the view that the poor and the miserable were responsible for their poverty and misery. Thomas Malthus's argument that the provision of aid and comfort to the disadvantaged was both unjustifiable and the surest way to build a society of lazy, imprudent, unambitious people was widely accepted and became the basis of governmental policy. Changes like this completed the denial of social responsibility and allowed for the creation of a national labor market and a reliable, methodical work force.

Once begun, the process of industrialization expanded without serious interruption. Progress, defined as continuous economic growth and industrial expansion, became the catchword of the nineteenth century. Larger and more complex machines and factories were built and, with them, new forms of transportation and communication. Industrial cities arose as more and more people settled around the growing manufacturing centers, and to coordinate the activities of and provide services to these people bureaucratic organizations were created. If the French Revolution produced the ideological and political conditions of modern society, the Industrial Revolution generated the material and the social conditions. Both were bourgeois revolutions which constituted the victory of the capitalist or middle class over the *ancien régime*, and together they established the political system of liberal democracy, the economic system of industrial capitalism, and the social system of bureaucratic organization which continue to shape the way we in Western society live.

Nineteenth-century Western thought is by and large a celebration of modern society, a society characterized by its absence of constraint and its emphasis on personal liberty. In the new society, it was argued, the individual is free to pursue his own interests without interference from others. Certainly, in the pursuit of these interests, the individual may find it to his advantage to agree freely to a contract which imposes on him certain obligations (for example to pay the rent or to work for one employer for a specified period of time), but these obligations and constraints are not imposed by society, whatever that is, they are imposed by the individual himself, acting freely and rationally. This individualistic position rested on a combination of social contract theory and utilitarianism.

Social contract theory, especially as it was formulated by Thomas Hobbes, views society as a contract, an agreement freely entered into by individuals. Fearing a destructive 'war of all against all', individuals rationally and willfully designed and accepted a set of rules, a contract, to regulate and order their interactions. Society, in short, is artificially created by individuals. Utilitarianism is basically a theory of motivation which claims that individuals are motivated by their desire for pleasure and avoidance of pain. Human interaction is nothing more than individuals seeking to maximize their pleasure or happiness. Taken together, social contract theory and utilitarianism see social relationships originating in and being shaped by the desire of individuals to increase their sum of happiness. To assure that their pursuit of happiness occurs freely, without force or fraud, individuals agree in advance to the obligations they will have as a party to the relationship. In light of this view, it was argued that social relationships in modern society are rooted not in the force of tradition and status, but in the voluntary and rational agreements made by individuals. The order and constraint that prevail are not independent of the individual, they were created by and are understandable only in terms of the individual's rational pursuit of pleasure. We are living in the Age of Contract, and thus we are living as individuals free from all obligations except those we impose on ourselves.

Early political economists, like Jeremy Bentham, justified industrial capitalism and the free market economy in terms of the principles of utilitarianism. Utilitarianism views the social as a series of exchange relationships determined by individual interests, desires, and motivations. In the free economy of modern society, the individual is left alone to selfishly pursue his own happiness. Whether or not the individual is successful in this effort to maximize self-interest is entirely dependent on his personal qualities and capabilities – how talented, skilled, prudent, thrifty, wise, and ambitious he is. According to utilitarianism, there is a natural inequality in the distribution of these traits. By nature, some people have a great abundance of talent and ambition, some have very little, while most people fall somewhere in the middle. It is only fair that the most capable receive the highest rewards and the least capable receive the lowest rewards. By assuring that social and economic inequalities correspond to the natural inequalities of individuals, the free market is thus just. In short, the utilitarian economists explained inequality in terms of individual personal qualities. 'Upper class' is just a name to describe the most able individuals, 'lower class' a name to describe the least able. Social classes, unlike the estates found in traditional society, are not legally closed, for individuals are able to move freely into or out of 'social classes' on the basis of their abilities. The worker in industrial capitalism is not bound to the land of the lord for life, he is free to become all that he is capable of becoming. Only laziness and personal inadequacy stand in the way of individual success. The new society may not be the best of all possible worlds, but it is a fairly close approximation.

The Conservative Response

Enlightenment thought had at its core the view that man is rational and thus capable of creating a just and free society. Liberated from the constraints of a hostile nature and oppressive social institutions reason would flourish, and progress toward a more perfect set of social arrangements would begin. In these terms, the French and Industrial Revolutions were justified – both had abolished the established constraints on reason and so permitted the expression of freedom and human progress.

Where was this increase in reason, freedom, and progress to be found? In the disorganization, misery, disease, and uncertainty of the expanding cities? In the noise and dampness of the new factories? In the blood, violence, and disorder that flowed through the streets? In the disorientation that accompanied the breakdown of the family and the community? These were the questions posed by the conservatives. In their view, the two revolutions, misguided by the stress on individual reason found in Enlightenment thought, had terribly weakened the fabric of social order and had produced not human betterment, but chaos and misery. This situation would be remedied only by replacing the Enlightenment stress on individual reason with an affirmation of the traditional and non-rational foundations of social order.

Initially, the conservative repudiation of the Enlightenment project was deeply religious and reactionary in character. Society, according to this theologically grounded conservatism, is created by God, not by rational individuals, and social relations are divine, expressive of God's will. The most divine of all social relations are those that appear to guide the interaction of the monarchy, the nobility, and their subjects. Only with the restoration of the lost medieval order and, with it, the recognition that people possess not natural rights but only social rights divine in origin, will we begin to overcome the widespread misery, frustration, and disorder that presently beset us. Affirming all that the Enlightenment rejected – traditional authority, hierarchy, inequality, religious revelation, sacred customs, and the sanctity of the group over the individual – the conservative response went beyond conservatism to become regressive (Zeitlin, 1968, pp. 34–5).

Two Frenchmen, Louis de Bonald and Joseph de Maistre, were essential to the early development of the conservative response. Both agreed that society, ordained as it is by God, is not reducible to its individual members nor completely knowable by individual reason. Thus Bonald noted throughout his work that 'the general will of society, of the social body, of social man, the nature of social beings or of society, the social will, the will of God are synonomous' (ibid., p. 49). Similarly, Maistre insisted that 'all imaginable institutions rest on a religious idea ... They are strong and durable in the measure in which they are divinized ... Human reason (or what one calls philosophy without knowing what one does) is no substitute for this basis (which one has called superstitious, again without knowing what one does); philosophy on the contrary is an essentially disorganizing force' (Voegelin, 1975, p. 183). The social order, God's order, must be shielded from the disruptive force of reason. God's will, His plan and purpose, surpass the reach of individual reason, it is mysterious, never entirely knowable. At best we acquire only incomplete knowledge, and acting to change society on this basis, no matter how noble and sincere our intentions, too often brings us into violation of God's plan. The fragile foundations of social harmony, the sacred supports of social order – denigrated in Enlightenment thought as unnecessary, backward, superstitious constraints – are quickly undermined. In the absence of society, that is, without God, man is not possible. Forgetting the divine origin of society, the Enlightenment thinkers wildly and irresponsibly wielded the sword of individual reason and severely damaged the bases of social stability – family, community, church, the status order. The wounds inflicted by these philosophical, speculative, negative swordsmen are vividly apparent in the chaos, frustration, loneliness, and general degradation of social life that define the new society.

When stripped of both its religious and theological assumptions and its regressive orientation (so that it defended the *status quo* and not the *status quo ante*) the conservative position formulated in response to the Enlightenment and the new society justified in its terms proved to be a significant impetus to development of sociological thought. Secularized conservatism made virtually the same arguments and claims as did the religious conservatism of Bonald and Maistre, but derived them from the principle of social realism which states that the social is a reality in and of itself, neither reducible to nor understandable with reference to the attributes of its individual members. In contrast to religious conservatism, secularized conservatism did not assume that society operates in accordance with God's law. Rather, the assumption is that society functions with respect to its own laws of development. The task is to know and to obey society's laws. The basic assumptions of this secular conservatism which so strongly influenced the rise of sociology have been carefully identified and discussed by Irving Zeitlin (1968) and, most especially, Robert Nisbet (1968, 1978).

First, society is an organic unity, greater than the sum of its individual members, with its own characteristics and dynamics. Society advances at its own pace and according to its inherent laws of development. Society, in short, is a reality unto itself with its own properties and attributes. According to this view, the individual is not the fundamental unit of society. Rather the basic units are the intimate groups that emerge around family, community, occupation, and religion. These units are interdependent (they constitute an organic unity) so that a change in one effects a change in all. As with any organic unity, society tends toward persistence, cohesion, and stability.

The second assumption is that society predates the individual and provides the context within which the individual develops as a human and moral being. Historically prior to and morally and ethically superior to the individual, the social reality sets the terms of human growth. Outside society, man is impossible.

Basic social institutions serve as necessary checks on man's insatiable and selfish needs, according to the third assumption. These institutions provide order, stability, and meaning to life. In the absence of regulating limits and constraints, frustration and unhappiness are bred. For in the never-ending quest to satisfy basically unsatisfiable needs, the more we have, the more we want. Contentment, personal order and stability require the restrictions imposed by social institutions.

The fourth assumption alerts us to the fragility and tenuousness of the social bond. Resting on tradition and custom, the social order will break whenever individuals, however high their ideals and sincere their motivation, seek to hasten the process of societal growth. Individual interference with the internal laws of society results in disorder and unhappiness.

The social order, its basic units and institutions, its dominant norms and values, is both non-rational in origin and sacred in character. By non-rational this fifth assumption refers to the emergent quality of the social. Aspects of the social are non-rational in that they were not rationally and deliberately designed and constructed as means to achieve a goal or resolve a problem. Rather, religious, familial, and ethnic institutions arise more or less naturally and without conscious deliberation from human interaction. They are indeed purposeful or functional, they enable society to acquire and maintain stability and cohesion, but their origin has nothing to do with individual reason and everything to do with the imperatives of society. This non-rational foundation of the social reality is the primary source of its sacredness. More powerful than the individual and existing over, above, and independent of him, society inspires in people a sense of fear and of deference, of awe, wonderment, and mystery, a sense of the divine. Society is not given by God. Indeed, it is just the reverse. Society is the source of the sacred.

The final defining assumption of conservatism stresses the importance of hierarchy and status. Hierarchy and status differentials are deeply rooted in and proceed from custom and tradition. Non-rational in origin, hierarchy imposes limits on needs and aspirations and restraints on people. Furthermore, it classifies functions, tasks, and people in a way to assure order and integration. Some are better able to lead than are others, and social harmony requires that they be given the opportunity to do so. Structured inequality is one avenue over which societies seek to persist as stable, integrated, organic unities. Social order rests on authority and this requires people who recognize and submit to the laws of development inherent in society.

The major implication of these assumptions is obvious: when time-honored social institutions are challenged, when the reality and moral superiority of the social is denied, social life is undermined. Adherence to conservative principles and abhorrence of Enlightenment principles is the first requirement of any effort to begin to reverse the trends brought by the disorganizing, disruptive forces unleashed by the Enlightenment project. In contrast to Enlightenment thought, conservatism affirmed social authority (obligations) over individual freedom (rights), natural hierarchy over equality, the power of the non-rational over that of individual reason, and stability over progress.

Saint-Simon and Comte take much from conservatism in their formulation of sociology. Yet, while the rise of sociology is best seen as being part and parcel of the general conservative response to the widespread dislocation of the time, the fact is that virtually all key sociological ideas, concepts, and assumptions initially developed represent a synthesis of conservative and Enlightenment thought. Building on the principle of social realism, early sociology seeks to construct a human science (an Enlightenment notion) to study a social reality resting on non-rational foundations and sacred supports (a conservative conception). Similarly, early sociology accepts whole-heartedly the idea of progress from the Enlightenment but joins it with the conservative emphasis on stability to argue that progress is possible only in the context of social order.

Our task now is to see how out of this synthesis of conservative and Enlightenment thought, Saint-Simon and Comte formulated a sociology which justified and came in its methodology to rely on instrumental reason.

Saint-Simon, Comte, and Sociological Positivism

Saint-Simon (1760–1825) takes as his primary task the formulation of a design for the reconstruction of society. He proposes a 'social physiology' (the word 'sociology' is coined later by Comte) to guide this process of reconstruction. Social physiology has as its basic premise that a new order can be established only with careful reference and deference to the dynamics and forces that inhere in the social reality. On the assumption that these properties of the social are open to scientific understanding and identification, Saint-Simon patterns the human science of social physiology after the natural sciences, and promotes it as an instrument of adaptation to the objective, independent, external reality of society. Reason is important to the harmonious realization of the new order, but it will be a reason constrained by the requirements of science. To acquire the happiness, abundance, security, and stability promised by this new order we have no need to go beyond the existing facts of society. We simply need to adjust ourselves to them. Through science we learn both what these facts are and how best to adapt to them.

The defining responsibility of the science of society, Saint-Simon insists, is to identify the laws of progress inherent in society. These inevitable, uncontrollable, absolute laws guide the process of societal development. 'The supreme law of progress of the human spirit carries along and dominates everything; men are but its instruments ... it is no more within our power to withdraw ourselves from its influence or to control its action than it is to change at our pleasure the primitive impulse which makes our planet circle the sun' (Saint-Simon in Kumar, 1978, p. 31). All we can hope to do is to know these laws of progress – and they are knowable only through science – and, in turn, support their course, adapt to their imperatives. Otherwise, we become either the blind victims of inevitable historial change or, worse, the agents of chaos and misery as we act contrary to the constitutive principles and elements of social reality. The effective establishment of the new order requires from the outset submission to these laws and to the scientific method by which they are discovered.

Saint-Simon's science of society is preoccupied with the search for utilities – what is useful given the existing requirements of society. The new social order is to be founded on these utilities, the most important of which have to do with science and technology. Now, Saint-Simon (in Durkheim, 1962, pp. 173–4) writes, 'all society rests on industry. Industry is the only guaranty of its existence ... The most favorable state of affairs for industry is, for this reason, the most favorable to society ... [Thus] the producers of useful things – being the only useful people in society – are the only ones who should cooperate to regulate its course.' If the producers are useful, the useless are the non-producers, the idlers and parasites who comprise both the remaining nobility and the new class of bourgeois owners. Saint-Simon (1964, pp. 72–3) makes this point forcefully.

> Suppose that France lost fifty of her best physicists, chemists, physiologists, mathematicians, poets, painters, sculptors, musicians, writers; fifty of her best mechanical engineers, artillery experts, architects, doctors, surgeons, apothecaries, seamen, clockmakers; fifty of her best bankers, two hundred of her best ironmasters, arms manufacturers, tanners, dyers, miners, clothmakers, cotton manufac-turers, silk-makers, linen-makers, manufacturers of hardware, of pottery and china, of crystal and glass, ship chandlers, carriers, painters, engravers, goldsmiths, and other metal-workers; her fifty best masons, carpenters, joiners, farmers, locksmiths, cutlers, smelters, and a hundred other persons of various unspecified occupations ... making in all three thousand leading scientists, artists, and artisans of France ... The nation would become a lifeless corpse as soon as it lost them.
>
> Suppose that France loses at the same time all the great officers of the royal household, all the ministers (with or without portfolio), all the councillors of state, all the chief magistrates, marshalls, cardinals, archbishops, vicars-general, and canons, all the prefects and sub-prefects, all the civil servants, and judges, and, in addition, ten

thousand of the richest proprietors who live in the style of nobles.

This mischance would certainly distress the French, because they are kindhearted ... But this loss of thirty thousand individuals, considered to be the most important in the state, would only grieve them for purely sentimental reasons and would result in no political evil for the State.

In an argument which later influences Marx, Saint-Simon maintains that a new, more just and decent society requires that power be taken from the non-producers and given to the producers, the useful. But Saint-Simon develops his argument substantially differently than Marx. For he is convinced that the crisis of European society ultimately can be resolved only with the rationalization of power, the transformation of politics into rational administration.

With the advancement of the science of society the ground will have been laid for the society of science, Saint-Simon (in Durkheim, 1962, p. 137) reasons, for 'politics will become a science of observation, and political questions handled by those who would have studied the positive science of man by the same method and in the same way that today one treats those relating to other phenomena ... Politics [must become] the science of production.' Only with the scientization or, in effect, the depoliticization of politics will the reconstruction of society be fully accomplished.

Politics is about power and it most essentially involves the opportunity to struggle over, debate, argue about, and participate in the formulation of the ends and purposes to which power will be put. To politicize people and issues is to bring them into this process of determination. For Saint-Simon, this process is too often volatile, unwieldy, and emotion-laden and too frequently mistaken in its results. In the new society, politics will be replaced by rational administration, politicians by a cadre of the most useful and creative people, scientists and industrialists. Saint-Simon accuses the Enlightenment thinkers and the leaders of the French Revolution of committing a grave mistake by devoting their energies to improving the 'governmental machine' when they should have concentrated on subordinating politics to administration.

They should have asked who ... are the men most fitted to manage the affairs of the nation. They would have been forced to recognize the fact that the scientists, artists, and industrialists, and the heads of industrial concerns are the men who possess the most eminent, varied, and most positively useful ability, for the guidance of men's minds at the present time ... [These] are the men who should be entrusted with administrative power, that is to say, with the responsibility for managing the national interests. (Saint-Simon in Kumar, 1978, pp. 35–6)

Not the most popular, the most pure, or the most socially influential, but the most capable, given the scientific-industrial character of the new order, will be accorded the responsibility of regulating society. And they will guide or administer the operation of society in accordance with scientific knowledge and understanding. Public opinion is an anachronism, made obsolete by the development of scientific truths not subject to political debate and disagreement. Decisions will be made on the basis of demonstrable facts and in a way consistent with the rational course of societal progress. The administrators of Saint-Simon's new society, in Durkheim's (1962, p. 19) words,

> do not dictate orders, they only declare what conforms to the nature of things. The [scientists] show what the laws of social hygiene are; then, from among the measures they propose as a result of these laws, the industrials choose those which experience has proved most practicable. The first will say what is healthful and what is not, what is normal and abnormal; the second will execute. The one will teach what is true; the others will draw from these teachings the practical consequences they imply.

Politics, in short, is to become scientized and rationalized, separated from questions of ends and objectives, reduced in the form of rational administration to an instrument of adaptation to the external social reality. The ends to which power is to be put, the purposes by which society is to be regulated, are given in the facts of existing society. The reorganization of society requires that we defer to those capable of identifying these facts and that they, in turn, submit to the facts themselves. In this new industrial order, Frank Manuel (1956, p. 304) notes, 'the real nobles would be industrial chiefs and the real priests would be scientists'.

In developing this point, Saint-Simon does not dispute the conservative claim that science and industry contributed greatly to the dissolution of the old order. He does, however, reject their call for a restoration of past arrangements. Society has to be reconstructed on the basis of scientific and industrial principles. But the new society in structural outline at least will resemble the old. It too will be hierarchical, stable, organic, and ruled by an elite. Science will do for the new society what religion did for the old. Compliance and submission will continue but in line with the authority and laws of science, not those of God. In the last analysis, the idea of God is wholly commensurate with the idea of scientific law – both give expression to the fundamental idea of unity, the idea most indispensable to the effort to re-establish social order at a higher level of development. In line with this view, Saint-Simon (in Manuel, 1956, p.

136) proclaims the need to reorganize and reconstitute the clergy and maintains that

> the reorganization of the clergy can only mean the reorganization of the scientific corps, because the clergy must be the scientific corps. The clergy can be useful, can only have strength, as long as it is composed of the most knowledgeable men, as long as the principles which it knows are unknown to the common people.

Apparent in this advocacy for reconstituting clergy as scientists is a strong defense of instrumental reason. Since Aquinas, Roman Catholicism (whose clergy by and large Saint-Simon is referring to) regarded reason as the capacity to go beyond the facts of this world and there to discover God's plan and purpose. The existing arrangements were to be understood and assessed with respect to how well they met the transcendent criteria grasped by reason. Reason, in this view, brings us at least partial knowledge of that which does not exist empirically, indeed, of that which we can use to evaluate the empirically given. The reason of Saint-Simon's scientists and industrialists, however, is purely instrumental. It is confined exclusively to the established universe. Truth, goodness, happiness, security, all are to be found in – not beyond – the facts of this universe. Above all, it is the willingness of the bearers of instrumental reason, the scientists and industrialists, to respect the laws of the social reality and to comply with the facts of this reality that warrants their participation in the administration of society. The new society would satisfy simultaneously the conservative demand for the subordination of individual freedom to social authority and the Enlightenment hope for a human science capable of guiding progressive development.

Auguste Comte (1798–1857) spent several years as Saint-Simon's personal secretary, and after the two separated amidst great acrimony Comte proceeded to perfect and elaborate most of Saint-Simon's ideas, often neglecting to credit the groundbreaking work of his former mentor. Like Saint-Simon, Comte is preoccupied with developing ideas that will guide the resolution of the crisis and the reorganization of society. He also insists that a science of society – 'sociology' he calls it – is indispensable to this task. The search for imaginary transcendental purposes has to be replaced by a full appreciation of the existing factual order. Society is a lawfully changing reality, and it is the responsibility of sociology to know these laws and, in turn, to use this knowledge both to formulate an appropriate strategy of reconstruction and to constrain the presently unchecked desires, aspirations, and ambitions of the populace.

While Comte echoes Saint-Simon's call for granting the representatives of the newly emerging forces of science and industry control over the governance of society, he believes that by itself rational administration is not enough to bring into being an effective, efficient, and integrated society. More important is a highly cohesive, firmly structured set of moral values similar to the collective nomos found in traditional society. For Comte, social scientific knowledge is to be used not only to create an appropriate strategy of reconstruction but also to forge a moral code capable of constraining the presently unbridled desires, aspirations, and ambitions of the populace, and of inspiring in people humility in the face of the objective requirements of social order. Sociology has to be simultaneously the science of society and the religion of humanity. In the positive polity Comte proposes, Saint-Simon's scientific-industrial elite is located within a hierocratic, corporate state (Giddens, 1971b, p. 479). In this system, 'the spiritual power will be confined to the hands of the *savants*, while the temporal power will belong to the heads of industrial works ... on the *savants* devolves the task of undertaking the first series of works and on the leaders of industry that of organizing, on the bases thus established, the administrative system' (Comte in Hawthorn, 1976, p. 76). Essentially the practitioners of the positive science of sociology, the *savants* would discover and convey the social rules and attendant moral code in terms of which the supervision of the scientists and industrialists would be carried out.

The essential theme of Comte's sociology is 'progress and order'. Progress is possible but only in the context of social order. Advancement results only from changes that take place within the established structures, changes consistent with the laws inherent in society. Changes of structure are the antithesis of progress. Progress issues from and, in turn, furthers the cause of social order. It is a process of harmonious evolution. Only when society is allowed to change at its own pace and in its own terms is improvement assured.

The progress and order theme is reflected in the two main components of Comte's sociology, dynamics and statics. Statics involves the study of social consensus, the non-rational foundations of organic unity and the bases of collective integration, that hold together a particular society. Where statics provides a recognition of the diversity of historical societies, dynamics enables an understanding of the principles that underlie every social order. Dynamics entails the examination of the laws of social progress and the successive and necessary stages of societal growth. Through dynamics we discover the pattern of evolutionary development. We learn through statics that this pattern is grounded in social solidarity. Taken as a whole, the science of sociology inspires in us a respect for social order and a faith in its future. Sociology, Comte immodestly claims, is the religion of humanity.

Comte identifies three stages in the development of the human mind and society, each distinguished by a particular mode of thought and explanation. The theological stage incorporates humanity's movement from fetishism to polytheism and eventually to monotheism. During this phase, the human mind accounts for events with reference to divine and supernatural forces. Priests arise as the dominant agent of explanation. The theological stage was superseded by a metaphysical stage where philosophers displace priests as the primary explainers. At this level, the human mind constructs explanations with a view toward essences and ideals, self-evident truths and inalienable rights. If the theological and metaphysical stages represent for Comte the *ancien régime* and the Enlightenment, the emerging positive state of development refers to the new scientific-industrial order (Lenzer, 1979, p. 69).

According to Comte, the human mind reaches full maturity during the positive stage. Explanations are made to correspond to empirical data and scientists and industrialists, subordinating their imagination to observation and preventing reason from straying from the facts, assume the role once occupied by priests and philosophers. In Comte's view, writes Leszek Kolakowski (1968), pp. 54–5),

> The positive mind no longer asks *why*, ceases to speculate on the hidden nature of things. It asks *how* phenomena arise and what course they take; it collects facts and is ready to submit to facts; it subjects [thinking] to the continuous control of 'objective' facts. It does not employ terms that have no counterpart in reality ... Humility in the face of compelling facts and practical inspiration – such are the distinctive features of the positive intellect.

Positivism is the doctrine Comte proposes as the foundation of the strategy for reconstructing society. Furthermore, he deems sociology the most positivistic of all the sciences and accords it the uppermost spot in the hierarchy of sciences. The 'ultimate, synthesizing science', the 'Queen of the sciences', sociology will be the most important for in the final analysis only sociological truths, based as they are on scientific knowledge of the laws of social progress, can guarantee the well-being of society and its members. Sociological positivism holds the key to any future progress.

Positivism relies on the scientific method and seeks to establish general laws on the basis of methodical observation and experimentation. In extreme form, positivism devolves into scientism by equating knowledge with scientific knowledge or technical information. For Comte, positivism denotes both certainty and utility. Positivism, he claims, provides information useful for expanding our certainty about and, in turn, our control over the course to be taken by the reconstruction of society. And it is able to do this by virtue of the respectful attitude it brings to its effort to know the factual order. The only source of knowledge is that which already exists. In the broader context of Comte's work, 'positive' has two additional meanings, 'good' and 'affirmative'. The established order is good in that it contains within itself tendencies toward order and progress. Positive thought recognizes this and thus is affirmative. In contrast to the negativism of Enlightenment thought, positive thought concentrates on what is, not to negate it, but to affirm and support its progressive capabilities. In formulating sociological positivism, Comte roundly repudiates the transcendental point of view. Affirmation and organization, not negation and destruction, are the foremost tasks. With this view, Marcuse (1941, p. 341) has written, the new sociology tied 'itself to the facts of the existing order and, though it [did] not reject the need for correction and improvement, it [did] exclude any move to overthrow or negate that order. As a result, the conceptual interest of the positive sociology [was] to be apologetic and justificatory.'

Sociological positivism became a major protector and defender of the established order, and submission and resignation emerged as its central themes. 'The habit of submission is the first condition of order in human affairs', Comte (1969, pp. 126–7) writes.

> For this habit the sense of an irresistible Fatality offers the only adequate training ... As soon as the development of Positive thought has proceeded far enough to bring this involuntary submission into due prominence, it creates a spirit of true humility, and thus becomes consciously to ourselves a most valuable agent of moral discipline. Our reason, naturally so proud, will then have no higher aim than to become a faithful mirror of the world without us, so as to dispense by its own internal workings with the necessity for external observation; for this is what is done by scientific prevision, a power which deserves our highest admiration. This combination of submission with power is one of our noblest achievements, and is at the same time a most effective agent in our moral training.

Positivism is useful not only for the technical knowledge it provides but also for the discipline, humility, and fatalistic resignation it imposes. The positive spirit teaches people to find satisfaction within the prevailing social order and promotes progress by securing 'universal submission to the necessity embodied in the predominant and rising social and economic forces – more specifically, the new industrial-economic order' (Lenzer, 1979, p. 83).

Comte's sociological positivism receives its impetus and its rationale from the logic of instrumental reason. Positive sociology is presented as a rational, calculative means to be used in the pursuit of societally-determined ends. Not surprisingly, then, the strategy Comte draws for the reconstruction of society from positive sociology entails a significant reduction of human freedom. Comte (in *ibid.*, p. 83) puts the matter this way:

> There are very few persons who consider themselves fit to sit in judgment on the astronomical, physical, and chemical ideas which are destined to enter into social circulation; and everybody is willing that those ideas should direct corresponding operations; and here we see the beginnings of intellectual government. Can it be supposed that the most delicate conceptions, and those which by their complexity are accessible to only a small number of highly-prepared understandings, are to be abandoned to the arbitrary and variable decisions of the least competent minds? If such an anomaly could be imagined permanent, a dissolution of the social state must ensue ... [Required for the reorganization of society is] the renunciation by the greater number of their right of individual inquiry on subjects above their qualifications ...

The Comtean vision entails the scientization of politics and the limitation of the freedoms of speech and conscience. It requires that key questions be taken from the realm of open public discourse and be given over to the scientists to be decided on the basis of expert knowledge. Scientific knowledge is an indisputable guide to the effective administration of society. In the form of science, reason becomes an instrument of adaptation to the factual order and, as such, an opponent of human freedom. In developing this vision, Comte basically elaborates on Saint-Simon's earlier work.

Together, Saint-Simon and Comte give sociology its name, its method, and its subject-matter. Sociology is the scientific study of society, most particularly of the laws of progress inherent in society. This sociology clearly is a product of the rise of industrial capitalist society. Like this society, positive sociology champions instrumental reason and fosters the instrumentalization of culture. Culture once contained, Norman Birnbaum (1969, p. 112) writes, 'possibilities unrealized or indeed impeded by the prevailing system of domination. Indeed, culture [had] as one of its essential meanings a continual struggle against domination, temporarily abated in privileged periods, but invariably resumed as human purposes old and new [failed] to find objectification in society.' In contrast, instrumentalized culture, Birnbaum (ibid., p. 113) continues, represents a 'system of symbols, of consciousness, of sensibility, of preconscious and unconscious meanings [which] has been assimilated to the imperatives of machine production, market organization, and bureaucratic power'.

Here, the human element in the making of culture disappears and the ends to be pursued appear beyond the reach of human choice, not amenable to influence by open public discourse. Rather, these ends seem to be given by the imperatives of mechanization, market, and bureaucracy.

Positive sociology was a product of this instrumentalized culture. In effect, Comte produces, in Gertrude Lenzer's (1979, p. 73) words, 'another Copernican reversal [where] man was once again displaced not only from the center of the universe but from the center of what he had believed to be his world – the human world. The idea of the freedom and autonomy of human beings or of any human claim to transcendence, was now held as cancelled.' Rationality without reason has its roots in these developments.

Sociology was formed during a period when the major beneficiaries of instrumental reason, the emerging bourgeoisie, though clearly in the ascendency, still confronted the relatively powerful remnants of the old order. The secret of sociology's initial appeal lay in its ability to speak to both sets of interest. Thus, Alvin Gouldner (1970, pp. 106–7) writes that sociology was 'at first the intellectual product of old strata that had lost their social power and of new ones that were still far from fully developed'. In the presence of a fundamental split between a restored yet weakened nobility and a still unorganized but increasingly powerful bourgeoisie, there arose

a set of collective public sentiments which was, on the one hand, detached from *both* major contending social alternatives – old regime traditionalism and middle class liberalism – and, on the other, expressed a need for a new social map to which men could attach themselves; that is, for a *positive* set of beliefs. It was this new structure of collective sentiment that Sociological Postivism congenially resonated and which, in part, enabled it to find public support ... [Sociology] was born of an effort to find an apolitical alternative to political conflicts over the fundamental character of society. (ibid., 1970, p. 101)

With its appreciation of conservative themes and respect for the conserving forces of social reality, positive sociology seemed to complement the emerging individualist utilitarian culture of the new society. Positive sociology focused on collective utilities, what is useful for maintaining cohesion, solidarity, and stability – the bases of societal progress. Yet it took pains to emphasize that collective utilities are not at all incompatible with individual utilities. Indeed, the maximization of self-interest and the attainment of individual happiness depend on social order. Concerned both with completing its own revolution and with discouraging popular unrest and resistance from below, the rising middle class took readily to the sociological argument that change is necessary and inevitable but must be tempered with a respect for stability and order if its consequences are to be beneficial. Not revolution, but the peaceful application of instrumental reason is the cornerstone of progress, societal well-being, and human happiness.

Emile Durkheim (1858–1917): Sociology, the Science of Ethics

Durkheim, notes Edward Tiryakian (1978, p. 190), shares Saint-Simon's and Comte's 'repugnance of political upheavals, of group struggles for power, of chicanery and civil strife' and he continues their effort 'to make sociology a healing and stabilizing science, one that will find a viable basis for restoring social consensus and for enhancing social integration'. Following the tradition of positive sociology, Durkheim adopts the principle of social realism, arguing that society, a reality in and of itself, tends toward cohesion, integration and persistence. Social life, according to Durkheim, rests on the commitment of people to the dominant norms and values of their society. If social well-being relies on commitment, human well-being requires constraint. Humans, Durkheim holds, differ from other animals in their insatiable needs and unlimited desires. If not checked by external forces – societal norms and values – these unbridled desires cause frustration and discontent. Human satisfaction is impossible in the absence of societal constraint, and constraint is simply the reverse side of commitment. 'What is needed if social order is to reign', Durkheim (1972, p. 177) argues, 'is that the mass of men be content with their lot. But what is needed for them to be content, is not that they have more or less but that they be convinced that they have a right to no more. And for this, it is absolutely essential that there be an authority whose superiority they acknowledge and which tells them what is right.' The superior authority Durkheim has in mind is society. Social order and human happiness require the limiting, constraining, and regulative force of society.

Social constraints for Durkheim are moral in character. Indeed, the source of morality is to be found only in the social reality. Moral acts, Durkheim maintains, are neither instinctually motivated nor carried out for purely personal and selfish reasons. Rather, the ends of moral acts are impersonal (and not infrequently at odds with personal aims) and require for their achievement pre-established normative rules. The disinterestedness (as opposed to self-interestedness) and devotion to a being superior to oneself that mark moral acts have their roots in group attachments.

People attain the stature of moral beings only by virtue of their attachments to the social. Thus, in this view, man is dependent on society not only for his happiness and physical well-being but also for his morality. The social is the moral.

Durkheim carefully identifies the subject-matter and methodological rules of scientific sociology in a way consistent with these assumptions about the relation of man and society. Social facts, Durkheim insists, constitute the subject-matter of sociology. 'A social fact is every way of acting, fixed or not, capable of exercising on the individual an external constraint; or again, every way of acting which is general throughout a given society, while at the same time existing in its own right independent of its individual manifestations' (Durkheim, 1938, p. 13). Social facts are external to and constraining of the individual. While independent of individual will, they impose themselves on and morally regulate this will.

The defining task of sociology is to interpret social facts, and for the successful completion of this task a distinctive sociological method is necessary. First, it must be 'entirely independent of philosophy'. Sociology must disavow the non-empirical concerns of philosophy and fully integrate itself within the circle of the natural sciences. Only as positive science will sociology properly develop. Secondly, the method must be 'objective, ... dominated entirely by the idea that social facts are things and must be treated as such'. By this rule, the sociologist is to treat his subject-matter exactly as the physicist, chemist, and physiologist treat theirs. Without preconceptions and biases, the sociologist attends exclusively to the objective, empirical characteristics of the facts under examination. Finally, 'if we consider social facts as things, we consider them as *social things*. The third trait that [must] characterize our method is that it [be] exclusively sociological' (ibid., pp. 141–6). Social facts can be explained only with reference to other social facts, or, in other words, the properties of society cannot be understood in terms of the attributes of its individual members. 'Sociology is, then, not an auxiliary of any other science; it is itself a distinct and autonomous science, and the feeling of specificity of social reality is indeed so necessary to the sociologist that only distinctly sociological training can prepare him to grasp social facts intelligently' (ibid., p. 145).

Given the connection Durkheim draws between the social and the moral, sociology as the science of society or social facts is in effect the science of morality and ethics. Through the science of sociology we acquire both respect for the moral reality and the means for improving it. Sociology, Durkheim maintains, is capable of establishing a scientific basis for distinguishing the pathological from the normal. Upon this distinction beneficial intervention in the course of societal development is possible. Pathological social facts are obstructive of the cohesive and progressive tendencies of society and they should be eliminated. Normal social facts, on the other hand, are essential to the elaboration of these tendencies and, no matter how horrible or unjust they may appear, no action should be taken against them.

'A social fact is normal', Durkheim (1938, p. 64) writes, 'in relation to a given societal type at a given phase of its development, when it is present in the average society of that species at the corresponding phase of its evolution.' Moreover, a normal social fact 'is bound up with the general conditions of collective life of the social type considered'. In other words, normal social facts meet the criteria of generality – they are shown to be common to societies of the same type – and functionality – their effects demonstrably satisfy the requirements of the society for order and progress. Should, for instance, the rate of poverty in the United States be shown to be both typical of the rate found in all societies of the advanced industrial capitalist type and functional for the stability and persistence of that type, it would be regarded as a normal social fact. Any effort to eliminate it would threaten the social order.

In effect, Durkheim argues that scientific sociological knowledge, particularly as it makes possible the distinction between the pathological and the normal, is indispensable to the betterment of the moral reality. While he never goes as far as Saint-Simon and Comte to promote a scientific-industrial elite, Durkheim (ibid., p. 75) does insist that 'the duty of the statesman is no longer to push society toward an ideal that seems attractive to him, but his role is that of the physician. He prevents the outbreak of illnesses by good hygiene, and he seeks to cure them when they have appeared.' In diagnosing these illnesses, in formulating the hygenic principles and cure, the statesman must rely closely on the sociologist.

Durkheim seeks to have reason replace 'subjective sentimentalism' as the ground for dealing with questions of morality. Not surprisingly, the reason to which he refers is instrumental reason.

> If what is meant by [reason] is a moral faculty which contains, in an immanent state, a moral ideal, the *true* ideal which it is able to oppose, and should oppose, to that which society follows at each moment of its history, I say that this *a priorism* is an arbitrary affirmation which all known facts contradict. The reason to which I make my appeal is reason applying itself to a given matter in a methodical manner in order to understand the nature of past and present morality, and which draws from this theoretical study its practical consequences. Reason thus understood is simply science, the science of morality. (Durkheim, 1974, pp. 66–7)

The only reason which has the right to intervene with an eye toward reforming the moral reality 'is not my reason nor yours; it is the impersonal human reason, only truly realized in science' (ibid., p. 65). The instrumental reason of science enhances people's control over both external nature and, equally important, their inner passions, the unlimited and aimless desires whose expression produces misery. The enlarged control made possible by instrumental reason, Durkheim claims, is a condition of freedom in modern society. Consistent with his basic assumptions, however, Durkheim defines freedom in terms of submission.

Human freedom cannot mean, in Durkheim's view, emancipation from society. In the absence of moral constraint and discipline, unbridled desire reigns and the result is dissatisfaction and unhappiness, if not worse. Whenever 'the individual disassociates himself from collective goals in order to seek only his own interests ... suicide increases. Man is the more vulnerable to self-destruction the more he is detached from any collectivity' (Durkheim, 1972, p. 113). Individual autonomy and freedom are attained only in and through society – or, more accurately, in and through modern society whose highly complex division of labor requires autonomy and freedom for its operation. The progressive emancipation of the individual results not from the destruction of social bonds but from their evolutionary and orderly transformation. To facilitate this transformation the individual must submit to society. Yet,

> this submission is the condition of his liberation. For man freedom consists in deliverance from blind, unthinking physical forces; this he achieves by opposing against them the great and intelligent force which is society, under whose protection he shelters. By putting himself under the wing of society, he makes himself also, to a certain extent, dependent upon it. But this is a liberating dependence. There is no paradox here. (Durkheim, 1974, p. 72)

There is no paradox here precisely because Durkheim defines freedom in instrumental terms as the capacity to control external and internal nature in light of the requirements of the 'great and intelligent force which is society'. Freedom as the capacity to discuss, debate, and formulate the ends and purposes of life, as the capacity to change the established facts, bringing them closer into line with normative ideals, receives no consideration in Durkheim's scheme of things. For Durkheim, the ends and purposes of human life as well as individual freedom itself are given by society.

Durkheim presents scientific sociology as an instrument of individual adaptation or submission to society. Writing fifty years after Comte,

Durkheim argues that the fundamental problem facing sociology and society is the absence of a morality appropriate to the new social conditions. The old traditions and practices have receded and nothing has arisen to take their place. A 'breakdown has occurred which can be repaired only when a new moral discipline comes into being and takes root. In short, our first obligation today is to forge a new morality for ourselves' (Durkheim, 1933, p. 409). The crisis of our time is a moral crisis, Durkheim maintains, and the state of normlessness or anomie from which this crisis originates is a pathological social fact which impedes both the harmonious operation of society and individual freedom. Sociology, the science of morality, has the responsibility of resolving this crisis on the basis of instrumental reason.

The individual must be ruled by a conscience superior to his own. His ambition must be regulated, his desire checked. 'To limit man, to place obstacles in the path of his free development ...', Durkheim (in Lukes, 1977, p. 83) observes, 'this limitation is a condition of our happiness and moral health. Man, in fact, is made for life in a determinate, limited environment.' In the absence of limitation, anomie prevails. When, often as a result of rapid social change, conventional meaning systems or mappings of the world break down or are discredited, the bases of social stability erode. People no longer know clearly how to go about getting what they want. Very often, they possess only a confused conception of what they want and where they are going. The anomic condition is one of low group cohesion and low collective regulation of personal needs and desires. The anomic experience is characterized by uncertainty, insecurity, hopelessness, fatalism, and despair. Anomie, Peter Berger (1969, p. 22) writes, 'is the nightmare par excellence, in which the individual is submerged in a world of disorder, senselessness, and madness ... To be in society is to be "sane" precisely in the sense of being shielded from the ultimate "insanity" of such anomic terror. Anomie is unbearable to the point where the individual may seek death in preference to it.' With the disruption of the collective nomos, people confront the nothing of chaotic meaninglessness.

Initially, Durkheim regards anomie as a by-product of the as yet uncompleted shift from traditional to modern society. Traditional society rested on a simple division of labor wherein tasks and responsibilities were differentiated and allocated largely on the basis of age and sex. Given the small degree of differentiation found in society, people shared the same basic values, and this value consensus served as the basis of social integration. The collective conscience was virtually identical with the individual consciences of every member of society. The collective conscience of simple society was distinguished by its strong emphasis on the tyranny of the group over the individual and its rigidly fixed moral boundaries. Repressive and obstructive of the development of the person as an individual, it is regarded by Durkheim as totally inappropriate to the complex division of labor which undergirds modern society.

The complex division of labor displays a vast multitude of specialized, narrowly defined, highly differentiated tasks which it is required to allocate with reference to individual ability, achievement, and merit. While its development has severely weakened the social bases of value consensus, the complex division of labor is not inherently disintegrative. Rather, Durkheim takes pains to argue, it has its own logic of integration, one which organizes differences by the principle of functional interdependence. The performance of each differentiated position is dependent on the performances of all other positions. Through this interrelatedness of services, the parts of the complex whole are brought together.

Appropriate to complex society is a collective conscience of moral individualism. Moral individualism is a societal injunction to tolerate, respect, and encourage the individuality of others (such individuality, particularly in the area of skill, being essential to the complex division of labor). Far from endorsing an ethos of egoism and selfishness, moral individualism imposes limits and constraints on the individual. The individual is restrained in his choice of goals and means by his respect for other individuals. Unacceptable are those aims and pursuits that violate this respect. The individual in modern society is made possible by the constraints and obligations of moral individualism.

Anomie prevails in modern society, according to Durkheim, in so far as the collective conscience of moral individualism remains under-developed. With the erosion of the repressive collective conscience of simple society, two tendencies have arisen which make difficult the establishment of moral individualism. The first, utilitarian individualism, replaces the tyranny of the group with the tyranny of the individual and urges not respect for the individuality of others but individual selfishness. The second and more prominent, anomie, represents the substitution of no moral boundaries whatsoever for the fixed moral boundaries that previously existed. Against these pathological tendencies, Durkheim sets out to propose a strategy for strengthening the bases of moral individualism.

Indispensable to this endeavor, Durkheim asserts, is the creation of a partially autonomous democratic-corporatist state capable of normatively regulating communal groups, bringing the economy under conscious and rational control, and implementing national and regional policies of economic exchange and growth – while all the time vigilantly safeguarding individual liberties. Durkheim regards corporatism as an integrative element indispensable to all post-agrarian societies, and he

seeks to demonstrate that democratic corporatism is commensurate with
the criteria of social normality consistent with modern complex society.
The primary aim of Durkheim's corporatist strategy, writes Dominick
LaCapra (1972, p. 232), is 'to establish a normative triangle of
community, individual rights, and state regulation under the general
guidance of universal, humanistic values'.

Durkheim's effort to discover a way of resolving the problem of anomie
begins with his observation that the 'first origins of all social processes of
any importance should be sought in the internal constitution of the social
group' (Durkheim, 1938, p. 113). Our concentration must be directed to
the dynamic density of the group, which Durkheim (ibid., p. 114) defines
'as the function of the number of individuals who are actually having not
only commercial but also social relations, i.e., who not only exchange
services or compete with one another but also have a common life'. Out of
the regular interaction between and among those who share a common life
emerges a collective nomos. Given the influences the complex division of
labor has on group dynamics in modern society, the emergent collective
nomos would be moral individualism. The basic remedy for anomie, then,
entails the creation of micro-social opportunities or centers for
interaction for those who are or should be living a common life (Marks,
1974). 'Within any political society', Durkheim (1958, pp. 23–4) writes,

> we get a number of individuals who share the same ideas and interests,
> sentiments and occupations, in which the rest of the population have no
> part ... They feel a mutual attraction, they seek one another ... Once
> the group is formed, nothing can hinder an appropriate moral life from
> evolving.

The main basis of the collective nomos in complex society, Durkheim
argues, is the occupational corporation.

Superficially similar to medieval guilds, the occupational corporations
Durkheim envisions are clearly defined, well-organized, internally
democratic groups existing as national public institutions. For each major
occupation in the division of labor there would be a corporation whose
members would be drawn from all those in that occupational category
throughout the country. While legally sanctioned by and responsible to
the state, these occupational corporations 'would have the authority to
resolve conflicts both within their own membership and in relation to
other occupational groups; and they would be the focus for a variety of
educational and recreational activities' (Giddens, 1971a, p. 103). In this
sense, the occupational corporation would closely resemble the
occupational community whose members regularly interact with one
another outside as well as inside the workplace. With each occupational

center generating its own emergent morality, the problem of anomie would begin to be brought under control.

Durkheim recognizes that to be effective the remedy for anomie found in the establishment of occupational corporations required an explicitly developed political dimension. The problem of anomie was not simply an occupational one, it was society-wide in character and scope. In addition, there would be a good probability that the morality produced by one occupational group would be different from if not antagonistic to that arising from a second. For social solidarity to predominate over a disputatious particularism, 'related groups would have to share a *conscience collective* containing norms which defined the justified modes of interaction, mutual expectation, and exchange with one another' (LaCapra, 1972, pp. 91–2). Anomie requires for its resolution a genuinely collective nomos, one representative of society as a whole. Such a collective nomos would emerge from the interaction of everyone with everyone else. The direct interaction of everyone with everyone else is obviously impossible in a large, complex society. However, the indirect interaction of each with all others is another matter (Marks, 1974, p. 338).

Being the most inclusive of all societal associations, the state becomes for Durkheim the most appropriate arena for the indirect interaction of everyone with everyone else in society. Democratically elected political representatives are small enough in number so that they could directly interact with each other. As long as public officials were truly representative of all the various differentiated segments of society, the morality that emerged from their direct interaction would constitute a collective nomos. To assure that this be the case, Durkheim insists that occupational corporations should replace territorially defined constituencies as the basic electoral units. The occupational association, Durkheim (1958, pp. 102–3) writes, 'is the true electoral unit, and because the links attaching us to one another derive from our calling rather than from any regional bonds of loyalty, it is natural that the political structure should reflect the way in which we ourselves form into groups of our own accord'. Public officials would become representatives of distinct occupational groups and all corporations would be represented in the state apparatus. Through their representative, the members of one occupational corporation would be indirectly interacting with the members of all others. From this cooperative political arrangement would arise a cure for the excesses of anomie – a civic morality which would endorse the principle of moral individualism and further the progressive emancipation of the individual. 'Our moral individuality', Durkheim (in Giddens, 1978, p. 64) concludes, 'far from being antagonistic to the state, has on the contrary been the product of it.'

For Durkheim, the steady expansion of the directive role of the state is normal in modern complex society so long as nothing is done to threaten the cultivation of intermediary corporative groups. Only the state is capable of formulating laws expressive of collective representations valid for society as a whole. Only the corporate group, on the other hand, is capable of providing both resistance to any absolutist tendencies the state may possess and the social interaction and experiences in which socially valid representations can be rooted. In this view, the state is a moral actor responsible not only for translating narrow particularistic concerns into coherent and meaningful collective representations, but also for assuming 'an active role in canalising and directing policies which translate these attitudes into practice. As such it leads as well as being led' (Giddens, 1972, p. 18). At the same time, as intermediaries between the state and the individual, occupational corporations 'are essential if the state is not to oppress the individual; they are also necessary if the state is to be sufficiently free of the individual ... They liberate the two confronting forces, while linking them at the same time' (Durkheim, 1958, pp. 96, 106).

Durkheim locates the foundation of democracy for modern society in the regular interaction between the directive state and occupational corporations. As he defines it, democracy possesses two central features: frequent institutionalized communication and consultation between the state and its citizens, and an influential, interventionist state with strong attachments to the key sectors of society. To the extent that the first condition obtains, the collective conscience of moral individualism will be firmly established and forcefully expressed. Guided by the morality of individualism, growing state intervention will serve to enhance individuality as it brings to society the rational coordination demanded by the complex division of labor. Given these circumstances, corporatist political structures, democracy, and individual liberty continuously feed and enlarge one another.

Despite the clear influence of Saint-Simon and Comte on Durkheim's thinking, the democratic corporatism he proposed substantially differs from the elitist corporatism advocated by his predecessors. Durkheim maintains that a society's mark of honor has little to do with its wealth and military greatness and everything to do with the justice of its organization and moral constitution. The basis of modern societal honor is the corporatist-democratic state characterized by the ever active participation of publicly interested citizens.

The planning of the social milieu so that the individual may realize himself more fully, and the management of the collective apparatus in a way that will bear less hard on the individual; an assured and amicable exchange of goods and services and the cooperation of all men of good will towards an ideal they shape without any conflict

– in these Durkheim (ibid., pp. 74–5) finds the ground of a decent and prosperous society. In this context, Prager (1981, p. 920) writes, Durkheim regards a properly functioning democracy as one which 'successfully promotes an active and reflective citizenry; it serves to transform citizens into increasingly more autonomous individuals responsibly participating as individuals in their political and social life'.

In one respect, Durkheim's model – especially its emphasis on the creation of occupational corporations or national peak associations licensed and recognized by a directive and partly autonomous state and substituted for territoriality as the basis of electoral units – anticipated well the corporatist arrangements developed and pursued in the twentieth century. In another, more crucial respect, however, Durkheim's vision has been repudiated. Corporatism appears antagonistic to and, not as Durkheim had it, necessary for democratic politics in modern industrial capitalist societies. Corporatism, as it has developed and continues to develop in this century (the subject of Chapter 5), expresses the logic of instrumental reason and displays the same antipathy toward democracy that we encounter in Saint-Simon and Comte.

Underlying Durkheim's concern with occupational corporations and political reform is the claim that sociology is able to secure the knowledge necessary for the rational amelioration of the prevailing anomic state of affairs. Durkheim eventually despairs of these rational proposals, and he concludes his career-long search for a solution to anomie by concentrating on non-rational periods of 'collective ferment' and 'creative effervescence' – liminal periods celebrative of the human bond. This solution to anomie, writes Mark (1974, pp. 358–9), requires that people 'seek each other out in uninstitutionalized contexts throughout the entire society so that the resulting interchanges would culminate in a new sympathy and affection of man for man ... which would spontaneously come to be relived in periodic celebrations and ceremonials'. In suggesting this as the only effective remedy, Durkheim in effect withdraws earlier claims concerning the ability of sociology to intervene in and mitigate the crisis of anomie, for, surely, sociology cannot be expected to initiate the 'great collective shock' presupposed by periods of ferment and creative effervescence.

Durkheim formulates the non-rational solution to anomie in his last major work, *The Elementary Forms of the Religious Life*, a study of the origin of religious beliefs and practices. Briefly, Durkheim argues that religious ideas are born during periods of collective effervescence marked by the euphoric experience of intense social interaction among people once dispersed and now closely reassembled. The very act of regrouping people and momentarily concentrating their interaction with one another produces excitement and joy. Durkheim describes these periods as sacred, for they provide the setting within which people experience an all-powerful being greater than themselves, a force they simultaneously fear and respect and ultimately come to worship. The all-powerful being experienced during these moments of collective ferment, Durkheim maintains, is not God, but society. It is unquestionable, Durkheim (1965, pp. 236–7) writes,

> that a society has all that is necessary to arouse the sensation of the divine in minds, merely by the power that it has over them; for to its members it is what god is to his worshippers. In fact, a god is, first of all, a being whom men think of as superior to themselves, and upon whom they feel that they depend ... Now society also gives us the sensation of a perpetual dependence ... It requires that, forgetful of our own interest, we make ourselves its servitors, and it submits us to every sort of inconvenience, privation, and sacrifice, without which social life would be impossible ... [Yet] the empire it holds over consciences is due much less to the physical supremacy of which it has the privilege than to the moral authority with which it is invested.

God is an object of venerable respect precisely because He is a symbol of society.

In worshipping God we in effect pay our respect to society; in experiencing God, we actually feel the sacred qualities and moral force of the social reality. During the sacred periods of collective effervescence, social attachments are strengthened and reaffirmed, the social bond is renewed, and new collective ideals are created. We celebrate as we submit to society, and out of this celebration and submission emerges a remedy for anomie, that 'state of incertitude and confused agitation' which presently engulfs us.

> A day will come when our societies will know again those hours of creative effervescence, in the course of which new ideas arise and new formulae are found which serve for a while as a guide to humanity; and when these hours shall have been passed through once, men will spontaneously feel the need of reliving them from time to time in thought, that is to say, of keeping alive their memory by means of celebrations which regularly reproduce their fruits. (ibid., p. 475)

Modern society, Durkheim concludes, requires creative ferment. With this conclusion, he identifies the limits of positive sociology's affirmation of instrumental reason. Fuelled by the expansion of science and technology, the rationalization of society undermined important bases of social solidarity and foreclosed opportunities for spontaneous inter-action. Instrumental reason contributed greatly to the moral crisis of anomie. Yet the practitioners of positive sociology long held that instrumental reason also had the capacity to produce the resolution to this crisis in the form of a scientific-industrial elite or scientific knowledge with which the normal could be distinguished from the pathological. Toward the end of his life, Durkheim devalues the efficacy and curative powers of instrumental reason and simply waits for the day when we would know again 'those hours of creative effervescence'.

Conclusion

The reason without rationality – calculative, scientific, positive and instrumental reason – which so worries C. Wright Mills is present in sociology from the start. Adopting the conservative principle of social realism, Saint-Simon and Comte develop sociology as an approach to the problem of societal reconstruction. Sociology's task is to know scientifically the laws of progress inherent in the social order and to assure consistency between them and programs of reorganization. In advocating the allocation of decision-making power to a scientific-elite comprised of those knowledgeable and respectful of the social reality, Saint-Simon and Comte seek to depoliticize politics, that is, to limit the freedoms of discussion and opinion as they bear upon the formulation of certain ends and purposes.

Following in this tradition, Durkheim promotes instrumental reason in the form of scientific sociology as the carrier of a solution to moral crisis and the bearer of guidelines leading to enhanced individual freedom. Both a remedy for anomie and the progressive emancipation of the individual require submission to a collective morality appropriate to complex society. Sociological knowledge, Durkheim initially thinks, is capable of facilitating the emergence of the necessary collective nomos. Ultimately, he despairs of this view and substitutes non-rational periods of collective effervescence for instrumental reason in his recommendations for alleviating the state of anomie. Once he recognizes the limitations of instrumental reason, Durkheim becomes exceedingly pessimistic about the prospects of effectively eliminating anomic conditions in modern society.

Writing outside the tradition of conservative positive sociology, Karl Marx and Max Weber also give very close and careful attention to the relation of reason and freedom and the impact the development of industrial capitalism had on it. Much more systematically than Durkheim,

Marx and Weber concentrate on the rationalization of society – the tendencies toward commodification, secularization, and bureaucratization – and its implications for human freedom. Marx's optimistic assessment of these developments is contrasted with Weber's more despairing evaluation in the next chapter.

3

Marx and Weber: Reason, Rationality and Emancipation

Karl Marx (1818–83) and Max Weber (1864–1920) agree that the key to understanding modern society is to be found in its rational features and rationalizing forces. They disagree substantially, however, on the character of modern rationality, the direction taken by the processes of rationalization, and the impact modern society ultimately would have on the relation of reason and freedom. For Marx, history is the movement toward greater reason and freedom, a movement which will culminate in the rise of socialism and the later evolution of communism. The rationalization of the productive forces, Marx claims, leads in a contradictory and conflict-ridden fashion to a reduction in socially necessary labor time and a corresponding increase in free time. The result of this historical process is reasonable people able to safeguard their freedom against the repressive aspects of instrumental reason. Weber rejects this view, arguing, first, that the rationalization of economic life necessarily entails the rational administration of people as well as things, and, secondly, that socialism would represent an extension and completion of the rationalizing tendencies found in industrial capitalism. The rationalization which is the fate of modern society, Weber claims, threatens to give rise to an iron cage whose rationality is without both reason and freedom.

Reason and Freedom in Marx's Theory of History

Marx's theory of history is both materialistic and dialectical. In its terms, he defines reason and freedom and the relation between them and proceeds to evaluate capitalism critically and to make a case, in the name of reason and freedom, for socialism and communism. An appreciation of Marx's treatment of reason and freedom is best begun by a consideration of his critique of Hegel.

Hegel Reversed

Hegel's idealist treatment of reason and freedom derives from his adherence to the Enlightenment belief that thought should rule society. The standards by which reality is governed should be constituted by what people believe to be true, good, and right. Despite the prevalence of highly varied, even contending, conceptions of true, good, and right, Hegel argues for the existence of universally valid principles of each. Only with their discovery will thought justifiably claim its place of prominence in the governance of reality. Taken together, these universally valid principles and ideas, expressive of what ought to be, comprise Reason. Reality and truth are defined in their terms: not everything which exists is real, only that which exists in accordance with the standards of Reason. Truth, accordingly, is a function of what should be rather than of what is. Something is true only when it has become what it can be; when, that is, it has fulfilled its inherent potentiality. Truth is a matter of self-fulfillment.

On these assumptions, Hegel regards human history as a movement toward self-fulfillment, one bound to culminate in freedom. Freedom, however, is also an idea and truly can exist only in pure thought. The movement toward freedom, then, is at one with the development of the Mind. History, in this view, is not a series of concrete occurrences and events but the ceaseless human effort to apprehend Reason – to understand what ought to be – and to change what already exists in light of this understanding. With the development of Mind, Reason – the potentiality of humanity for freedom – is ever more revealed. This knowledge of what ought to be comes to guide the transformation of the existing order, enhancing its reasonableness and freedom.

History, for Hegel, is Reason coming to consciousness of itself. Reason acquires this self-consciousness only in the mind of the free individual. Freedom is the essence of Reason, the primary, if not only, form in which Reason can be. Only by interacting with the world and finding itself there can Reason be realized, and it is realized by coming to consciousness of itself within the freely acting human subject. Reason is actualized, and what is true, good, and right is realized, in the expanding autonomy of the individual.

History as the life of Reason and freedom is fraught with conflict and struggle, but this discord is initiated and largely takes place on the level of ideas. As the standards of Reason become more completely and clearly known, new ideas, more closely approximating potentiality, contradict established ideas, and ultimately this contradiction is resolved when arrangements compatible with the new ideas replace those justified by the old. Hegel's appreciation of the contradictory character of historical development is at the base of his dialectical approach.

Very simply, dialectical analysis concentrates on the discrepancies, the tensions, the contradictions between actuality (what already exists) and potentiality (what should be). The master assumption of this view is that everything is always undergoing change and movement, is always in the process of becoming something else – becoming its opposite. A is always in the process of becoming non-A, actuality moving toward its opposite, potentiality, what is becoming what ought to be. Reality, then, is a unity of opposites, for that which already exists has potentiality; it contains the basis of that which does not yet but should exist. Reality, in short, is contradictory. For Hegel, contradictions are ideational in character. What ought to be is given by the spirit of Reason; what is is represented by existing ideas. The resolution of the contradiction between the two takes the form of new ideas which have a truth-value higher than that of the old ideas. In terms of these ideas, concrete social changes are made.

Marx finds considerable merit in Hegel's dialectical approach, but regards the idealist assumptions on which it rests as profoundly mistaken. Hegel must be set 'right side up', and this requires the substitution of materialist for idealist assumptions. Following Ludwig Feuerbach, Marx insists that the understanding of history must start with real people living in the real material world. Ideas, thoughts, and spirit emanate from material existence; they are not real but simply reflections of what is real. 'It is not the consciousness of men that determines their existence', Marx (1970, p. 21) writes, 'but their social existence that determines their consciousness.' Ideas are a function of the way people make a living. Accordingly, the effort to understand history must begin with real human beings and their efforts to exist in the world. What people do is crucial, not what they think.

While accepting Feuerbach's materialist premises, Marx rejects his claim that something is real only if it exists empirically and is subject to sense-experience. Here, Marx sides with Hegel to argue against sense-certainty as the ultimate criterion of truth. In effect, Marx's effort is to invert Hegel's dialectic so that its categories and assumptions make reference to the concrete activity of people. Thus contradiction and conflict are expressed not on the level of ideas but in the relationship between the dominant class (whose interest is to preserve that which already exists) and an oppressed class (whose interests are satisfiable only in those arrangements which do not yet but should exist). Actuality is represented concretely and materially by one class, potentiality by another. What negates the established arrangements is not the idea of what ought to be but concrete socio-historical conditions.

Similarly, Marx's materialist dialectic gives reason and freedom a materialist basis. Reason is grounded in the objectification process of human labor. Freedom is associated with the social organization of that labor – the mode of production – and varies inversely with the rate of socially necessary labor time. Like Hegel, Marx regards history as the life of reason and freedom. Unlike Hegel, Marx locates this history in the way people socially produce the material conditions of their existence.

Marx's theory of history

Marx's master assumption, the root of both his materialism and his dialectical approach, is that people make society and society, in turn, makes people. As the active creators of their social existence, people are limited by previous social constructions. 'Men make their own history', Marx (1963, p. 15) asserts, 'but they do not make it just as they please; they do not make it under circumstances chosen by themselves, but under circumstances directly encountered, given and transmitted from the past.' Joining together person and society in this mutually influencing interaction is productive activity. Societies are socially produced; they are the result of human labor. The 'first premise of all human existence and, therefore, of all history ... [is] that men must be in a position to live in order to be able to "make history". But life involves before everything else eating and drinking, a habitation, clothing and many other things. The first historical act is thus the production of the means to satisfy these needs, the production of material life itself' (Marx and Engels, 1970a, p. 48). To satisfy their needs, people develop productive capacities and forces and these shape the social relations people have. 'The totality of these relations of production constitutes the economic structure of society, the real foundation, on which arises a legal and political superstructure and to which correspond definite forms of social consciousness. The mode of production of material life conditions the general process of social, political, and intellectual life' (Marx, 1970, p. 20). Society thus consists of an economic structure or mode of production – the forces of production and the social relations appropriate to them – and a superstructure comprised of the dominant ideas which influence individual consciousness.

As people construct society, they simultaneously make history. For Marx, history is the 'process of the continuous creation, satisfaction, and re-creation of human needs' (Giddens, 1971a, p. 22). A particular mode of production becomes obsolete once it accomplishes the satisfaction of needs for which it was developed. With the gratification of these needs, a new and higher set of needs emerges. These new needs give material expression to what should be. They come into contradiction with the already existing productive order, for their satisfaction requires the creation of a qualitatively improved mode of production. Once the more highly developed productive arrangements meet the new needs, still newer needs arise (expressive of greater potentiality), again necessitating the qualitative transformation of society. In short, in the social production of their existence, people change themselves (their needs) and their society (beginning with the mode of production) and these changes are what the making of history is all about.

Clearly, human labor is at the very center of Marx's view. Through their labor, people do not simply produce the means of their existence. Beyond this, they fulfill their potentialities, they realize themselves as human beings. Indispensable to self-fulfillment and realization is the objectifying character of human labor. As humans go about satisfying their needs, they objectify their essential powers by projecting them on to socially produced objects, the consumption of which brings need-satisfaction. The objects come to express the human powers that went into their construction. Through objectification nature is humanized, brought into the socially constructed world where it serves human purposes. In the same way, people are humanized, their lower, animal-like needs giving way to higher, more fully human needs. More to the point, reason is grounded in the process of objectification.

Objectification enhances self-control and self-reflection, the two key aspects of reason. In their objectified form, human powers are more easily seen and felt. People find themselves in the objects they produce, yet they do so at a distance which allows them to reflect upon their powers and the uses to which they should be put. At the same time, the experience permits them to recognize the transformative effect of their actions. People learn that they have the capacity to control nature for human purposes. Reason as self-control guided by self-reflection is thus made possible by objectification. To become more reasonable, Robert Paul Wolff (1968, p. 90) observes, 'means to transform into ends things which previously were not ends. A man becomes more [reasonable] just insofar as he brings within the scope of his will some datum of experience which previously confronted him as independent of his will.' As more and more of the world is humanized, so to that extent does it become open to human control and reflection. As a consequence, people are better able to recognize both their needs and potentialities and their capacity to make history in a way compatible with them.

The process of objectification and need-satisfaction and recreation are the basis of the movement from natural man to species man (Ollman, 1971, pp. 75–115). Man's natural powers and needs are those he has in common with other animals. In contrast, his species powers and needs are distinctively human and only with their fulfillment does man become himself. As a natural being, man, like other animals, strives to satisfy his physical needs. He does what he does as a matter of necessity, under the compulsion of physical need, and without awareness and reflection. Once man has realized his species character – free and conscious activity – all this changes. As a species-being, man's productive activity and thus his history is made an object of his will and consciousness. Species man acts not merely out of compulsion but as a self-determining and self-reflecting productive being. Species man is man become himself, and represents the culmination of the historical movement toward self-fulfillment.

Obviously, the gradual shift from natural man to species man involves the movement from the realm of necessity to the realm of freedom. Freedom, like reason, is grounded in the material world by Marx. Simply, freedom expands as socially necessary labor time – the time for the production of goods and services necessary for existence – contracts. With each new mode of production, socially necessary labor time is reduced and free time correspondingly enlarged. The shift away from necessity and toward freedom which accompanies the advancement of the mode of production brings people greater control over nature, themselves, and the course of human evolution.

Underlying this progressive movement, according to Marx, is the contradiction that arises in modes of production between the productive forces and the relations of production. The productive forces undergo continuous improvement and reach a point where they come into conflict with the established social relations. In other words, the forces of production outrun, or make obsolete, the relations of production in the sense that the potential for greater freedom found in the more technologically developed productive forces can be realized only with the creation of new social relations. In this way, quantitative changes – the measurable technological improvements of the productive forces – give rise to qualitative change – the transformation of social interaction. Each successive mode of production, then, represents a qualitative advancement over its predecessor.

Marx begins his analysis of this movement with what he calls primitive communism. Primitive societies were characterized by a communal mode of production. The basic means of production – land – was collectively owned. As a consequence, these societies were classless, democratic, and egalitarian. It would be wrong, however, to romanticize life in these societies, for in the presence of the least technologically developed productive capacities, work was tedious, hard, and often unrewarding, diets were frequently inadequate, and the life-span usually short. Primitive societies initially engaged in hunting and gathering and subsisted on the uneven provisions of nature. While there were no classes, everyone was dependent on nature and, in effect, a slave to necessity. Under the pressure of population increase, the technological basis of these societies gradually improved. The result was a permanent surplus which made possible a more settled existence. Horticulture, the cultivation of food, and animal herding replaced hunting and gathering as the primary productive activities. As skill, knowledge, and technology continued to advance in the form of crop cultivation, soil fertilization, and metallurgy, food supply and economic surplus expanded.

The production of surplus gave rise to a division between direct producers and those involved in non-producing, supervisory activities, for the former now had the technological capacity to produce for the latter as well as themselves. From this division of labor emerged the class societies – the slave, feudal, and capitalist modes of production – which followed primitive communism. The emergence of class society was a progressive development for it signified the expansion of the realm of freedom. 'Primitive societies', write Howard Sherman and James Wood (1979, p. 357), 'create neither pyramids nor vast irrigation projects; neither Plato's philosophy nor Euclid's geometry.' The creation of each requires that some people be free from the necessity of direct production and this freedom from necessity is brought about by advances in the mode of production that permit more and more people to devote less and less time to socially necessary labor.

At their highest level of development, primitive societies were highly specialized and, as a result, reliant on other equally specialized societies. This reliance came to take the form of both commerce and conquest and enslavement. Taking the members of a conquered society as slaves was made possible by the technological development of the productive forces for it makes sense to keep slaves only when they are able to produce a surplus for their owners. Primitive communism was replaced by a new mode of production, slavery, characterized by the private ownership of land and people. Communal, democratic, and egalitarian relations of production gave way to class relations between masters (non-producers) and slaves (direct producers) who produced the surplus which supported their owners. Slavery was superior to primitive communism in that its mode of production provided freedom to a larger number of people. In primitive communism everyone was a slave to necessity; in slave society some – the masters – are free. Similarly, the feudal mode of production which subsequently arose was an improvement over slavery. In feudalism, the non-producers or lords controlled but did not own in body the direct producers or serfs. Though bound to the land through a series of feudal obligations, the serfs possessed a far greater degree of autonomy than did their counterparts under slavery.

As the technological development of the productive forces proceeded, serfs in ever increasing numbers were forced from the land. Without their own means of production, they made a living by selling their labor power to those who privately held these means in the form of capital – land, factories, equipment. The capitalist mode of production succeeded the feudal mode, and its development further enlarged the realm of freedom. There were more non-producers (capitalists) here than in the previous modes and, furthermore, the direct producers or proletarians had substantially greater formal freedoms than had any previous group of direct producers. But, Marx argues, as with the earlier modes of production, capitalism will promote the development of the productive forces to a point where they will contradict capitalist social relations. The tremendous potential embedded in the productive forces developed by capitalism will be realized only with the creation of socialist social relations, which require the elimination of private ownership and social classes. In socialism and in the advanced communism that will peacefully evolve from it, the realm of freedom will have been enlarged to such an extent that people will make their productive activity the object of their will and consciousness. In these circumstances, man becomes himself, reasonable and free. Marx's defense of socialism and communism, discussed in greater detail below, is a defense of reason and freedom.

In contrast to Hegel, Marx treats reason and freedom in very concrete terms, locating each in human productive activity. As the productive forces are rationalized, life becomes for increasing numbers of people more reasonable, more under the sway of self-reflection and self-control, and more free. In this light, Marx views the capitalist mode of production as superior to those that preceded it. Nevertheless, at the time he wrote, Marx regarded this once progressive force as an obstacle to the further movement toward reason and freedom promised by socialism and communism.

Reason and Freedom in Capitalism

Marx argues that capitalism is organized around the alienation of labor and perverts the objectification process to such an extent that labor becomes an obstacle to, no longer the basis of, the growth of reason. Fuelled by the exploitation of alienated labor, the development of capitalist productive forces follows a course of proletarianization which obstructs the exercise of formal freedoms. Capitalism is incapable of realizing the tremendous possibilities for the growth of reason and freedom it creates.

Marx's chief criticism of the capitalist mode of production is that it systematically promotes and strengthens the basis of alienated labor. It thus distorts the one activity through which human self-realization is able to take place. Alienated labor, as Marx (1964, p. 110) describes it, 'is *external* to the worker, i.e., it does not belong to his essential being; ... in his work, therefore, he does not affirm himself but denies himself, does not feel content but unhappy, does not develop freely his physical and mental energy but mortifies his body and ruins his mind.' Alienated labor results from the distortion of the process of objectification. In their productive activity, people continue to objectify their human powers but these powers are no longer experienced as their own. Rather, these powers and the objects they constitute are experienced as alien or foreign forces beyond the control of people. People lose sight of the connection between their labor and the objects created by that labor. They no longer find themselves in these objects. Indeed, people become slaves to these objects, to their powers experienced in alienated form. 'The _alienation_ of the worker in his product', Marx (ibid., p. 108) states, 'means not only that his labor becomes an object, an _external_ existence, but that it exists _outside him_, independently, as something alien to him and that it becomes a power on its own confronting him. It means that the life which he has conferred on the object confronts him as something hostile and alien.'

The expanse of alienated labor is broad including as it does the totality of social relations in capitalism. The worker loses control of the product which is appropriated by and produced to satisfy the needs of others. Productive activity also is under the control of others. Stripped of intrinsic meaning, productive activity becomes for the worker merely a necessary means for making a living. In addition, workers are alienated from one another and from their species-being, caught in a labor process where they are unable to express their social character and develop their full abilities. Man is alienated from himself.

Marx identifies three conditions of the capitalist mode of production which he takes to be the primary contributors to the alienation of labor: the division of labor, the market system, and the institution of private property. The division of labor in capitalism divides work tasks into narrowly defined, routine roles whose incumbents in turn are divided, allowed to develop only those limited capacities required for the adequate performance of their roles. These detailed laborers have imposed on them the activities they undertake. Characterized by a separation of mental and manual labor and by a tendency toward job simplification and deskilling (both of which facilitate mechanization and, in turn, the subordination of the worker to the demands of machine technology), the capitalist division of labor dehumanizes as it prevents workers from fully exercising all their capabilities – that is, as it alienates them from their unused human potentialities.

Governed by seemingly impersonal and objective economic laws beyond human control, the capitalist market transforms labor into a commodity. In the commodity form, labor is no longer experienced as a life-power. Under the market system, producers as wage laborers are compelled to disregard the human needs their products do or do not satisfy in order to concentrate on the saleability – the market or exchange value – of their products. The commodification of labor is also advanced by the capitalist set of property relations which entails private ownership of the productive forces. Under the system of private property, control over the productive process and the product belongs not to the producers but to those who own the means of production. Private property is both an expression of and a means of furthering alienated labor. On the one hand, Marx (ibid., p. 117) observes, private property 'is the *product* of alienated labor, and ... on the other it is the *means* by which labor alienates itself, the *realization of this alienation*'. Wage laborers possess private property in the form of their labor-power. Separated from the means of production, they are constrained to surrender their control over their labor-power. To make a living, they must exchange this commodity for a wage. In capitalism, then, labor, like other private property, is alienable. Wage labor represents the realization of this possibility; wage labor is alienated labor.

Corrupted by these defining components of the capitalist mode of production, the labor process becomes an avenue of self-denial and obstructs the cultivation of human reason, blocks the development of the intellectual faculties, awareness, consciousness and will that set people apart from the rest of the animal world. Alienated labor makes people less human. 'What is animal becomes human', Marx (ibid., p. 11) claims, 'and what is human becomes animal.'

Freedom, like reason, is debased in capitalism. Like those before it, the capitalist mode of production is exploitative. The non-producing capitalists make their living by extracting the surplus directly produced by the proletariat. Indeed, this surplus value is the source of profit. In light of the aim of profit-maximization, the profit brought by exploitation is invested in the rationalization of the productive forces (on the assumption that technological improvement increases efficiency, productivity, and profitability). Underlying the rationalization of the productive forces in capitalism is the process of proletarianization, which combines appropriation with centralization. More and more people have taken from them their means of production which, then, are placed in the hands of a smaller group comprised of those able to afford the increasingly more expensive productive forces. As capitalism develops, greater numbers of people are forced to become wage laborers or proletarians. By stripping people of their means of production, the process of proletarianization concretely limits their exercise of freedom and enlarges the pool of exploitable labor. But, Marx argues, this limitation occurs with respect to a freedom already constrained by the institution of private property.

Capitalist economies are predicated on private property. At the center of capitalism is the freedom to buy and sell, and people exercise this freedom only with regard to what they privately own or come to own. By locating freedom in the institution of private property, capitalism withholds it precisely as it is granted. For the giving of property rights to certain goods to one person precludes all other people from freely using those goods. Accordingly, G. A. Cohen (1979, p. 16) argues, capitalism 'does not protect liberty in general, but only those liberties built into private property, an institution which also limits liberty'.

Marx treats the question of human freedom in terms of man's relation to nature, to others, and to himself. How does a given form of property-relations, he asks, contribute to or detract from man's freedom from natural necessity, freedom from interference from others, and freedom to develop his essential powers? Focusing on capitalist property-relations, Marx argues that while they doubtlessly encourage a significant extension of technological control over nature, they also subject people to the experience of alienation. The necessity of obeying nature is replaced by the necessity of obeying the products of alienated labor: the state, the market, and God. More clearly, the necessity of working for others is a constitutive feature of capitalism. Furthermore, while capitalism has undermined political bondage and other bases of forceful intervention in people's lives, the institution of private property enables owners to interfere with the freedom of non-owners to benefit from their property. Finally, capitalist property-relations foster a division of labor and a labor process which prevent the worker from comprehensively developing his human capacities. The worker does not exercise his essential powers in these circumstances; rather, he becomes alienated from them. In all these ways, capitalist property-relations constitute 'the negation of human freedom' (Meszaros, 1970, p. 154).

In capitalism the degradation of labor occurs alongside the progressive development of the productive forces. Labor's capacity to make people reasonable and free is held in check so as not to impede the pursuit of profit. Yet, this very pursuit of profit is indispensable to the extraordinary growth of the productive forces in capitalism. Under capitalism, Marx argues, the productive forces have been developed to the extent where they make possible the reduction of socially necessary labor time for all. This potential for expanded freedom, however, cannot be realized within the context of capitalist social relations, for such realization requires the abolition of private property and the elimination of the class structure. In the presence of capitalist property-relations, the reduction of socially necessary labor time expands not freedom but the rate of unemployment. A contradiction arises between the potentiality of capitalist productive forces and the existing property-relations of capitalism.

Marx is fairly confident that this contradiction will be recognized as the process of proletarianization introduces more and more people to the ranks of the immiserated. As the objective conditions of their life worsen, members of the proletariat will acquire a class consciousness through which they will understand the necessity to become free, the need to realize the potential residing in the forces of production by struggling to create a socialist mode of production. Class consciousness is true consciousness in that it enables its possessors to cut through illusory appearances to discover, first, the existing bases of their misery, second, their capacity to alter these bases, and third, what can be or what the established mode of production makes possible. Class consciousness is the equivalent of Hegel's Reason. In its terms what should be becomes conscious of itself; man begins to recognize himself as species-man.

For Marx, the struggle which moves the transition from the capitalist to the socialist mode of production will be led by the class conscious proletariat. A direct outgrowth of the rise and development of capitalism, the proletariat is fundamentally different from all other social classes in that it is always progressive. The proletariat's uniqueness is that

> to realize its own individual interests, it must bring about the total destruction of the class structure. The complete abolition of class distinctions ... is its vested interest. In this way, its special interest becomes coextensive with the common interest of mankind – to free itself from the inhuman, alienating social situation generated by the existence of class structure, to attain universal human emancipation. (Sztompka, 1979, p. 237)

Two important implications reside in this argument. First, potentiality is represented by the objective interests of the proletariat; these interests are the material ground of reason and freedom. Knowledge of reality – of the existing order and the emerging order which arises from and contradicts it – is achieved from the standpoint of proletariat interests. Second, the proletariat revolution will be the final revolution for it will eliminate the basis of class society and thereby the source of class repression and class struggle.

Reason and Freedom in Socialism and Communism
Communism is described eloquently by Marx as:

> the *positive* transcendence of *private property*, or *human self-estrangement*, and therefore as the real *appropriation of the human essence* by and for man; communism therefore as the complete returning of man to himself as a *social* (i.e., human) being – a return become conscious, and accomplished within the entire wealth of previous development ... [It] is the *genuine* resolution of the conflict between man and nature and between man and man – the true resolution of the strife between ... freedom and necessity ... Communism is the riddle of history solved, and it knows itself to be this solution. (Marx, 1964, p. 135)

In communism, people acquire the freedom to make their history as they choose, and their choice will be made reasonably, with self-control and self-reflection.

Communism will emerge naturally from the socialist mode of production instituted with the demise of capitalism. Marx regards socialism as a transitional stage between capitalism and communism, one required by the continued presence of capitalist tendencies, inclinations, and attitudes. During the socialist stage, the primary objectives are the elimination of these remnants of capitalism and the establishment of the material foundation of communism.

In Marx's view, the socialist mode of production is characterized by collective ownership of the decisive forces of production; comprehensive planning of the economy to assure the availability of socially useful though economically unprofitable goods and services; and workers' control over the organization of production and the division of labor. Associated with these features is the dictatorship of the proletariat, the most distinctive structural aspect of socialism. Any political state is a dictatorship in Marx's terms. Socialism requires a centralized and coercive state to accomplish the goals mentioned above. However, the socialist dictatorship differs from all previous ones in two fundamental ways. First, it is a dictatorship of the majority; it operates to satisfy the interests of the proletariat where earlier states defended the privileges and the interests of the ruling minority. Second, the dictatorship of the proletariat guides a process of development which will culminate in the disappearance of the state. Other states strive to reproduce themselves; the socialist state seeks to 'wither away'. Toward this end, the socialist state is responsible for the immediate implementation of the following measures.

1. Abolition of property in land and application of all rents of land to public purposes. 2. A heavy progressive or graduated income tax. 3. Abolition of all rights of inheritance. 4. Confiscation of the property of all emigrants and rebels. 5. Centralization of credit in the hands of the State, by means of a national bank with State capital and as exclusive monopoly. 6. Centralization of the means of communication and transport in the hands of the State. 7. Extension of factories and instruments of production owned by the State; the bringing into cultivation of waste lands, and the improvement of the soil generally in accordance with a common plan. 8. Equal liability of all to labour ... 9. Combination of agriculture with manufacturing industries ... 10. Free education for all children in public schools. Abolition of children's factory labour in its present form. (Marx and Engels, 1970b, pp. 57–8)

Implied in these measures is the imperative to move dramatically, though not completely at this stage, from market to plan and from private to collective ownership, and in the process to continue the productive advances begun under capitalism. Absolutely crucial to this movement is the fortification of the social bases of equality. Distribution by the principle 'from each according to his ability, to each according to his needs' awaits the rise of communism. In socialism, deductions from the total social product are to be made in order, first, to replace worn out or used up means of production; second, to advance the productive forces; third, to create a reserve fund as protection against accidents and disasters; and, fourth, to provide for the satisfaction of social needs (for example education, medical care, housing and diet). What remains is available for individual consumption and can be distributed according to any number of criteria (Marx, 1966b, pp. 6–10). This distributive scheme provides equality of condition by establishing a level of social consumption below which no one may fall. Those goods and services necessary for freedom cannot be bought and sold; they are acquired by everyone equally. Other goods and services, say, a yacht or piano lessons, can be purchased by funds people earn by working longer hours or in dangerous, onerous, or difficult jobs. Whether or not people do this is their own decision, for equality of condition permits people to choose freely how they will make use of their free time. Guaranteed the basic conditions of a decent life, people will become, over time, more reasonable and free and eventually make unnecessary the centralized guidance proferred by the dictatorship of the proletariat. The dissolution of the dictatorship will occur simultaneously with the emergence of communism.

The evolution to communism will be initiated by the accomplishments of socialism, particularly the extirpation of capitalist tendencies and personality traits and the unprecedented technological development of the productive forces. By bringing about an abundance of material goods, the humanization of the workplace and the reduction of working hours, these achievements provide the material basis of communism.

In communism, private property will be completely abolished, replaced by a 'community of goods' in terms of which 'we shall have the utilization of all the instruments of production and the distribution of the products among all members of society by common agreement' (Engels, 1981, p. 456). With the elimination of private ownership, industrial and agricultural production will increase to 'provide a quantity of products sufficient to gratify the needs of all' (ibid., p. 458). The detailed division of labor which subdivides people and permits the development of only limited capacities will be dismantled. Occupational differences will disappear and so too will differences based upon religion, race, nation, and family. Social relationships will become highly cooperative and intrinsically satisfying and the need for external forms of coercion, control, and discipline will cease to exist.

Most importantly, in these circumstances labor will become the object of will and consciousness. In communism, Marx (1981a, p. 435) writes, 'my labour would be a *free manifestation of life* and an *enjoyment of life...* Furthermore, in my labour the *particularity* of my individuality would be affirmed because my individual life is affirmed. Labour then would be *true, active property.*' Labor will become a mode of self-realization, and productive activity something people will wish to engage in. Nevertheless, productive activity in communism will remain in the realm of necessity for people must always work in order to live. Marx (1981b, pp. 464–5) makes the point this way:

> The freedom in this field cannot consist of anything else but the fact that socialized man, the associated producers, regulate their interchange with nature rationally, bring it under their common control, instead of being ruled by it as by some blind power; that they accomplish their task with the least expenditure of energy and under conditions most adequate to their human nature and most worthy of it. But it always remains a realm of necessity. Beyond it begins that development of human power, which is its own end, the true realm of freedom, which, however, can flourish only upon that realm of necessity as its basis.

In communism, the realm of necessity will be reduced and the realm of freedom expanded as far as possible and the socially necessary labor which remains, far from constituting an obstacle to freedom, will be a 'free manifestation and affirmation of individual life'.

Against this background, Marx claims that communism will enable the full and conscious restoration of man to himself. With this restoration will come the individual, in Bertell Ollman's (1977, p. 80) words,

> who is highly and consistently cooperative, who conceives of all objects in terms of 'ours', who shares with his fellow men a masterful control over the forces of nature, who regulates his activities without the help of externally imposed rules, and who is indistinguishable from his fellows when viewed from the perspective of existing social divisions. He (she) is, in short, a brilliant, highly rational and socialized, humane, and successful creator.

In the life of this individual, reason and freedom will come together.

Marx is firmly optimistic about the future course of history. While unrelentingly critical of the suffering caused by the capitalist mode of production, Marx regards capitalism as vastly superior to previous socioeconomic formations. After charging the bourgeoisie with having 'left remaining no other nexus between man and man than naked self-interest ..., [having] substituted naked, shameless, direct, brutal exploitation' for exploitation veiled by religious and political illusion, Marx and Engels (1970b, pp. 33–4) go on to insist that the capitalist mode of production the bourgeoisie have advanced 'has been the first to show what man's activity can bring about. It has accomplished wonders far surpassing Egyptian pyramids, Roman aqueducts and Gothic cathedrals.' Capitalism undermines ancient prejudices and rescues a substantial segment of the population from the 'idiocy of rural life', it destroys local seclusion and backwardness, obliterates national narrow-mindedness, and 'draws all, even the most barbarian, ... into civilization' (ibid., p. 36). According to Marx and Engels (ibid., pp. 34–5), these progressive qualities are to be understood simply with respect to the fact that the 'bourgeoisie cannot exist without constantly revolutionizing the instruments of production, and with them the whole relations of society ... constant revolutionizing of production ... distinguish[es] the bourgeois epoch from all earlier ones ... All that is solid melts into air, all that is holy is profaned, and man is at last compelled to face with sober senses his real conditions of life, and his relations with his kind.' By advancing the productive forces more extensively 'than have all preceding generations together', the bourgeoisie have established the potential for substantially reducing socially necessary labor time. The realization of this potential awaits the rise of socialism and communism. Currently, in the midst of capitalist property relations, this basis for a more decent society is expressed not as potentiality but as irrationality. For the developed productive forces are used to further exploitation, alienation and 'free time' in the form of unemployment. But just as the bourgeoisie arose to resolve the contradictions of feudalism, so will the proletariat emerge to overcome the irrationality of capitalism.

Weber's assessment of future prospects is not as hopeful as Marx's. Indeed, in important places it is harsh and bleak. Weber, too, sees a connection between reason and freedom, but one which leads in the direction of rational domination, not human emancipation.

Reason and Freedom in Weber's Theory

'The reason envisaged by Weber', Marcuse (1968, p. 205) notes, is '*technical* reason, [involved in] the production and transformation of material (things and men) through the methodical-scientific apparatus. This apparatus has been built with the aim of calculable efficiency; its rationality organizes and controls things and men, factory and bureaucracy, work and leisure.' For Weber, reason or Western rationalism appears in the modern world as a technical rationality which brings to the selection of means of action methodical calculation, quantification, and predictability. Action which occurs consistent with this rationality is rational. Rational action, as Weber defines it, involves choosing the most appropriate means available for the achievement of a given goal. Purposive, planned, and calculated, rational action is predicated upon the separation of means and ends and, on another level, facts and values. Means and facts are subject to rational assessment and organization; values and ends are not. As sentiment, feeling, and custom are subordinated to deliberate calculation, rational action proceeds. Weber takes its development as the fundamental characteristic of modern society.

Daniel Levine notes that rational action is manifested both subjectively and objectively. Subjective rationality is located in the mental processes of actors and 'is taken to refer to action that is conscious and deliberate ... and/or action that is oriented to means that are *regarded* as correct for a given end' (Levine, 1981, p. 10). Objective rationality resides in institutionalized courses of action and refers 'to action that uses technically correct means in accord with scientific knowledge and/or has been subjected to some process of external systematization' (ibid., p. 10). In each case, the emphasis is on the exact calculation of appropriate means for the efficient and methodical acquisition of a given end.

Weber frequently argues that rational action is an indispensable basis of freedom. He regards the institutional forms of objective rationality as conducive to equality before the law, the protection of individual rights and the creation of a free labor market. Similarly, he takes subjective rationality to be an essential precondition of freedom of choice, particularly when compared to mental processes dominated by tradition or emotion. 'The characteristic of incalculability', Weber (1949, pp. 124–5) writes,

is the privilege of – the insane. On the other hand, we associate the highest measure of an empirical 'feeling of freedom' with those actions which we are conscious of performing rationally – i.e., *in the absence of physical and psychic 'coercion', emotional 'affects' and accidental disturbances of the clarity of judgment,* in which we pursue a clearly perceived end by 'means' which are the most adequate in accordance with the extent of our knowledge, i.e., in accordance with empirical *rules.*

Weber's position seems clear enough: the growth of rational action makes for an increase in freedom. Yet this position is at odds with Weber's other, more fully elaborated claim that the spread of rational action –

rationalization – restricts human freedom by enslaving people in a cold, impersonal, rationally insensitive iron cage.

Calculability, predictability, and methodical routine are the key consequences of rationalization. Increased rationalization, in Weber's (1946, p. 139) words, 'means that principally there are no mysterious incalculable forces that come into play, but rather that one can, in principle, master all things by calculation … One need no longer have recourse to magical means in order to master or implore the spirits, as did the savage, for whom such mysterious powers existed. Technical means and calculations perform the service.' With rationalization, criteria of rational decision-making and instrumental action are injected into increasingly larger areas of social life. The demystification of beliefs, the disenchantment of nature, the secularization of meaning, the scientization of thought, the formalization of law and organization – all are accomplished in the name of rationalization. Fostering a stronger reliance on instrumental criteria and technical control, rationalization shields the processes of work and decision-making from non-rational pressures and considerations. It entails the separation of the home, sentiment and politics from work, calculation and administration on which the journey to the modern world is initiated. The technical efficiency and material progress promised by rationalization, Weber points out, require a new form of domination, one where human freedom is restricted by the chains of impersonal procedure and formal rules of conduct.

The Origin and Spread of Rationalization
In the doctrines of ascetic Protestantism formulated in the sixteenth and seventeenth centuries Weber finds the source of the capitalist spirit – the rational attitude, ethic, and orientation to everyday life peculiar to the modern era. The capitalist spirit values hard, steady work and deems success in this area a sign of moral rectitude and personal virtue. A methodically disciplined life is both the key to this success and intrinsically proper and right, particularly as it has people forego immediate pleasure for future gain. By accounting for the spirit of capitalism with reference to the ethic of Protestantism, Weber gives considerably more attention to the role of ideas in the making of history than does Marx. He does so, however, while recognizing the importance of material conditions. Weber argues that the rationalism embedded in the Protestant ethic furthered the already continuing development of the material conditions of modern capitalism.

In his *General Economic History*, Weber (1927, pp. 276–7) identifies six essential conditions of rational capitalist enterprise: 'The appropriation of all physical means of production … as disposable property of autonomous private industrial enterprises'; 'freedom of the market';

'rational technology, ... one reduced to calculation to the largest possible degree, which implies mechanization'; 'calculable adjudication and administration'; 'free labor – persons must be present who are not only legally in the position, but also are economically compelled, to sell their labor on the market without restriction'; 'the commercialization of economic life'. To one degree or another, these conditions had been developing in various areas throughout the globe. However, Weber claims, they first appeared in modern rational capitalism where the religious ethic of ascetic Protestantism prevailed.

According to Weber, the Protestant ethic was instrumental in weakening traditional opposition to the development of the material bases of rational capitalism. It dissolved both the older religious resistance to commercial profit-making and the long-established popular indifference towards making money for the sake of making money, and provided in their stead a religious sanctification of the profit-motive and achievement-orientation. Along the way, the Protestant ethic inculcated in people the personality traits necessary for economic success and achievement. Weber finds this ethic most forcefully expressed in the beliefs of Calvinism.

At the center of Calvinism is the belief in an absolute, infinite God, a God who has predestined each of us, at the moment of our birth, to be among the elect or the damned. We can never know for certain what our fate is, nor is it possible through the performance of good works to change the status God has determined for us. The only thing we are sure of is that man has been placed on earth to create God's kingdom, and this requires constant and hard work. Leisure and luxury, idleness and vanity, detract from hard work and methodical habits and thus are sinful. Clearly, these beliefs promote 'intense worldly activity' and the methodical organization of life appropriate to such activity.

The logical outcome of adherence to these beliefs appears to be fatalism – if nothing can be done to alter one's fate, why try? Weber argues, however, that the result was just the reverse, for steady, disciplined, reliable work was tied 'to faith such that only the systematic and relentless practice of appropriate worldly activity can permit the individual to draw the conclusion that his or her faith is true and therefore saving ... [As a result] the psychological consequences of Calvinism are made dynamic rather than passive' (Marshall, 1982, p. 75). Hard work, as the way people both demonstrated to themselves the depth of their faith and minimized the anxiety they experienced as a consequence of not knowing their fate, is thus encouraged. In the same way, Calvinism encouraged curtailed consumption, forced savings and reinvestment and promoted a code of conduct suitable to rational capitalist enterprise. In Weber's (1958, p. 172, p. 174) words, the religious valuation of restless, continuous, systematic work in a worldly calling, as the highest means to asceticism, and at the same time the surest and most evident proof of rebirth and genuine faith, must have been the most powerful conceivable lever for the expansion of that attitude toward life which we have here called the spirit of capitalism. When the limitation of consumption is combined with this release of acquisitive activity, the inevitable practical result is obvious: accumulation of capital through ascetic compulsion to save ... [Yet,] much more important than the mere encouragement of capital accumulation, it favoured the development of a rational bourgeois economic life: it was the most important and above all the only consistent influence in the development of that life. It stood at the cradle of the modern economic man.

The rationality which resides at the core of the capitalist spirit and which is the fundamental basis of the development of modern society received its first systematic expression in ascetic Protestantism. At bottom, ascetic Protestantism provided the context for the cultivation of rational action.

Weber regards the religious ethic of ascetic Protestantism as a major 'turning point of the whole cultural development of the West' (Schlucter, 1981, p. 143). The other-worldly asceticism characteristic of other religions defined religious self-sacrifice in terms which took people from this world and saw secular self-denial as the moral equivalent of purely religious pain and sacrifice. 'Only ascetic Protestantism', Weber (1968, p. 630) writes, 'completely eliminated magic and the supernatural quest for salvation, of which the highest form was intellectualist, contemplative illumination. It alone created the religious motivation for seeking salvation primarily through immersion in one's worldly vocation.' The ethical principles of this-worldly asceticism, clearly manifested in the beliefs of Calvinism, are: 'diligence in worldly callings or vocations; strict asceticism with respect to the use of material goods and the indulgence of worldly pleasures; and systematic use of time' (Marshall, 1982, p. 71). In their terms, the 'godly life' was available to all who engaged in hard, reliable, and methodical work, to all who denied themselves the pleasures of this world in order better to practice their faith and contribute to the making of God's kingdom on earth.

Ascetic Protestantism is most significant in its justification of rational outlook and rational action, each of which contributed mightily to the development of capitalism. As capitalism expanded – as it became more rationalized – this justification was shed of its religious trappings and became embedded in the 'spirit of capitalism'. In this secularized form, it promoted the further rationalization of social life, most particularly through the process of bureaucratization.

Weber sees modern bureaucracy as the foremost social expression of formal rationality. Formal rationality designates 'the extent of quantitative calculation or accounting which is technically possible and which is actually applied' (Weber, 1968, p. 85). Exclusively concerned with means, formal rationality fosters a procedural as opposed to moral outlook. Based on the separation of rulers from rules, of people from positions, and of sentiment and beliefs from procedures and regulations, formally rational bureaucracy exhibits a centralized, specialized, and hierarchical structure which, by demoralizing and impersonalizing, severs performance from dependence on the non-rational and the irrational, and thereby promotes technical efficiency and effectiveness. The vast technical superiority which bureaucracy possesses over other forms of organization is the decisive fact underlying its steady, uninterrupted advance.

'Precision, speed, unambiguity, knowledge of files, continuity, unity, strict subordination, reduction of friction, and of material and personal costs', asserts Weber (1946, pp. 214–16), 'These are raised to the optimum point in the strictly bureaucratic administration ... Bureaucracy offers the attitudes demanded by the external apparatus of modern culture in the most favorable combination.' Given these capacities, bureaucracy is the most appropriate organizational form for modern capitalism 'which demands the official business of administration be discharged precisely, unambiguously, continuously, and with as much speed as possible' (ibid., p. 215). The logic of bureaucracy is highly compatible with that of capital accounting, and both succeed to the extent they are able to eliminate 'from official business love, hatred, and all purely personal, irrational, and emotional elements which escape calculation' (Weber, 1968, p. 975). Capable of efficient coordination in the face of complex problems and consituted by rationally determined rules which prescribe the immediate and long-range (or career) actions expected of members, bureaucracy is furthered by and furthers the spread of rationalization.

In Weber's view, bureaucracy is above all a structure of rational domination. The 'maximum of formal rationality in capital accounting', Weber claims, 'is possible only where workers are subjected to domination by entrepreneurs' (ibid., p. 138). Entrepreneurial domination is most rational when bureaucratic in form. 'Rationally regulated association within a structure of domination finds its typical expression in bureaucracy ... [where] the discharge of business [occurs] according to calculable rules and "without regard for persons"' (ibid., pp. 954, 975). Domination in bureaucracy rests on rational-legal authority with respect to which power is legitimate only when its exercise is consistent with the formal, impersonal rules and regulations which define the organization. In this setting, people give their allegiance not to ultimate values or particular individuals but to the organization itself – its rules, regulations and procedures. Compliance, discipline and domination take place rationally and legally through these rules, regulations and procedures.

Weber identifies several features which enable bureaucratic organization both to promote the rational action of its members and to become itself a rational actor. Among the most important of these features are the following: complex division of labor – precisely defined areas of responsibility and competence along with carefully delineated offices whose explicitly defined responsibilities require specialized training and expertise; hierarchy – the differentiated offices are arranged according to the principle of unity of command so that each is under the control of a higher one; formality – duties are performed, performances are assessed, and interactions occur in accordance with written rules and regulations; technical and professional qualifications – recruitment to and promotion within the bureaucracy are determined on the basis of certified qualifications; career and tenure – members are afforded the opportunity of a career within the organization and are awarded job security if their performance and qualifications so warrant.

To the extent that bureaucracies manifest these characteristics, Weber argues, they are capable of rational action. Some of these features directly promote rational action on the part of the members of the bureaucracy. For instance, the possibility of a career encourages people to comply with formal rules of conduct while hierarchical structure confines decision-making to a small group of a highly qualified people. Other features serve to shield the bureaucracy from non-rational influences. The granting of tenure insulates people from political pressures while reliance on technical and professional qualifications minimizes the impact which sentiment, kinship, love and hate can have on recruitment and promotion. Bureaucracy becomes more rational as its reliance on human sentiment declines. Technical efficiency is the result of rational dehumanization.

Weber describes bureaucracy as one of the great social inventions of all time. Capable of regulating the activities of extraordinarily large numbers of people with maximum efficiency and minimum interpersonal friction, bureaucratic organization is the very embodiment of rational action – an instrument deliberately created for the efficient attainment of complex goals. In addition to its technical superiority, bureaucracy also provides people with equal treatment and protection against arbitrary uses of power. These are undoubtedly significant. Yet, Weber urges, they should not detract from the recognition that bureaucratic organization arises and expands primarily because it is a most efficient instrument of discipline and domination, a peculiarly modern source of 'unfreedom'.

With the spread of rationalization in the form of capitalism and bureaucracy, modern society becomes technologically advanced. It is able to produce more in less time and with less effort, and manages to reduce hunger and toil and to keep more people alive for longer periods of time. Modern society has minimized material impoverishment, Weber argued, but it has done so in such a way that the impoverishment of the human spirit has been increased. Rationalization has produced 'specialists without spirit, pleasure-seeking beings without a heart – these no-ones make themselves believe that they have risen to heights never before reached in the development of the human species' (Weber, 1958, p. 339). Man's participation in modern society is guided more by rational calculation and less by particular social attachments. Freed from these sentimental attachments, the individual becomes more responsive to the demands of modern institutions for mobility, for adherence to the impersonal rules and regulations of bureaucratic organization and the market, and for regular, disciplined, methodical action in pursuit of clearly stated goals. Modern society tends to transform man into an agent of depersonalized organization, and the more it gives him, the more disenchanted he becomes. Rational action is efficient precisely because it lacks human purpose and social meaning, precisely because it is emptied of enchantment. Weber's concern with the loss of human purpose is captured well in J. L. and Barbara Hammond's (1936, p. 381) history of the rise of bureaucratic capitalism: 'In an age of such rapid invention and development it was easy to slip into the belief that the one task of the human race was to wrest her secrets from nature, and to forget how much of the history of mankind is a history of the effort to find a tolerable basis for a common life.'

Weber's identification of the dehumanizing consequences of rationalization has much in common with Marx's analysis of alienation. However, unlike Marx, Weber discovers in rationalization the fate of modern society, whether the society be capitalist or socialist. Far from being unique to capitalism, rational bureaucratic organization is indispensable to any effort to foster economic and social development. Technical efficiency, regardless of the operative political ideology, presupposes a rational, formally specialized administrative apparatus. Accordingly, to the extent that socialism is predicated upon further economic development and centralized planning, Weber (1947, p. 339) asserts, it 'would, in fact, require a still higher degree of formal bureaucratization than capitalism'. Socialism does not reverse the trends towards rationalization found in capitalism, it extends and completes them. In short, socialist society can be either a modern society or a free, non-alienating, humanly satisfying society, but it cannot be both; and if it is to be a modern society, then rationalized, bureaucratized, efficient, and impersonal domination – much more extensive than that generated by capitalism – will be its characteristic feature. Where Marx sees reason expanding in socialism, Weber envisions the spread of rationalization. Where Marx's firm optimism is grounded in the prospects of class struggle and proletarian enlightenment, Weber's hope, as weak and tentative as it is, finds a basis in the non-rational qualities of charisma.

Disenchantment and Charisma

The dynamic and apparently inexorable spread of rationalization brings about the disenchantment of the world. 'Not summer's bloom lies ahead of us', Weber (1946, p. 128) writes, 'but rather a polar night of icy darkness and hardness, no matter which group may triumph externally now.' The disenchanted world has lost its magical and mysterious qualities. It is a world without superstition, religious tradition, and myth, a cold and barren world bereft of charm and meaning. Disenchantment signifies not merely secularization and scientization, calculation and rational administration, but as well the wounding of the human spirit – the erosion of dignity, grace and personal honor (Mitzman, 1970, pp. 182–91; Greisman, 1976, pp. 495–507).

Weber's concern with the disenchanting consequences of rationalization is hardly novel in the context of German social thought where, going back one hundred years, the relation between reason or rationality and human improvement was a major theme. By the mid nineteenth century, the initial view that rationalization promised significant human and social progress was replaced by another, one which associated rationalization with the degradation of the human spirit. Ferdinand Toinnes gives clear expression to this view in his discussion of the shift from *Gemeinschaft* to *Gesellschaft* (Mitzman, 1973, pp. 3–131).

Gemeinschaft refers to a small, traditional, close-knit, community-based society; *Gesellschaft* to a large, complex, impersonal, bureaucratic society. In Toinnes's view, the technological and organizational breakthroughs which culminated in modern *Gesellschaft* came at heavy cost. The routinization engendered by rational organization and technique has sapped the will and constrained impulse, spontaneity and creativity, the fundamental sources of human freedom and vitality. Values have been relativized to such a degree that criteria of right and wrong, good and bad, moral and immoral are murky or even non-existent; society literally has been de-moralized. In contrast to the culture of *Gemeinschaft*, that in *Gesellschaft* does not express human qualities. As a consequence, people feel estranged from their cultural products, finding in them neither themselves nor meaningful purpose. The result is resentment – the spirit-breaking, life-draining experience of meaninglessness. Technical advance does little to compensate for the devitalization of life, the loss of the sense of enchantment, brought by rationalization.

In contrast to Toinnes, Friedrich Nietzsche finds in the disenchantment of the world cause for celebration. At the center of Nietzsche's celebration is the 'death of God' – the loss of faith, morality, ethical precepts, and belief in eternal, absolute verities produced by the rationalizing tendencies of the modern age. With the disappearance of their highest values, people find their lives without purpose and justification. Experiencing themselves and their world as absurd, most people become anxious, insecure, and afraid. In the absence of meaning, the profound questions of life go unanswered.

Nietzsche regards these developments as positive, for without God, morality and eternally fixed values people are in a position to go 'beyond good and evil' and there realize their human essence. Informed by the Judeo-Christian ethic and liberal precepts of reason and compassion, the morality destroyed by rationalization 'blessed the meek' and cultivated weakness, passivity and vulnerability. Originating in man's inability to face the actual absurdity of his existence, it was a slave morality transforming into sin the dark, dominating, at once creative and destructive life-energies which make up human essence. In the absence of ethical and religious ideals, people are free to release these energies, to exercise their will to power by seeking power for the sake of power, by striving to conquer and to dominate for no purpose other than the dissipation of energy.

Not all, Nietzsche recognizes, are capable of acting on their will to power. Most are too wretched, too cowardly, too weak, at home only in the slave morality. Some, however, possess the necessary courage, strength, and pride. These 'supermen' represent the highest expression of the human essence. Hard on themselves, ruthless on others, they are cleansed by the pain and suffering they endure in their creative striving to overcome and dominate. For the vast majority, the disenchantment of the world means a life of terrible anxiety and intolerable fright. For the few, the supermen, the death of God and the loss of meaning mean the chance to become truly human.

Weber is sympathetic to Toinnes's position. He too recognizes that the scientific, rational, methodical organization of life has reduced ignorance, disease, danger, and toil while damaging the bases of a meaningful, spirit-enhancing existence. Yet, in the last analysis, Weber sides with Nietzsche, agreeing with him that life is ultimately without absolute purpose and meaning and, more importantly, that hope for the future resides in a small number of extraordinary people. Weber's 'charismatic heroes' are the first cousins of Nietzsche's 'supermen'.

Weber (1968, p. 241) defines charisma as

> a certain quality of an individual personality by virtue of which he is considered extraordinary and treated as endowed with supernatural, superhuman, or at least specifically exceptional powers or qualities. These are such as are not accessible to the ordinary person, but are regarded as of divine origin or as exemplary, and on the basis of them the individual concerned is treated as a 'leader'.

Charismatic leaders are viewed by their followers or disciples as special, extraordinary, gifted, and in possession of heroic qualities and spiritual grace. Not merely an attribute of individual personality, charisma requires for its existence social confirmation. Only in a particular social context is the 'gift of grace' regarded as such. Important here is the leader's ability to give clear articulation and meaning to widely held yet heretofore vaguely expressed feelings and sentiments. To the extent that the leader successfully overcomes the threats to personal well-being that greet his pronouncements and actions, his charismatic qualities are magnified, becoming the basis of a movement of people committed to the grand mission he represents.

At every opportunity, Weber (ibid., p. 241) insists that charisma 'transforms all values and breaks all traditional and rational norms'; it 'is indeed the specifically creative revolutionary force of history'. An essentially irrational phenomenon, charisma 'is a driving, creative force which surges through the established rules, whether traditional or legal, which govern an existing order' (Giddens, 1971a, p. 161). Though its revolutionary implications receive most forceful expression in the context of traditional forms of domination, charisma remains a significant rebellious force in rational society. Charisma, Weber argues, is sharply opposed to the methodical and the rational. 'Specifically irrational in the sense of being foreign to all rules', charisma is the direct antithesis of bureaucratic authority and 'rejects all rational economic conduct' (Weber, 1968, p. 244). Charisma is an irrational counter-force to rationalization.

In charismatic leaders and movements, Weber finds the prospect for occasional periods of human renewal and revitalization within the iron cage. For Weber, the this-worldly mysticism and dynamic force of charisma, notes Arthur Mitzman (1970, p. 190), 'promised intrinsic meaning to lives which otherwise existed only as means to unknown and unknowable ends'. Not necessarily as ruthless, aggressive, and conquering as Nietzsche's superman, Weber's charismatic hero shares with him the courage to confront head on the meaninglessness of life in rational bureaucratic capitalist society. In this potentially hazardous act, the charismatic hero gives expression to widely shared fears and anxieties and, by symbolizing the meaning of meaninglessness, provides people, however temporarily, with some purpose for being. Only charisma, unstable, impermanent, and irrational in character, can re-enchant the world, can personalize, humanize, and emotionalize rational society. How often and for how long it could do so without itself becoming rationalized or routinized is a question Weber is not prepared to answer.

In the final analysis, Weber shares Durkheim's historical pessimism with respect to the future course of human development. Unlike Marx, whose optimism rested on the conviction that progress toward a better society would emerge from an enlightened and reasoned class consciousness, Durkheim and Weber lose faith in the progressive aspects of reason. Reason, for them, comes to mean instrumental reason, a source of control and domination antithetical to the non-rational bases of social stability and the irrational bases of human impulse. Thus, Durkheim seeks a partial solution to anomie in non-rational periods of collective effervescence as Weber looks for a temporary cure for disenchantment in irrational periods of charismatic mysticism. Of the three, only Marx is able to sustain commitment to the values of reason and freedom. With their concept of instrumental reason, Durkheim and Weber find the bases of freedom in modern society becoming more fragile and fewer in number. Eventually, they seek to counter reason with the non-rational and the irrational and to substitute escape for freedom – escape through moments of collective ferment or periods of charismatic heroism.

Rationality and Bureaucracy: Weber, Marx, and Lenin

In 1917, as Weber was completing his sociological analysis of the dynamics and structures of the modern bureaucratic state, V. I. Lenin was perfecting, both conceptually and in practice, the Vanguard Party. A highly centralized, formal organization, the Vanguard Party was designed to bring consciousness and direction to a working-class revolution in part geared to the destruction of the bureaucratic state which Weber regards as the distinguishing feature of modern society. After the Russian Revolution, Lenin, claiming to follow the blueprint prepared by Marx, supervised the evolution of the Vanguard Party into the dictatorship of the proletariat, a 'temporary bureaucracy' intended to facilitate the transition to communism and the 'withering away of the state'. Over the past seventy years or so, this dictatorship of the proletariat has expanded into a stable and massive state bureaucracy which undergirds a system of rational domination that insults and denies Marx's vision of socialism.

Weber, as we know, fully expects the rationalization of domination in socialism. This development appears to substantiate Weber's view while repudiating Marx's. Yet there are good grounds for arguing that in initiating this development, Lenin relied on a category of rationality that is clearly more Weberian than Marxist in character. A careful consideration of this argument should result in a fuller appreciation of the differences between Weber's and Marx's treatments of reason and rationality. The dynamics of modern bureaucracy receive limited attention in Marx's critique of industrial capitalism. Generally, Marx views bureaucracy in its political rather than industrial setting and, as a consequence, he treats bureaucratic organization as a transitory social form. An aspect of bourgeois state administration, bureaucracy is both a manifestation of the centralizing tendencies of capitalism and an instrument of class domination. This assessment is accepted by Lenin whose analysis of bureaucracy, as Wright (1974, p. 83) notes, begins with the assumption that not only is bureaucracy 'the basic structure through which the capitalist class rules ... [but] bureaucratic organization is suited only for capitalist domination'. Dependent on the bourgeoisie and separated from and not accountable to the people, bureaucratic organization is ultimately an instrument of coercion and control, and is unnecessary in – indeed, is contradictory to – a communist society free of class antagonisms. Until the 'higher' phase of communism arrives, however, 'the socialists demand the *strictest* control ... [and] this control must *start* with the expropriation of the capitalists, with the establishment of workers' control over the capitalists' (Lenin, 1949, p. 89). During the transition to communist society, bureaucratic organization – a workers' or socialist bureaucracy – is maintained; bureaucratic domination continues, but in a different form, as the majority comes to dominate the minority.

The bureaucratic structures inherited from capitalism cannot be abolished overnight, but they can be transformed gradually from a repressive to an emancipatory instrument. 'The working class cannot simply lay hold of the ready-made state machinery', Marx (1966a, p. 64) writes, 'and wield it for its own purposes.' Instead, a transitional bureaucracy, representative of and responsive to the workers, must be created. Chosen as a model for the transitional bureaucracy was the short-lived Paris Commune of 1871. The significance of the Commune for Marx is that, by establishing the conditions for the direct participation of the workers in the decision-making process, it democratized the administrative functions of bureaucracy. A 'self-government of the producers', the Commune staffed its administrative apparatus with elected representatives of the workers who were subject to immediate recall and received wages and benefits equal to those of other workers. The Commune supplied in embryonic form a prototype of bureaucracy controlled by political initiatives from below.

The Paris Commune figures centrally in Lenin's effort to formulate a more comprehensive and detailed conception of socialist bureaucracy. It is important to recognize, however, that for Lenin the 'Commune had a narrow polemical meaning. It proved there could be no peaceable transition from capitalism to socialism and the "old state machine must be smashed"' (Lenin, 1949, p. 81). Comprised of professional revolutionaries and possessing a centralized and specialized structure, the vanguard is assigned the leadership role in the workers' bureaucracy. To combat the potential for elitism which resides in this situation, Lenin proposes a democratization of the administrative functions of bureaucracy similar to that which occurred in the Paris Commune. Bureaucratic functions of control and accounting, Lenin (ibid., p. 41) claims,

> have become so simplified and have been reduced to such exceedingly simple operations of registration, filing and checking that they can be easily performed by every literate person, can quite easily be performed for ordinary 'workmen's wages', and that these functions can (and must) be stripped of every shadow of privilege, of every semblance of 'official grandeur'.

As knowledge of and the ability to administer social production spreads, control of bureaucracy comes to be vested not in the upper positions of the hierarchy, but in the social producers themselves. Since power is no longer a property of position, the threat of the emergence of a bureaucratic elite rapidly diminishes.

The fundamental problem with Lenin's formulation is that it confines workers' control to the administrative sphere of bureaucratic organization. Technical services and operations, which Lenin regards as non-bureaucratic and, hence, not a possible source of elitist structures, are not subject to political control. 'The question of control and accounting', Lenin (1969, p. 337) states quite explicitly, 'should not be confused with the question of the scientifically trained staff of engineers.' The first question is concerned with political necessity, the second with technical necessity.

Control and accounting functions comprise the power dimension of bureaucracy, and to the extent they are democratized, bureaucratic domination is precluded. Technical functions are independent of this political dimension, and therefore technically determined subordination is not open to political challenge. The technique of modern, industrial enterprise, Lenin (ibid., p. 342) comments, 'makes absolutely imperative the strictest discipline, the utmost precision on the part of everyone carrying out his allotted task, for otherwise the whole enterprise may come to a stop, or machinery or the finished product may be damaged'.

The advancement of the technical means of production, although internally an undemocratic and apolitical process, further simplifies administrative tasks, thus facilitating greater worker control over the bureaucratic apparatus, and generates the material prerequisites of a classless society. Rationalization in socialist society brings not the extension of formal structures of domination, but just the reverse, as people, in the absence of class restrictions, acquire the knowledge and understanding that enables them individually and collectively to master their social life.

Lenin's conception of socialist bureaucracy resided among the central elements of the Bolshevik policy on industrial growth and modernization, and, in the years immediately following the revolution, was used to justify and to guide not only the steady expansion of bureaucratic offices and growing attacks on autonomous, self-governing unions, but also the incorporation of the technical achievements of capitalism, ranging from modern industrial technology to the managerial program of labor discipline developed by Frederick Taylor. Technical necessity came to dominate more and more spheres of activity in the bureaucracy and beyond. Concurrently, there was a narrowing of those areas of concern subject to political control. This is evident in a series of proposals Lenin offered in 1918 which, as summarized by Bendix (1956, p. 193), proclaim that

> The masses of the people must participate actively in planning the policies which should govern production and distribution, but during the workday they must observe iron discipline and subordinate themselves unconditionally to the dictatorial will of one man, the Soviet manager ... [Toward this end] the Courts must be used to inculcate labor-discipline. Anyone who violated the demands of labor-discipline must be discovered, brought before the courts, and punished.

Technically necessary subordination, required for the development of the 'higher' phases of communism, underlay the progressive depoliticization of socialist society. And the political sphere diminished in socialist Russia, not with the abolition of private property but with the emergence of a technically expert bureaucracy. Detached from the political will of the masses by 'technical necessity', the experts in industry and in the party successfully and efficiently supervised the modernization of Russian society. But they did so as Weber predicted, by establishing a highly repressive and an immensely powerful bureaucratic organization.

Rationality Reconsidered
The contending assessments of the relationship between socialism and bureaucracy that arise from Weberian and Marxist social theories rest on different conceptualizations of rationality. While Marxist theory marks a distinction between the 'rationality of technique' and the 'rationality of

consciousness', Weberian theory, as Giddens (1973, p. 275) notes, draws a clear connection between 'technique, and the application of instrumental rationality to the material world, and bureaucratic organization as the application of technical reason to social activity'. In his concept of bureaucratization, Weber assimilates both aspects of rationality with the result that rationalization appears as an inexorable process by which the administration of things eventuates in the administration or domination of people. By distinguishing the two aspects of rationality, Marxist theory envisages the possibility of a society where the application of instrumental rationality and technical reason is confined to the material world, and critical rationality or political consciousness permeates every other sphere of life to the degree that domination, whether it be rooted in the means of production or the means of administration, becomes virtually impossible. In Giddens's (ibid., p. 277) words, ' "rationalization", in the sense of the rational transmutation of the modern cultural ethos, provides men with the understanding necessary to control [and to prevent] "rationalization" in the sense of the dominance of technical rationality in social life'.

From the Marxist viewpoint, the class structure of capitalism impedes the rationalization of understanding and consciousness, the growth of reason. As a result, the rationalization of technique, although furthered by the development of capitalism, defies rational control and strengthens the irrational domination of social life. Only with the removal of class barriers is the rationalization of consciousness and the limitation of instrumental rationality to the material world possible. Thus, the central problem concerns the eradication of class restrictions. In responding to this problem Marxist theory ultimately conjoined the two aspects of rationality – and thereby narrowed its distance from the Weberian position – by presuming that the transformation of the capitalist economy engendered by the rationalization of technique, the progressive development of productive forces, ignites the revolutionary action that liberates individuals and society from the constraints of class domination. The rationalization of technique, then, is seen to establish the material conditions necessary for the rationalization of consciousness. In more familiar terms, ideological changes are dependent on substructural changes, the realm of freedom is contingent upon the realm of necessity.

The convergence of the two aspects of rationality is especially clear in Lenin's analysis of the technical and political realms of bureaucracy. Technically determined subordination is legitimate as long as it, first, occurs within an organization stripped of its class, that is, control and punishment, functions, and, second, establishes the material conditions of classlessness which permit the acquisition of rational understanding and consciousness. What Lenin fails to realize, however, is that 'it is not only class power but *any* source of societal domination that inhibits dialogue and undermines rationality' (Gouldner, 1976, p. 98). Domination and unfreedom, whether technically or politically determined, inhibits dialogue, understanding and consciousness, and this inhibition allows the rationalization of technique to penetrate unchallenged throughout society. The extension of technology and technocratic bureaucracy severely delimits the space where communication free from domination is possible and thus impairs the conditions of the growth of reason. Political goals are transformed into technical problems whose solution require not public discussion, but subordination to the technically necessary.

Lenin's 'Weberianization' of Marx's treatment of rationality must be challenged. The two categories of rationality found in Marx's work need to be clarified and the distinction between them re-established. Habermas proposes just such a clarification with his distinction between technical and practical rationality (discussed in Chapter 1). Technical rationality refers to the efficient and calculated pursuit of given goals, practical rationality to a process of enlightenment or of generalized reflection in terms of which goals are chosen in the context of non-distorted public (that is, political) communication. Practical rationality, Gouldner (ibid., p. 51) observes, suggests that people are '*properly* bound only by rules they can articulately justify ... [and this] premises an ecology of speakers who cannot give one another orders, because they have relative equality; who have some means of enabling them to resist compulsion and who must therefore be persuaded "rationally"'. Thus, where technical rationalization involves the extension of instrumental action and is expressed in the continuing growth of productive forces, practical rationalization results in the enlargement of the sphere of action guided by social norms, formulated in and through non-distorted communication, and subject to conscious reflection. Rationalization in this sense involves the transformation into ends or objects of decision features of social life which previously were not ends.

The expansion of purposive rational subsystems that result from technical rationalization leads to the more efficient functioning of society, but there is no automatic connection between the technical advance of the productive forces and human emancipation. Human emancipation as a practical matter – a matter of choice requiring reflection and consciousness – is not attainable by technical means alone. Practical rationalization, the rationalization of consciousness, the growth of reason, must accompany, not be expected to follow, the rationalization of technique, and such can occur, Habermas (1970, p. 118) writes, only

through removing *restrictions on communication*. Public unrestricted discussion, free from domination, of the suitability and desirability of action-orienting principles and norms in the light of the sociocultural repercussions of developing subsystems of purposive-rational action – such communication at all levels of political and repoliticized decision-making processes is the only medium in which anything like 'rationalization' is possible.

Practical rationality or the rationality of consciousness rests not on technical rationalization but on the expansion of the space and the time available for political discourse and critical dialogue.

By reopening the distinction between the rationality of technique and the rationality of consciousness and redrawing their relation such that each mutually interprets the other, Habermas overcomes many of the objectivistic and elitist tendencies found in Leninism, and thus enables the Marxian category of rationality to regain its distance from the Weberian category. Suggested by Habermas's treatment of the two aspects of rationality is the importance of having the rationalization of organization and technique accompanied by the rationalization of culture and consciousness, so that the practical questions associated with the free and conscious selection of ends are never subordinated to the imperatives of formal, instrumental rationality.

To sum up, Weber identifies reason with rational action, formal rationality, and the process of rationalization. The growth of such instrumental reason can only mean the extension of rational domination; the administration of things leads to the administration of people. Marx, in contrast, regards reason in a twofold way. Reason as technical rationality expresses itself in the advancement of the productive forces, an advance which makes possible both the reduction of socially necessary labor time and the formalization of domination. This latter, regressive side of technical rationality could be prevented from developing, Marx is convinced, by the expansion of reason as practical rationality, the growth of reason in culture and consciousness. Reasonable people would want to, know how to, and be capable of subordinating technical achievements to human purposes. For Marx, then, reason is the essential precondition of freedom; for Weber, reason as it it is expressed in the modern world is freedom's enemy.

Conclusion

Marx's category of reason allows him to assess ends and values as well as means rationally – to account for the rationalization of both consciousness and technique. Social theory committed to reason, according to Marx, is necessarily political and normative in the sense of being concerned with the formulation of ends and purposes. Indeed, Marx offers his social theory as a guide to political practice, arguing that the values embodied therein are rational. Normative statements – statements of what ought to be – derive from the commitment to reason. Social theory has a political responsibility.

Weber's category of reason precludes ends, values, and grand human purposes from rational evaluation. These, along with politics, religion, and philosophy, are essentially matters of faith, taste and preference; questions of opinion, not fact. What should be cannot be rationally known. Social theory committed to reason is necessarily value-neutral and has no political responsibility. Weber's social theory stands at a dispassionate distance from and devalues political activity; Marx's is grounded in and salutes politics. On the question of the role of values in social theory, Weber and Marx are in substantial opposition.

Weber's entire work was guided by the supposition that at any one moment only a selected and incomplete portion of the 'meaningless infinity of the world process' can be the object of scientific analysis. What gives meaning to this 'meaningless infinity', that is, what provides scientific analysis with its object of investigation, is the relevance a particular segment of reality has for the values of the investigator. Here, Weber is merely restating Kant's contention that the phenomenal world presents itself as a series of chaotic and unconnected impressions, knowledge of which is possible only in terms of some value-orientation which can arrange these impressions in a meaningful, that is conceptual, manner. Because they reflect the values of the investigator, concepts do not produce mirror-images of cultural reality; they are at best heuristic tools useful for organizing the infinite processes of the real world. Knowledge of the 'thing-in-itself', as Kant demonstrated, is impossible, and, as a consequence, concepts and reality must always remain distinct. Given this necessarily strong dependence of scientific research on value-relevance, Weber cautions the social scientist, first, to clarify the standards which comprise his or her value-position and, secondly, to identify where in the process of argumentation a shift occurs from analytical and scientific discussion to one based on sentiment. In suggesting this distinction between empirical and normative knowledge, Weber is not asserting that value-judgements be kept completely divorced from social scientific discourse, for, as we have seen, it is his position that sociological investigation takes its departure from some standpoint rooted in the realm of values.

Although knowledge of cultural reality is always knowledge from a particular viewpoint, the social sciences are still capable of acquiring objectivity. Indeed, objectivity – as meaningful knowledge of the concrete reality – is initially possible only on the basis of the evaluative ideas of the investigator. Weber (1949, p. 11) writes,

The 'objectivity' of the social sciences depends ... on the fact that the empirical data are always related to those evaluative ideas which alone make them worth knowing and the significance of the empirical data is derived from these evaluative ideas. But these data can never become the foundation for the empirically impossible proof of the validity of the evaluative ideas.

Given this, objectivity is possible only as a property of method.

Weber proposed the 'ideal type' method with the intention of providing the social sciences with an adequate technique for acquiring and assessing the objective validity of empirical knowledge of the socio-cultural world. While expressing the social scientist's ability to form constructs in line with particular values, the ideal type simultaneously provides procedures which, if properly employed, prohibit these values from intruding on the ensuing investigation. In Weber's eyes, the ideal type is indispensable if the social sciences are to maintain the distinction between empirical and normative knowledge. In short, the ideal type concisely reflects Weber's argument that sociological investigation must be restricted to assessing the appropriateness of various means for achieving a given end and, in turn, to estimating the probable cost or impact the attainment of the desired end will have on other goals. Objective validity requires that scientific choice be confined to the realm of method. Decisions regarding the establishment of particular goals or, on another level, choices between contending viewpoints brought to bear on the infinite richness of the cultural world cannot be guided by scientific analysis. Scientific postulates cannot be used either to derive an 'ought' from the phenomenal world or to validate value-judgements used to gain access to that world. Accordingly, the findings acquired through sociological analysis are used to tell people what they can do, not what they should do. 'Whoever lacks the capacity to put on blinders', Weber (1946, p. 135) remarks, '[has] no calling for sciences and ... should do something else.'

Rejecting Weber's claim that knowledge of social reality is necessarily elusive, Marx maintains that knowledge is the product of the dialectical interplay between man in society and the objective world, and since man participates in the construction of social reality he can know it. The acquisition of knowledge is a practical activity: the existence that determines consciousness is an ever-changing existence which itself is determined by and is accessible to the knowledge of man. Social reality, in this view, comprises not only existence but the tendencies contained therein. Recognition of these tendencies simultaneously constitutes accurate knowledge and a critical evaluation of the existing order. Thus true knowledge and critical or normative assessment of the prevailing arrangements are one, since the evaluative ideas used in the assessment are materially rooted in these arrangements.

For Marx, truth presupposes knowledge of the totality – knowledge which critically evaluates the existing structures and relationships in terms of the tendencies and potentialities they deny. As we saw previously, Marx claims that knowledge of the totality is only possible from the standpoint of proletariat interests, since these interests are compatible with – indeed, expressive of – potentiality. Where for Weber objectively depends on value-neutrality, for Marx, objectivity requires commitment to particular interests, those he regards as demonstrably consistent with the historical movement toward reason and freedom.

PART 2

In light of Mills's theoretical project, Part 1 examined the conceptualization of the relation of reason and freedom in classical sociological thought. In Part 2, the primary aim is to show the contemporary and practical relevance of this theoretical concern. If Mills's theme – that with the development of modern society reason is reduced to a rationality which diminishes the bases of human freedom – can be employed, as it was in Part 1, to facilitate our appreciation of the central concerns of classical sociological thought, it can also be used, as it is in Part 2, to heighten our understanding of some of the key historical developments and social forces that lead to and presently help define advanced industrial society. The shift from an analysis of changes in sociological thought to an analysis of changes in society takes place initially by way of an examination of recent work in the area of social criticism, work which locates the major contemporary obstacles to human freedom in the social forms of instrumental reason: scientism, bureaucracy, market rationalization and administrative politics.

Chapter 4 begins by continuing the concern displayed in Part 1 with theoretical and philosophical expressions of the reason–freedom relation. Here, the focus is on the development of modernism, broadly conceived, and its rejection of reason in the name of freedom. Equating reason with its prevailing form of expression, instrumental reason, modernist thought insists that freedom is found away from reason in impulse, spontaneity, and the irrational. A discussion of key modernist themes and modes of expression and an examination of the important contributions of Nietzsche and Freud to the distinctively modernist currents of contemporary culture serve to elaborate and illustrate this view. In turn, the work of two contemporary social critics, the sociologist, Daniel Bell, and the historian, Christopher Lasch, is taken as a basis to show that modernist thought, and the culture and consciousness associated with it, are as much products as they are negations of instrumental reason. With the spread of rationalization, modernism quickly filters into popular culture and consciousness in the form of a narcissistic ethos and personality type. In the narcissistic freedoms of emotional expression, experiential exploration, and impulse satisfaction reside the seeds of a new form of rational domination where submission to a rational but unreasonable reality occurs. This is the fundamental irony of modernism and its narcissistic form of expression – under the banner of repudiating instrumental reason, they promote a 'freedom' compatible with instrumental reason, a 'freedom' which requires the very eclipse of the individual wrought by the spread of rationality without reason.

Against this background, Chapter 5 assesses the relation of reason and freedom in modern society by analyzing the spread of capitalist rationalization (a major form taken by instrumental reason) and its impact on the definition and practice of democracy (a form of freedom). After examining the spread of capitalist rationalization from the marketplace to the workplace to the family and then to the state, Chapter 5 goes on to assess how this development brought about a narrowing down of the democratic ethos and practice. Liberal democracy was associated with marketplace rationality, democratic elitism with the rationalization of workplace and family. The present rationalization of state power is accompanied by the emergence of corporatist democracy. Corporatism is based on highly rationalized political structures and requires a further restriction of democratic freedoms. It is the political arrangement anticipated by Saint-Simon, Comte, and Durkheim.

In summary, by tracing out the relationship between the rationalization of social life and the eclipse of the individual (in Chapter 4) and the weakening of democracy (in Chapter 5), Part 2 intends to demonstrate the present-day importance of the classical concern with reason and freedom in light of the concrete socio-historical developments which have given us modern society. The central point of each chapter is that many of these developments have impoverished our capacity for critical thought, a capacity sustainable only in the individual, and perfectable only in democratic participation. Reason as rationality becomes an enemy of freedom not only on the abstract level of social thought but in actuality, in the real world, as well.

4

Modernism: Freedom Without Reason

The Enlightenment faith in reason and rationality dominated the nineteenth century. Marx, Durkheim, and Weber are influenced strongly by and make important contributions to the expansion of the scientific outlook. Each finds the key to the understanding of modern society in rational organization; each sees deliberate, calculated rational action as a characteristic feature of modern man. Of the three, only Marx retains the Enlightenment conviction that the growth of reason makes for the enlargement of freedom. Durkheim and Weber, instead, regard reason as a threat to freedom, its spread underlying anomie and disenchantment. In opposition to reason, they recognize the non-rational and the irrational as sources of relief from the anxiety and hopelessness that accompany rationalization. By finding some ground for hope in collective effervescence and charismatic mysticism, Durkheim and Weber partly join in the repudiation of the Western commitment to reason and rationality that is at the heart of modernism.

Modernist thought arises forcefully in the period between 1890 and 1920 and its influence is profoundly and thoroughly felt in physics, philosophy, the social sciences, art, literature, dance, architecture and, finally, popular consciousness. Modernism shifts the focus of social thought from reason and rational action to sentiments, vital impulses, will and the unconscious. Subjective authenticity replaces objective validity as the basis of truth; repressed feelings replace rational thought as the locus of motivation. The changes brought by the modernist movement, H. Stuart Hughes observes, are immense.

Psychological process has replaced external reality as the most pressing topic for investigation. It was no longer what actually existed that seemed most important: it was what men thought existed. And what they felt on the unconscious level had become rather more interesting than what they had consciously rationalized. Or ... since it had apparently been proved impossible to arrive at any sure knowledge of human behaviour – if one must rely on flashes of subjective intuition or on the creation of convenient fictions – then the mind had indeed been freed from the bonds of positivist method: it was at liberty to speculate, to imagine, to create. At one stroke, the realm of human understanding had been drastically reduced and immensely broadened. (Hughes, 1958, p. 66)

Modernism celebrates freedom as it derogates reason; indeed, the two acts are one, for freedom – the freedom to discover and to express the authentic self heretofore hidden by rational assumptions and repressed by rational conventions and structures – is acquired away from reason and rationality. While modernism is a reaction to and an attack on instrumental reason, it is, at the same time, a product of the development of instrumental reason. Before developing this thesis, it is necessary first to distinguish modernism from, and show how it is related to, modernity and modernization.

Modernism, Perry Anderson (1984, pp. 112–13) writes, 'is the emptiest of all cultural categories ... what is concealed beneath the label is a wide variety of very diverse – indeed incompatible – practices, claims, outlooks, and aims'. The treatment of modernism's key sources and modes of expression offered below may seem to support Anderson's observation. Nietzsche's existentialism, Freud's theory of psychoanalysis, Einstein's theory of relativity, modern art and cultural relativism – all are examined to convey and illustrate the constitutive themes and distinctive character of modernist thought. No doubt, fundamental differences and incongruities are to be found between and among these representatives of or contributors to modernism. However, what they share in common – for instance, a distrust of reason, an appreciation of the power of inner irrational forces, a denial of the existence of fixed, objective, universal verities – is sufficiently strong to enable the category 'modernism' to carry the weight of their differences and inconsistencies.

Modernism is the cultural vision and vocabulary that arises with modernity, the historical experience of modernization (ibid., pp. 97–109). Modernity and modernization each imply development, the former the self-development made possible by the enlargement and diversification of human experience, the latter the economic development concomitant with market, technological, and bureaucratic rationalization. Modernity as the experience of modernization which fosters modernism is essentially ambiguous, combining as it does insecurity, fear, and disorientation with elation and exhilaration. The ambiguity of this simultaneous experience of emancipation and ordeal is a reflection of the ambiguity of the modernizing process itself. Modernization as rationalization liberates people from rigidly enforced statuses and role expectations and from narrowly conceived and repressive moral boundaries, as it 'generates a brutally alienated and atomized society, riven by callous economic exploitation, destructive of every cultural or political value whose potential it has itself brought into being' (ibid., p. 98).

Modernism as the vision (or the point of convergence for the set of various visions) which arises out of modernity ultimately seeks to overcome this ambiguity, in part by uncoupling modernity from its source – the rationalizing forces and tendencies of modernization. Modernist thought does this by opposing unlimited self-development, a main precondition of which is the exploration and unleashing of the innermost material of the psyche, to the restraining power of the instrumental reason which is at the center of modernization.

Modernism

Modernism, writes James McFarlane (1976, p. 82), is 'born of the irrational, and obeying a logic much closer to the subjective and associative promptings of the unconscious mind than to the formal progression of scientific inquiry ... [employs] a vocabulary of chaos – disintegration, fragmentation, dislocation ...'. Modernism as a state of mind, a type of mentality, a way of thinking and feeling, expresses a new mode of seeing, experiencing, and understanding the world, one which deprecates rational judgements and congnitive capacities, abandons morality and restraint, and celebrates as life-affirming the instinctual, the impulsive and spontaneous, desire and pleasure. Subversive of constraint, modernism is at war with the established order.

The modernist attitude is a result of the process of modernization or rationalization. It has its roots in that which it opposes: modern institutions and rational organization. Daniel Bell rightly notes that modernism emerges in response to two developments occurring at the end of the nineteenth and the beginning of the twentieth century, one having to do with perception of the social environment, the other with consciousness of the self.

> In the world of sense impressions, there was a disorientation of the sense of space and time derived from the new awareness of motion and speed, light, and sound, which came from communication and transport. The crisis in self-consciousness arose from the loss of religious certitude, of belief in an afterlife, in heaven or hell, and the consciousness of an immutable void beyond life, the nothingness of death. (Bell, 1980, pp. 276–7)

The first change occurs as the pace of life is suddenly and significantly quickened. Improvements in communications and transport shortened distances and altered the sense of time and space; the phenomenal growth of large cities found more and more people caught up in the dizzingly rapid rhythm of urban life. The second change arises as scientific skepticism undermines religious certitude and unquestioned purpose.

Consider some of the major technological developments made during the thirty years overlapping the turn of the century:

the internal combustion engine, the diesel engine and the steam turbine;
electricity, oil, and petroleum as the new sources of power;
the automobile, the motor bus, the tractor and the aeroplane;
the telephone, the typewriter and the tape machine, the foundation of modern office organization;
the production by the chemical industry of snythetic materials – dyes, man-made fibres and plastics. (Bullock, 1976, p. 59)

Equally profound are the alterations on the social and cultural plane. The continued erosion of the sacred and loss of belief in eternal verities and stable referentials; the growth of science and, with it, the conviction that all is to be questioned; the growth of population and the ensuing explosion of urbanization; the emergence of mass production and mass consumption; the relativization of values; the bureaucratization of social life and the proliferation of anonymous, impersonal, emotionless social relations; the increase in geographical and social mobility – these developments combined to destroy the time-honored sense of permanence, place, and continuity. They made man homeless, without stable and secure anchorage, and set up his encounter with nothingness. These are the sources of the personal confusion, chaos, and dislocation, the cultural uncertainty and meaninglessness, and the social instability which underlie the central themes of modernist thought.

The distrust of reason occupies the central position in the major themes of modernism. Reason is an inadequate guide to the conduct of human affairs and a poor basis for understanding human action. Of far greater import are the irrational forces of human nature. Expressed in art, poetry, dreams and the like, they are the primary impetus to action and the ground of authenticity. They defy rational understanding. In short, rational judgement distorts, impulse clarifies; calculation restrains, spontaneity releases; reason dominates, emotion frees.

The rejection of reason entails an aversion to hierarchy. As a result, the derogation of rational judgement is joined with the repudiation of criteria of assessment and evaluation. There are no acceptable grounds for distinguishing the superior from the inferior, good from evil, right from wrong, moral from immoral. Certainty, truth, beauty – all are fictions of the rational mind. There are no objective standards by which such determination can be made. There is no certainty, truth, or beauty; we are 'beyond good and evil'.

In this view, the idea of progress is abandoned. To regard a development as progressive is to evaluate it in light of criteria which are baseless. There is no improvement, no movement toward something better – who can say what 'improvement' and 'better' are? There is just change, continuous change and impermanence, and this never changes. Change without purpose, uncertainty and instability, there is much of, but no progress. Without purpose and meaning, beauty and truth, life is absurd. In the impulsive and the momentary we find not the good and the noble but life itself – excitement, newness and authenticity. Here we are true to our feelings and desires and, thus, true to ourselves.

Each of these themes is marked by a thorough-going relativism which denies both the existence of absolute, eternally stable referentials and the possibility of criteria by which rational judgements and moral interdictions can be made with any degree of certainty. All we can say is that one thing differs from another, not that it is better or worse than, superior or inferior to, the other. The emphasis on relativism so distinctive of modernism has an important root in the revolution in physics which begins at the start of the twentieth century with the achievements of Einstein, Bohr, and Heisenberg.

The momentous developments in physics during the first two decades of the century call into serious question both the possibility of acquiring with certainty knowledge of reality, and the assumption that the universe is inherently rational and orderly. The newly emerging physics gives support to the view that existence is absurd with its discovery that matter is comprised of waves and particles and, while having the appearance of stability, is actually in constant flux. Matter is always changing, yet remains the same. Accordingly, reality never can be completely and accurately known. Reality can be apprehended only from a particular position, one which produces not simply a partial but a distorted understanding of the whole. Thus there are no fixed criteria, no objective standards, for determining time and space. The temporal and spatial properties of a body can be established only relative to the 'whenness' and the 'whereness' of other bodies.

This view of reality, Charles Lemert notes, combines the principles of complementarity, indeterminacy and relativity. Complementarity asserts that whether we know matter as waves or particles depends on the method of observation we use. Full knowledge of one necessarily entails incomplete knowledge of the other; a rational understanding of the whole is impossible. Indeterminacy states that what is observed is invariably disturbed by the instrument of observation. Reality cannot be known as such and all knowledge we have of it is necessarily distorted. Together, Lemert (1974, p. 96) writes, these two principles are 'the core of the quantum physics which may be summarized crudely as the conclusion that the micro-particles of which all matter is composed cannot be said to "exist" in any traditionally rational (Newtonian) static sense'. While these principles abolish the rationalist distinction between knower and known, the principle of relativity jettisons the rationalist assumption of hierarchical order with its distinctions between higher and lower. Relativity denies the existence of fixed referential standards and emphasizes once again that reality is knowable only from particular standpoints, each of which affords incomplete and, in places, distorted knowledge. The key point is that the world is too complex, too unstable and impermanent, too absurd, to be grasped rationally. Rational method and rational principles provide a distorted appreciation of the world. Indeed, any approach will necessarily result in distortion. Yet there are no bases, no criteria, for saying that the rational scientific distortion is any better or any worse than the distortions produced by other approaches.

Modernist themes take a number of different forms. In the social sciences, anthropology in particular, the modernist current takes hold at the time in the form of cultural relativism. In contrast to the long-dominant evolutionary theory which claimed that modern societies are superior to, more highly evolved than, primitive societies, cultural relativism asserts that the values used in making such judgements are relative to the cultures of the judges. Denying the existence of trans-cultural standards of assessment, cultural relativism charges those who evaluate the practices of one culture in the terms of their own with the sin of ethnocentricism. Values and meanings vary from one culture to the next, and while it is possible to show how they differ, it is impossible to determine which are better or worse. In this context, truth is made to be relative and subjective, a matter internal to particular cultures or meaning-systems and dependent on what people believe to be the case as opposed to what the case actually is. What is true in one culture may not be true in another. Facts, then, are

> dependent on the way people think, and no room is left for the idea that things can be the case whether anyone thinks they are or not. In other words, the possibility of something being objectively the case is ruled out ... All this means that it is impossible to conceive of any kind of independent reality. Reality becomes merely what people think it is, and as different people have different conceptions of it, there must be different realities. (Trigg, 1973, p. 2)

Cultural relativism expresses the modernist claim that there are no absolute standards, no universal morality, no objective criteria for determining truth and beauty. Standards, moral precepts, and evaluative criteria are culture-bound. Ethical relativism, which develops at the same time, focuses on individual taste, not cultural meaning, and states that there are no grounds for comparing the value-preferences of individuals in order to conclude which are better. Matters of taste are beyond dispute, and should disagreements on this score arise, there are no ethical guidelines by which resolution is possible. According to this view, ethical tenets vary not simply from culture to culture but also within cultures from individual to individual.

Modern art – in the words of Bradbury and McFarlane (1976, p. 27), 'The art consequent on Heisenberg's "Uncertainty principle", of the destruction of civilization and reason in the First World War, of the world changed and reinterpreted by Marx, Freud, and Darwin, of capitalism and constant industrial acceleration, of existential exposure to meaninglessness or absurdity' – also emerges in the early twentieth century and gives what is the most forceful expression to the modernist impulse. Based on the conviction that reality is much too elusive and incoherent to be captured by formal representation, modern art seeks to destroy traditional forms, styles, and conventions. Its aim is not photographic resemblance but the release of inner feeling, the revelation of the soul.

Modern art subordinates the cognitive to the emotional and is a consequence of feeling rather than perceiving reality. The result is not formal representation but twisted, disrupted, and disjointed images – distortions, no doubt, but distortions equal to those provided by science. The classical ideas of climax and plot are flaunted deliberately in modern art, as figures are disassembled, their parts scattered about, no part of the canvas regarded as more important than another, no mode of representation more valid than all the others. Similarly, modernist literature violates grammatical form and rules of punctuation and abandons the conventions of chronological order and logical connections. The world is absurd and ultimately unintelligible and modern art and literature emerge to express and to celebrate the chaos which surrounds us.

This view, as William Barrett (1962, p. 57) clearly explains, represents a full-fledged rejection of the previously long-dominant tradition of Western art

which distinguishes sharply between the sublime and the banal and requires that the highest art treat the most sublime subjects. The mind of the West has always been hierarchical: the cosmos has been understood as a great chain of Being, from highest to lowest, which has at the same time operated as a scale of values, from lowest to highest ...

By now, the heirarchical scheme has been abolished altogether ... Now the painter dispenses with objects altogether: the colored shape on his canvas is itself an absolute reality, perhaps more so than the imaginary scene, the great battle, which in a traditional canvas it might serve to depict. Thus we arrive at last at [brute art] ... which seeks to abolish not only the ironclad distinction between the sublime and the banal but that between the beautiful and the ugly as well.

The modern artist sides with the child, the primitive, the insane, with all those whose inner being eludes the restraints of reason. Freedom is found away from reason, the most repressive and mutilating force in the modern world.

In philosophy the modernist current takes root in the birth of existentialism. Existentialism presumes that people possess absolute freedom of choice; people are free in all circumstances to choose to act or refuse to act in a certain way and thus must take final responsibility for their actions and lives. Dread and anxiety – existential *angst* – accompany this freedom, however, for there are no rational criteria for choosing how to act and live. The world is absurd, and to experience it is to experience emptiness and nothingness. Nietzsche is the most important influence on the early development of existentialism and it is important to consider once again the thrust of his argument.

Recall that Nietzsche regards the morality of nineteenth-century Western society as a herd morality, one which sanctions meekness, submissiveness, conformism, and mediocrity. The source of bad conscience and self-torture, the herd morality inverts the normal order of development and coops up man's animal nature, the fount of creativity, by transforming virtue into vice, strength and courage into evil. Christianity, by protecting the weak from the strong, and liberal democracy, by discouraging excellence and rewarding mediocrity, are especially corrupting forces. Modernization, the spread of rationalization, has weakened considerably the slave morality, but it must be overcome completely and this, according to Nietzsche, is the task of the man of the future. He who can accept the awful responsibility of existential choice is to 'deliver us both from a lapsed ideal and from all that this ideal has spawned – violent loathing, the will to extinction, nihilism – ... [and to] make the will free once more and restore to the earth its aim, and to man his hope' (Nietzsche, 1971, p. 61).

A kind of existentialist hero, this superman struggles to reveal the very essence of life, 'the intrinsic superiority of the spontaneous, aggressive, overreaching, reinterpreting and re-establishing forces', knowing that 'everything evil, terrible, tyrannical in man, everything in him that is kin to beasts of prey and serpents, serves the enhancement of the species "man" as much as its opposite does' (Nietzsche, 1966, pp. 54–5). The task as Nietzsche sees it is the transvaluation of values so that what is presently viewed as vice becomes virtue: peace, humility, and pity must give way to struggle, arrogance, and ruthlessness; will must come to dominate reason, for its full expression purifies and strengthens life. Only with the Dionysian release of inner energy will there be hope for man in the age of anxiety and nihilism. Modernism glorifies this release and in important respects seeks to accomplish in its destruction of form and convention a transvaluation of values. Nietzsche's attack on prudence, humility, and civic responsibility, his derogation of reason, his association of freedom with instinctual liberation, fuel the modernist impulse and help to define modernist thought.

Resting on the defamation of reason, the modernist location of freedom in the impulsive, in feelings, in the inner life has had paradoxical consequences. Twentieth-century modernism, Marshall Berman (1982, pp. 23–4) writes,

> has thrived and grown beyond its own wildest hopes. In painting and sculpture, in poetry and the novel, in architecture and design, in a whole array of electronic media and a wide range of scientific disciplines that didn't even exist a century ago, our century has produced an amazing plentitude of works and ideas of the highest quality. The twentieth century may well be the most brilliantly creative in the history of the world, not least because its creative energies have burst out in every part of the world. The brilliance and depth of living modernism ... give us a great deal to be proud of, in a world where there is so much to be ashamed and afraid of.

Modernism does more than release the sources of artistic creativity. In the name of emotional liberation and in the form of narcissism, discussed in detail later on, modernism has entered into popular culture and consciousness as a movement against social restraints and obligations and communal rules, a movement which justifies the refusal to sacrifice personal pleasure for collective ends. In this form, modernism calls on the individual to deny all renunciations of pleasure and desire, particularly those imposed by the requirements for social order. Freedom is found outside of social obligations, in the creativity of emotional expression.

Yet this is just one side of the modernist impulse. The other is loaded with authoritarian proclivities. Elements of modernism appeared prominently in the ideology of the fascist movements which arose in every major country in the two decades following World War I. In Italy and Germany, of course, these movements achieved their greatest success: Mussolini came to power in 1922, Hitler in 1933. While Italian fascism and German Nazism differ substantially in several important respects, they have much in common. Each arose in highly chaotic and disorganized social circumstances, each spoke primarily to an insecure, confused, rootless, and frightened middle class, making their appeals to emotion, not reason, and each drew freely from the modernist current, especially the work of Nietzsche (Stern, 1978; Herf, 1981). The Nazis made Nietzsche, who died in 1900, a national hero and actively sought to popularize his ideas, particularly those which encouraged the distrust of reason and valued intuition, will, irrationalism and militarism. Nietzsche's damnation of liberal individualism, democracy, Christianity, pacifism and humanitarianism, his glorification of strength, impulse, warrior spirit, and the dominating, power-seeking man of the future matched well the themes of Nazi ideology.

The reactionary modernism of fascism and Nazism blunted the artistically creative and self-absorbing narcissistic qualities of freedom defined in opposition to reason. Instead, it cultivated the dread, anxiety, uneasiness and fright associated with existential freedom. Reactionary modernism offered, in Erich Fromm's (1941) words, an escape from freedom, a flight from the terrors of modernity. The modern sensibility, Berman (1982, p. 18) observes, is born in the atmosphere 'of agitation and turbulence, psychic dizziness and drunkenness, expansion of experiential possibilities and destruction of moral boundaries and personal bonds, self-enlargement and self-derangement, phantoms in the street and in the soul ...'. The fascist sensibility often shares this atmosphere. It arises in a way to allow people to flee from the experience of nothingness out of which this atmosphere develops. Fascism is successful when people experience their freedom as threatening, burdensome, and frightening, for by justifying subordination to the superman or the charismatic leader, it legitimates the surrender of freedom. Fascism, no doubt, would have emerged even in the absence of Nietzsche's thought, but not in the absence of what his thought represents – the abrogation of reason.

The steady increase in the influence and appeal of modernist thought during the twentieth century owes an immeasurable debt to the work of Sigmund Freud. That Freud's work contributed so greatly to the acceptance of modernist ideas is ironic, for from the very start Freud was strongly opposed to the modernist effort to liberate the instinctual by disrupting the restraining power of convention, morality, and reason.

Freud: Modernity and its Discontents

The concept of man offered by Freud is at once, writes Marcuse (1955, p. 11), 'the most irrefutable indictment of Western civilization ... [and]

the most unshakable defense of this civilization'. Civilization, in Freud's view, rests upon the renunciation of individual pleasure. Repression, facilitated and justified by the grand illusions of moral restraint and cultural prohibition, is the predicate of civilized life and, as well, the prime source of human unhappiness and misery. Here, of course, Freud is consistent with the main currents of modernist thought. But unlike the modernists, in particular Nietzsche, with whom he otherwise has much in common, Freud is a moralist, an ardent defender of repressive morality. Civilization, as it produces unhappiness, protects us against the three fundamental sources of human suffering:

> the superior power of nature, the feebleness of our own bodies and the inadequacy of the regulations which adjust the mutual relationships of human beings ... [The] contention ... that we should be much happier if we gave [civilization] up and returned to primitive conditions ... is astonishing because ... it is a certain fact that all the things with which we seek to protect ourselves against the threats that emanate from the sources of suffering are part of that very civilization. (Freud, 1961, p. 33)

The restrictions imposed by civilized life are the bases of order, survival, and what we have come to know as individuality. For these, Freud is willing to live with, while through psychoanalysis he seeks to mitigate the more severe consequences of, the discontents produced by civilization.

Clearly at the core of Freud's view is the assumption that there exists a profound and irreconcilable tension between nature and culture, between the requirements of human satisfaction and those of civilization, between psychological man and social man. In protecting us from nature – including our own nature – civilization restrains the pursuit of individual pleasure with the result that each of us in the very core of our being becomes an enemy of civilization. Though we need society in order to live, our basic nature is anti-social. Culture and civilization (Freud uses the terms interchangeably) develop not by altering this anti-social nature, for this is impossible, but by transforming the opposition of person and society into a conflict between two parts of the person. Civilization develops by dividing man against himself so that his ego and conscience emerge in opposition to his basic nature. With the growth of civilization, Freud (1964, p. 13) explains, 'external coercion gradually becomes internalized ... only by [this] means does [man] become a moral and social being. Such a strengthening of the super-ego [or the conscience] is a most precious cultural asset in the psychological field. Those in whom it has taken place are turned from being opponents of civilization into being its vehicles.' But they are internally divided vehicles, for by becoming civilized they do not eliminate their opposition to civilization, they internalize it.

The internalization of repression is the basis of the process of humanization. To understand this we must examine how Freud draws the relation of person and society and, before this, briefly consider his well-known model of personality structure. Freud describes the personality as consisting of three related systems: the unconscious id, the largely conscious ego, and the superego constituted by the internalized prohibitions of the outside world. The id is the original system, the bodily bedrock of human nature, and, as the reservoir of human energy, the source of all drives and of the power of the other two systems. Existing at the level of the unconscious, and oblivious to the demands of external reality, the id houses wishful images and impulses and, in compliance with the pleasure principle, aims 'at an absence of pain and unpleasure and ... at the experiencing of strong feelings of pleasure' (Freud, 1961, p. 23). The task of the id is immediate satisfaction – tension-reduction or drive-discharge – and it accomplishes this task either by simple reflex action or by working through the primary process. The primary process entails creating an image of an object whose possession would satisfy a drive presently expressed. Such wishful thinking serves to abate tension temporarily, but is, of course, no long-run solution. Ultimately, satisfaction requires not the image but the object itself and this necessitates interaction with external reality. For gratification to occur the primary process must be joined with a secondary process.

The secondary process involves reality-testing, entering into and negotiating with external reality in search of desired objects, and serves to enhance the ability to distinguish internal from external phenomena. The 'transition from primary to secondary process is the most basic – the most biological and universal-cultural, the least historical – of repressions ... because it is inseparable from the specifically human characteristics ... the secondary process ... transforms the mobile energy of the id into the bound energy of the ego' (Horowitz, 1977, pp. 22, 18). The ego, which draws its energy from the id, is the conscious, rational, adaptive part of the personality. Drive-restraint, not drive-discharge, is the way the ego meets the task of need-satisfaction. The ego, the locus of reason, is in conflict with the id. Indeed, 'in its relation to the id it is like a man on horseback, who has to hold in check the superior strength of the horse; with this difference, that the rider tries to do so with his own strength while the ego uses borrowed forces' (Freud, 1960, p. 15). Obedient to the reality principle, the ego is compelled to deflect the pleasure-seeking passions of the id.

The logic of the pleasure principle is expressed in the dreams, hallucinations, and wishful thoughts of the primary process – all inadequate to the requirements of need-satisfaction. With the secondary process, Freud claims,

> the psychical apparatus had to decide to form a conception of the real circumstances in the external world and to endeavor to make a real alteration in them. A new principle of mental functioning was thus introduced; what was presented in the mind was no longer what was agreeable but what was real, even if it happened to be disagreeable. The setting up of the reality principle proved to be a momentous step. (Freud, 1948, p. 219)

Based on the recognition of the scarcity of external reality, an awareness that the world is unable regularly, fully, and immediately to satisfy inner needs, the reality principle constrains and modifies rather than denies the pleasure principle. It is the principle of law and order, and under its guidance, the ego seeks to delay gratification, to restrain the passions, to control emotions, to become productive and secure – in short, to adapt to the necessary restraints of reality. As the ego and the reality principle rise to prominence in the personality, the form and content as well as the timing of pleasure is altered to become consistent with the exigencies of civilization.

The superego contains the internalized standards of external authority and offers guidelines which both prescribe and prohibit. Through the superego, civilization 'obtains mastery over the individual's dangerous desire[s] ... by setting up an agency within him to watch over [them], like a garrison in a conquered city' (Freud, 1961, p. 61). A harsh and severe, overly rigid and repressive conscience is capable of seriously damaging the ego. Normally, however, the superego fortifies the ego and assists it in the effort to comply with the requirements of civilized life by containing the id.

In the civilized or socialized adult, the personality or psychic structure is dominated by the ego which, with the vigilant assistance of a moralizing superego, keeps the id in check and adapts the pursuit of need-gratification to the demands of the natural and social environment. Yet civilized man is not at peace with himself, for the objectives of the seemingly defeated pleasure principle remain influentially alive in the unconscious. Indeed, much of what civilized man does and thinks is symptomatic of repressed drives, impulses, and wishes which constantly threaten the sense of order and security, the semblance of control and reason, brought by the strengthening of the ego. Civilized man differs from the psychotic whose ego has collapsed under the unremitting pressure from the id only in degree and not in kind. The irrevocable conflict between nature and culture continues within civilized man, and as civilization advances, the conflict intensifies.

Freud offers a hydraulic model of the relation between person and society. This model asserts that the development of civilization proceeds at the expense of individual pleasure and happiness, for the energy which otherwise should be expended on pleasure pursuits is put to work in the building of civilization. Renunciation of instincts is the condition of civilized life, and the stronger the restraints are, the higher will be the level of civilization. 'The liberty of the individual is no gift of civilization', Freud (1961, pp. 42–3) writes. 'It was greatest before there was any civilization ... The development of civilization imposes restrictions on [the individual], and justice demands that no one shall escape those restrictions.' Civilization deflates the social bases of liberty and happiness – yet Marcuse (1955, p. 17) makes the important point that 'the equation of freedom and happiness tabooed by the conscious is upheld by the unconscious ... [and] continues to haunt the mind'.

The key to the hydraulic relation between person and society is repressive sublimation. The building of civilization requires, first, the repression of the wishes and ideas formulated in accordance with the pleasure principle and the instinctual energy called forth to satisfy them, and, secondly, the sublimation or rechannelling of that bottled up energy into socially acceptable activities. For instance, the libidinal energy derived from the life instincts is directed away from sexual and sensual objects and released in activities that create the symbolic and material bases of civilization. The repressed wishes and thoughts (repressed because they are in violation of the reality principle) are pushed into the unconscious while the repressed energy is channelled into the construction of culture and civilization. Culture, in short, is sublimation, both a consequence of and the prime contributor to repression. The moral injunctions, ethical and religious interdictions, legal prohibitions and symbolic boundaries and limits which make up culture serve to justify the repression necessary for the continuation of civilization and progress.

Freud discerns the repressive character of culture in what he takes to be the origin of the first moral prohibition, the incest taboo. Initially, in the absence of organized social life, Freud claims, people lived in primal family hordes dominated by a powerfully tyrannical father who owned and controlled all goods and monopolized the female members. Despite the love and respect they had for their father, the sons came to experience the situation as intolerable, particularly as the paternal rule over women greatly restricted the satisfaction of their sexual urges. Ultimately, the sons banded together and killed their father. Soon after, they experienced remorse over this act and decided to punish themselves by re-establishing the code of the father in the form of the incest taboo – a moral regulation which restricted the number and types of women with whom the sons could satisfy their sexual desires. Religion and morality – culture – is thus born out of the effort to punish and repress. With the internalization of this external prohibition, conscience originates, and it shares the aim of punishment and repression (Freud, 1962; Nachman, 1981).

The slaying of the father that results in culture, Freud argues, is symbolically re-enacted in the psychological development of the sons in civilization. The recapitulation of the historical act of patricide in the individual is at the center of the 'Oedipus complex'. Freud (1971, p. 71) describes it concisely in the following way:

> The relation of a boy to his father is ... an 'ambivalent' one. In addition to the hate which seeks to get rid of the father as a rival, a measure of tenderness for him is also habitually present. The two attitudes of mind combine to produce identification with the father; the boy wants to be in his father's place because he admires him and wants to be like him, and also because he wants to put him out of the way. This whole development now comes up against a powerful obstacle. At a certain moment the child comes to understand that an attempt to remove his father as a rival would be punished by him with castration. So from fear of castration ... he gives up this wish to possess his mother and get rid of his father. In so far as this wish remains in his unconscious it forms the basis of the sense of guilt.

Thus the son resolves the Oedipus complex by becoming like his father – that is, by internalizing his father's (and society's) standards, by making them his own. In light of these standards, the son's sexual desire for his mother is found to be repugnant and whenever this desire gains conscious expression the son punishes himself by feeling guilty. Guilt is the consequence of the internalization of external and repressive standards.

Freud (1961, p. 81) takes guilt to be the fundamental experience of civilized man – 'the price we pay for our advance in civilization is a loss of happiness through the heightening of the sense of guilt'. A form of self-inflicted punishment, guilt reveals clearly the internal division in man brought by civilization. Very often these feelings of guilt give rise to neurosis. When battered by both a surging id and a rigidly punitive superego, the ego strives to protect itself by forming defense mechanisms or neurotic symptoms which deflect or contain the conflicting demands for immediate pleasure, on the one hand, and adherence to high moral standards on the other. Civilized man is both guilt-ridden and neurotic.

Yet, Freud emphasizes, the same developments that produce guilt and neurosis also make possible the autonomous individual, for the internalization of controls enables a substantial reduction of dependence on external authority. As internal controls expand, external controls decrease and individuality is promoted. The moralizing conscience which fosters guilt and neurosis is at the same time the inner resources – the basis of the so-called inner-directed personality – that makes for the autonomous individual. Civilized man, Freud has no doubt, is a damaged, mutilated, guilt-ridden, and neurotic individual, but an individual nonetheless.

Freud goes beyond Weber's analysis in associating progress in civilization with instinctual renunciation and neurosis. Yet, like Weber, he sees this progress and the attendant subordination of human activity to the imperatives of rationalization as resulting in increasing joylessness and unhappiness. The similarity of the two views is a consequence of the inability of each, in Horowitz's (1977, p. 158) words, 'to imagine the detachment of the technological apparatus and its rationality from the interest in domination and their subordination to "valuational postulates of freely associated individuals", that is, to Reason properly so called'. Reason, for Weber and Freud, is the instrumental reason, the technical rationality, of industrial capitalism. Reason is ultimately repressive, the antithesis of joy, happiness and freedom.

Theory and Therapy: Freud on Reason and Freedom
Freud's account of freedom is seemingly contradictory. He offers a notion of freedom whose psychic content is unfreedom. Civilized freedom has at its core, he implies, rational domination. Marcuse (1970, p. 12) describes Freud's conflation of freedom and rational domination well:

> As soon as civilized society establishes itself the repressive transformation of the instincts becomes the psychological basis of a *threefold domination*: first, domination over one's self, over one's nature, over the sensual drives that want only pleasure and gratification; second, domination of the labor achieved by such disciplined and controlled individuals; and third, domination over outward nature, science, and technology. And to domination subdivided in this way belongs the *threefold freedom* proper to it: first, freedom from the mere necessity of satisfying one's drives, that is, freedom for renunciation and thus for socially acceptable pleasure – moral freedom; second, freedom from arbitrary violence and from the anarchy of the struggle for existence, social freedom ..., with legal rights and duties – political freedom; and third, freedom from the power of nature, that is the mastery of nature, freedom to change the world through human reason – intellectual freedom.

Freud's concern with the basic unfreedom of civilized freedom can be clarified by considering his view of psychoanalysis as both theory and therapy.

Freud conceives psychoanalysis as both a social theory of civilization – its origins, development and dynamics – and a therapeutic method for treating the individual in civilization. The two aspects of psychoanalysis, Freud recognizes, exist in contradiction to one another. 'Psychoanalysis as individual therapy necessarily participates within the realm of social unfreedom', Russell Jacoby (1975, p. 120) notes, 'while psychoanalysis as theory is to transcend and criticize this same realm.' As theory, psychoanalysis constitutes a basis for radical critique; as therapy, it is a method to facilitate individual adjustment, to accomplish, in Freud's words, the transformation of 'hysterical misery into everyday unhappiness' (ibid., p. 122). From the perspective of theory, the equation of freedom and happiness is upheld in the unconscious; from that of therapy, the unconscious, that repository of the repressed and the irrational, continually threatens the individual's freedom. Thus Freud can argue, Peter Gay (1979, p. 55) writes, that the unconscious 'is at once the great agent of, and the strongest fetter on, human freedom'.

The social theory of psychoanalysis reveals the many substantial restrictions placed on the individual in the name of civilization and thus disabuses civilized man of the notion that freedom has expanded with the development of society. Reason, in this theory, appears as the denial of the pleasure principle, of the freedom to gratify natural urges and desires. The freedom we possess in civilization is the freedom from the overwhelming power of instinctual forces. While the theory highlights the restrictions imposed on freedom, therapy, in a kind of reversal, seeks to expand the area of freedom available to the individual, and it regards reason as indispensable to this task.

The task of therapy, according to Freud, is 'to enable the ego to push its conquest of id further still'; to 'give the patient's ego freedom to choose one way or the other'; and, thus, to help assure that 'Where id was, there ego shall be' (Freud, 1965, p. 80). Therapeutic intervention strives to bring the material of the unconscious into the conscious where the once repressed wishes and conflicts become subject to rational processes, that is, where the unconscious can be brought 'under the domination' of reason. 'Freud's choice of the word domination is telling here', writes Stan Draenos (1982a, p. 71).

In Freud, reason becomes an instrument of psychical domination rather than the realization of a rationally determined harmony of the soul because it has lost its metaphysical sanction ..., all substantive content, all norm-giving force, and becomes merely a necessity-imposed regulative function of the 'mental apparatus' – a means among means in the technique of living that is unable itself to determine the sense of living.

The reason of the rational ego is technical reason, devoid of all concern with ends and purposes, simply a means of adaptation to repressive civilization, a means of acquiring freedom within unfreedom.

Through therapy the primary aim of reason is to dilute the severely harsh and redundant moral controls of the superego which make for neurosis and other psychic disturbances and character disorders. In this setting, 'reason aspires to no final solutions, but is capable of engineering a judicious easing of overwrought moral ... demands' (Rieff, 1959, p. 92). In this way, therapy intends to strengthen reason, the intellect, the ego, and to bring under their control the passionate forces of instinct. The individual for whom therapy has succeeded is able to understand rationally the tensions between nature and culture existing within him, and has the capacity to choose freely and accept everyday unhappiness over the hysterical misery of guilt and neurosis.

To summarize, in Freud's theory, reason has the aims of repression, domination, and control and is firmly opposed to the freedoms required for psychic satisfaction, personal pleasure, and individual happiness. Reason clearly is an enemy of freedom. Yet, in Freud's therapy, reason as ego-control, a rational means of denial, is taken as the essential precondition of freedom – the freedom from instinctual compulsion, the freedom to abide by the reality principle, the freedom to be civilized and unhappy. The opposition between reason and freedom found in theory disappears in therapy. It does so, of course, because the freedom defined in therapy has as its basis rational domination.

Freud and Modernism

Freud, Phillip Rieff (1959, p. 76) emphasizes, is 'a defender of the beleaguered power of reason ..., a critic of the passions'. Yet Freud is aware that reason is a fragile force, never quite able to dominate entirely the irrational substance of our being, and less a factor of motivation than a check on the unconscious wishful impulses which are the primary motivators of human action. Freud champions repressive culture and moral restraints, knowledgeable of the guilt and unhappiness they provoke, as illusions indispensable to civilized life.

Under the influence of modernism, Freud's moralism is lost, and his position reinterpreted to be consistent with the repudiation of reason and the celebration of inner passions. 'All Freud's work demonstrates', claims one such reinterpretation (Brown, 1959, p. 57), 'that the allegiance of the human psyche to the pleasure-principle is indestructible and that the path of instinctual renunciation is the path of sickness and self-destruction.' Why abide by repressive illusions, particularly when, as Freud so clearly shows, they cause so much suffering and unhappiness? Freud's answer to this question – we must comply in order to live in society, and we must have society in order to live as human beings – is forgotten, and the modernist response – we need not and should not conform to repressive illusions – prevails.

Reinterpreted in these terms, Freud's work contributes greatly to the evolution of modernist thought into a modernist culture which fosters, in Marcuse's (1970, p. 44) words, 'the obsolescence of the Freudian concept of man'. Modernist culture forbids nothing and encourages the exploration of all feelings and experiences. In its denial of constraints of any kind, modernist culture promotes the development of the narcissistic personality – possessive of a weakly bounded ego and few inner resources – and the disappearance of guilt-ridden, neurotic Freudian man. In Rieff's (1959, p. 392) terms, narcissistic man lives 'beyond reason – reason having proved no adequate guide to his safe conduct through the meaningless experience of life'; he lives 'beyond conscience – conscience having proved no adequate guide ... and furthermore to have added absurd burdens of meaning to the experience of life'; and he lives 'with the knowledge that [his] dreams ... cannot be fulfilled'. Taught not to feel guilty for expressing natural desires, narcissistic man goes with his feelings, 'lets it all hang out', and lives for the moment, all as part of the search for the pleasure denied Freudian man. With the development of narcissism, psychoanalysis becomes obsolete, for its very object – the individual – is made obsolete. Modernist culture, the culture of narcissism, rises with the eclipse of the individual.

The question of narcissism is broad and complex, involving as it does issues of authority, meaning, civility, family, community, and character structure. In examining this question, we come to confront those concrete socio-historical forces and developments which accompany and express the spread of rationality without reason and which lead to the eclipse of the individual. We thus shift our focus from the re-orientation of thought and theory to the re-orientation of society, culture, and personality. In so doing, our task is to see how the social forms and historical processes taken by instrumental reason emaciate human freedom by depriving it of its most essential source of sustenance – the individual. Below, the characteristic features of narcissism, particularly those most corrosive of individuality, are examined and, in turn, related to the rationalizing processes which underlie the development of capitalism.

Narcissism and the Modernist Impulse

When the modernist impulse spreads from the realm of art, fantasy, and imagination to become a dynamic force in social life, the result is narcissism. Narcissism is the contemporary expression of modernism and, in important respects, represents the most forceful and significant articulation of the modernist way of life. The modernist thrust of the narcissistic tendencies found in modern society is seen most clearly, perhaps, in the decline of civility. Civility, writes Robert Coles (1980, pp. 139–41), is bound up with

> a sense that one's behavior ought to be, under a range of circumstances, responsive to, and respectful of, certain standards ... [It] means all of us subordinating our feelings to certain shared imperatives ... [and] giving up impulse. For what? For the sake of procedure, order, restraint; for the sake of a thankful absence of the other person's torrent of emotional impulses ... The gift for the act of renunciation (civility) is, of course, civilization.

Richard Sennett (1974, pp. 264–5) similarly defines civility as 'activity which protects people from each other and yet allows them to enjoy each other's company', and proceeds to consider its reverse, incivility, as the 'burdening [of] others with oneself ... [and] the decrease in sociability with others this burden of personality creates'. Coles and Sennett agree that incivility has become a constitutive feature of modern society, helping to define it as an intimate society which structures narcissism and sanctions the disclosure of innermost feelings in a way that destroys public life, meaningful social relations, and a coherent sense of self. Arising in seeming opposition to the discontents of civilization, narcissistic incivility is accompanied by its own discontents and anxiety.

Two major and conflicting interpretations of this development are offered by Daniel Bell and Christopher Lasch. Influenced by Weber's analysis of rationalization and Durkheim's discussion of the sacred, non-rational supports of social order, Bell views narcissism as threatening to the requirements of advanced capitalism, a consequence of modernism's antagonism to bourgeois life and aims. Lasch's analysis of narcissism is informed by Marx's assessment of proletarianization and Freud's psychoanalytic concept of culture as sublimation. According to Lasch, narcissism develops not in contradiction to advanced capitalism but as a clear reflection of what this society has become.

The modernist impulse from the very start expressed and defined itself in opposition to the bourgeois impulse for order, cleanliness, reliability, and restraint. Nevertheless, Bell notes, modernism always has been most at home in bourgeois culture. Here, modernism in art and imagination has been approved, and, often, the uneasy tension between the bourgeois and the modern was a source of constructive creativity. However, once the distinction between art and life is overcome so that what is permitted in the former is also allowed in the latter, the two impulses enter into mutual rage, each seeking the destruction of the other. As the techniques of mass production and mass consumption were advanced after the 1920s, the rage intensified, mass production requiring the steady methodical, restrained worker, mass consumption the impulsive, pleasure-seeking consumer. Yet, the rationalization of society entailed by the development of these techniques ultimately weakened the Protestant ethic and shifted the balance in favor of the modernist impulse for instant gratification. Now, Bell (1976, pp. 21–2) argues, the 'cultural ... justification of capitalism has become hedonism, the idea of pleasure as a way of life. And in the ... ethos that now prevails, the model for a cultural imago has become the modernist impulse, with its ideological rationale of the impulse quest as a mode of conduct. It is this which is the cultural contradiction of capitalism.'

At the basis of this fateful contradiction is a radical disjunction of culture and economy. The standards of the economy are those of formal rationality, and they value efficiency, calculation, and the rational organization and ordering of things and people. In contrast, the standards of modernist culture are hedonistic, anti-rational, promiscuous, and in favor of instinctual sources of expression. The guiding principles of the two realms lead in contrary directions, and the contradiction they constitute threatens to tear apart the social fabric.

'Modernism', Bell (ibid., pp. 19–20) insists, has 'been the seducer. Its power derived from the idolatry of the self. Its appeal stemmed from the idea that life itself should be a work of art, and that art could only express itself against the conventions of a society, particularly bourgeois society.' In the form of narcissism, modernism is broadened to become an attack on all conventions and artifices, all restraints and boundaries, not simply those of bourgeois culture. Modernism as narcissism is a rejection of society itself. It is a freedom from society that results in the anomie which underlies identity crisis, cultural crisis, crisis of authority and governance, and the very crisis of advanced capitalism itself.

Lasch agrees with Bell that narcissism represents a denial of bourgeois values, but it is a denial, he claims, which emerges from developments promoted by those very values, a denial which is also a culmination of bourgeois values. Narcissism, according to Lasch, is the psychological outcome of the growing dependence on bureaucratic structure entailed by the rationalization of capitalism. Proletarianization, which initially stripped people of their means of production, now strips them of their ordinary competences – the skills and the knowledge of everyday life – and thus increases dependence on the state and the corporation. Narcissism originates in this 'new kind of paternalism, which has risen from the ruins of the old paternalism of kings, priests, authoritarian fathers, slavemasters, and landed overlords. Capitalism has severed the ties of personal dependence only to revive dependence under cover of bureaucratic rationality' (Lasch, 1978, p. 218). Narcissism is the psychological expression of this dependency, both a defense against the feelings of helplessness it provokes and a yearning for attention and care where neither seems to exist. Capitalism, Lasch (1979a, pp. 194–5) writes in a summary of his argument,

> has steadily eroded the capacity for self-help and self-discipline ... As more and more people find themselves disqualified, in effect, from their performance of adult responsibilities, the psychology of narcissistic dependence begins to pervade American culture, to replace the pursuit of gain with the more desperate goal of psychic survival, and to encourage a strategy of living for the moment, keeping your options open, and avoiding moral or emotional commitments.

For Lasch, then, narcissism is not the consequence of a modernism antagonistic to the rational requirements of advanced capitalism. It is, rather, a product of the rationalizing forces released by the development of capitalism. The connection between narcissism and modern capitalism is not a contradictory one but a complementary one. Where Bell worries that the hedonistic fall-out from cultural modernism will prevent people from adequately performing the tasks demanded by a rational and efficient economic realm, Lasch (1978, pp. 43–4) notes the consistency between narcissism and the expectations of contemporary work: 'the narcissist has many traits that make for success in bureaucratic institutions, which put a premium on the manipulation of interpersonal relations, discourage the formation of deep personal attachments, and at the same time provide the narcissist with the approval he needs in order to validate his self-esteem'. In Lasch's view, narcissism, far from contradicting advanced capitalism, stands as one of its characteristic features.

Despite their differences, both Bell and Lasch attribute narcissism to the spread of instrumental reason or technical rationality. This aspect of their arguments is important and deserves to be highlighted for the light it sheds on the implications of the modernist and narcissistic views of the relation between reason and freedom.

Instrumental Reason and Narcissistic Freedom

In a world where it is difficult to care for others, each looks to care for oneself, and the result is flight from public life and search for psychic survival. Narcissists experience life as impoverished, empty, and purposeless; they find interpersonal relations cold and manipulative. The narcissistic preoccupation with the self – relating to objects as extensions of the self, defining others as objects existing to serve its self – rests on and fosters a devaluation of others. The inability to care that is characteristic of narcissism, the sense that there is no one to turn to for support in time of need, furthers the effort to create a self-absorption that will enable the person to need no one at all. Finding no meaning in relationships with others, the narcissist turns inward.

The perspective of narcissism is without boundaries, admitting no reflective self-awareness. In the absence of firm ego boundaries, the world and the people and things in it are experienced as pictures of the self. Weak ego boundaries allow for openness and sensitivity, but they come directly at the expense of a meaningful and coherent identity. Without a stable identity, the narcissist loses everything when the quest for intimacy fails. As a safeguard against this possibility, the narcissist looks for the risk-free, painless intimacy of non-binding commitments.

The intense preoccupation with self that defines narcissism represents not merely self-love but also a hatred for the external world or object, a hatred whose outward discharge the person fears. Thus, while actively searching for intimate and open relationships, the narcissist fears these relationships for the inner rage, anger, and hostility they might unleash. Close involvement and commitment, caring and tenderness, are typically seen as signs of a manipulative dependency, emotional disaster, and potential self-destruction. The 'fear that being deeply involved [means] being "slaughtered" keeps the narcissist from making the commitments that are necessary for close relationships' (Hendin, 1975, p. 25).

The solution to the narcissist's search for sensory experience without emotional involvement, intimacy without feeling, is the casual, 'no-strings-attached' relationship. Although the casual relationship helps to avoid the pain and anger associated with close relationships, it also intensifies the experience of emptiness and meaninglessness, the sense of despair, that accompanies narcissism. This is especially the case with sexual relations. Given the narcissistic tenor of the times, Sennett (1974, p. 7) writes, 'there has ... been a reaction against the idea that physical love is an action people engage in, and like any other social action might have rules, limits, and necessary fictions which give the action a specific meaning. Instead, sex is a revelation of the self.' The sexual partner becomes an oject of self-validation, a source of pleasure to be taken while it is there. Casual sex requires no commitment and thus is free of the risk of loss the narcissist fears. Yet, like all forms of narcissistic intimacy, it promotes isolation in the midst of openness and impairs emotional involvement in the name of emotional liberation. 'Narcissism', Sennett (ibid., p. 8) finds, 'thus has the double quality of being a voracious absorption in self needs and the block to their fulfillment'.

The above loosely describes clinical or pathological narcissism, not the emerging narcissistic character structure which is increasingly, though certainly not exclusively, found among well-to-do, educated young adults.

This 'normal' narcissism embodies in much more qualified, less intense form many of the traits and tendencies found in the clinically diagnosed narcissistic personality, but arises, Morgenthau and Person (1978, p. 337) note, 'adaptively in response to cultural dilemmas and not primarily out of disordered individual development'. Adaptive narcissism is not the newest synonym for the rugged individualism of an earlier capitalism. The relatively autonomous subject of rugged individualism defined his self and his individuality in a cultural context of consensually validated values. In contrast, narcissistic individuality is 'seen as the legitimacy of the expression of the individual's needs against the demands of society, as opposed to the view of individuality that expresses itself through preeminence within an established order' (ibid., p. 342). Arising in the absence of durable relationships, meaningful standards and consensual values, adaptive narcissism testifies to individual impotence and inner emptiness, to the damaged self, not the ascendent self.

In Ralph Turner's (1976) terms, bourgeois individuality is defined with respect to an institutional self, narcissistic individuality with reference to an impulsive self. The institutional self is achieved, created, forged in the often painful interaction between personal desires and social demands. It is the result of an overcoming of external constraints that is made possible by the internalization of constraints or institutional expectations. The impulsive self is discovered in feelings and emotions, and its discovery takes place away from social constraints, far from those institutional barriers to impulse expression. For the institutional self, personal integrity means rigorous adherence to high standards of conduct and requires the capacity to keep emotions subordinated to these standards even in the most difficult circumstances. At all times, behavior must be in accord with the institutional prescriptions taken as one's own. Integrity for the impulsive self requires that behavior be consistent with feelings. Adherence to standards when the required behavior is at odds with what one wants to do is the epitome of hypocrisy. Only when inhibitions are abandoned is it possible to be true to one's real self. Where the individual promoted by the institutional self remains committed to principles even in the face of strong temptations to do otherwise, the individual fostered by the impulsive self continues to act on feelings and impulses and to disregard duties and obligations despite pressure to do the reverse.

The institutional self has much in common with ego-dominated, instinctually repressed Freudian man. Conversely, the impulsive self, in Freudian terms, exhibits a personality with a shrunken ego, one which has regressed into the id, and a harsh, punitive superego which acquires its psychic energy from the more destructive impulses of the id. The punitive, hostile, and aggressive side of the superego prevails when experience of loved and respected models of social conduct, a major modifying influence, is lacking. Emerging at the direct expense of conscience, the destructive superego facilitates the manipulation, exploitation, and appropriation of others. In the impulsive self the superego is put to work in the service of the id, the ego is weak, and consciousness and conscience are underdeveloped. If, as Freud argues, the individual requires a strong ego and inner resources, the impulsive self rests on the decline of the individual.

Narcissism has its roots in the rationalizing processes of capitalism. Resting on continuous economic growth, capitalism as an economic system derives its ultimate justification less from moral principle than from its efficiency and effectiveness in raising the material standard of living. The productive process of developed capitalism makes possible – indeed requires – mass consumption, and its rise, according to Bell, underlies hedonistic culture. Initiated in the 1920s and extended from then on, the techniques of mass culture – mass marketing, installment buying, advertisement – promote the 'buy now, pay later' attitude reflected in the narcissistic tendency to live for the moment and to grab solitary gratifications.

The rationalization of the state followed upon the rationalization of the economy, and one result was the erosion of public life and the civic affections and sentiments it sustained. The rational state, like the rational corporation, bases its appeal for mass loyalty on its capacity to deliver the goods. Incivility begins here, for it means very little to be a citizen of a rational, efficient system, particularly when that system is unable morally to justify the sacrifice of narcissism that is fundamental to the cultivation of a firm, coherent identity. What results is a culture without public life, a culture 'marked by a self-interest and egocentrism that increasingly reduce all relations to the question: What am I getting out of it?' (Hendin, 1975, p. 13).

Through the corporation and the state, the logic of rationality eventually penetrated the family, where it directly influenced patterns of socialization. The bourgeois family of earlier capitalism was privatized and offered a refuge from the cold rationality and impersonal harshness of outside society. In advanced capitalism, as Lasch shows in some detail, the same forces that impoverished work and civic life and made necessary the development of the family as a warm haven

invade the private realm and its last stronghold, the family. The tension between the family and the economic and political order, which in an earlier stage of bourgeois society protected children and adolescents from the full impact of the market, gradually abates. The family, drained of the emotional intensity that formerly characterized domestic relations, socializes the young into the easygoing, low-keyed encounters that predominate in the outside world ... (Lasch, 1977, p. xvii)

Under the pressure of mass consumption, the family became a conduit between consumers and the external agents of rationality once precluded from entering the home. Later, familial responsibility was further reduced as the family became increasingly dependent on expanded state services. Bureaucratic rationality replaced the family as the mediator between subjective and objective existence.

The contemporary family, in Sennett's (1977, p. 185) words, has become a 'destructive gemeinschaft'. Reflected in the celebrated permissiveness of the contemporary middle-class family is an effort, partly encouraged by the loss of parental authority, to avoid emotional entanglements and psychic conflicts, to escape those painful confrontations between parents and children whose resolution, according to Freud, appears necessary to the formation of strong, self-reliant identities. As emotional involvement in the family declines, children are acceded to, encouraged to be their own persons, provided with little more than material comforts. Lacking a morally grounded authority, the family, like the economy and the state, tends to concentrate more on delivering the goods than on warmth and shared concerns, and it creates a painless environment for growing up. Yet this painless pattern of childrearing is ultimately painful, for it produces children who 'have suffered a profound narcissistic injury that either numbs them or drives them toward the perpetual pursuit of pleasure detached from emotion' (Hendin, 1975, p. 313).

Narcissism involves an acting out rather than a repression or sublimation of psychic conflicts and urges. At first glance, this freedom to act out inner feelings appears inconsistent with the demands of rationality. This seeming contradiction disappears once it is recognized that narcissistic freedom is not only produced by but is compatible with the administrative logic of instrumental reason. The desublimation of psychic energy which underlies narcissistic freedom is repressive in character, for the released energy is governed by and placed in the service of rationalized organizational structures rather than a rational ego. Accordingly, narcissistic freedom is a rationally administered freedom in terms of which impulses receive immediate gratification, and sex devoid of meaning and intimacy emptied of feeling are freely pursued. Administrative desublimation produces much individual distress but little in the way of social distress.

By permitting the open acting out of psychic conflicts, this institutionalized desublimation eliminates not distress but the form and the meaning of distress. It both generates and masks submission to reality: 'The individual must adapt himself to a world which does not seem to demand the denial of his innermost needs – a world which is not necessarily hostile' (Marcuse, 1964, p. 74). Marcuse offers this observation in his discussion of one-dimensional man. Narcissism might very well be a response to or a way of coping with the loss of subjectivity and self which one-dimensional man represents. But narcissism is merely a subjective search for subjectivity, a meaningless quest for meaning.

Writing in 1955, Marcuse carefully describes the emancipatory political implications of narcissism and sexuality. 'Narcissistic Eros', Marcuse (1955, p. 156) writes, 'is to the end the negation of this order – the Great Refusal.' The Great Refusal promises not an end to society or culture, not simply the release of libidinal energies and impulses, but their transformation, one made possible by replacing repressive sublimation by non-repressive sublimation (sublimation under the control of critical, self-reflective reason). Narcissistic Eros promotes a non-repressive mode of sublimation which challenges, struggles against, and seeks to *overcome* the opposition between man and nature, subject and object, potentiality and actuality, in order to create a more satisfying culture. The reactivation of narcissistic sexuality is culture-building only when part of a common, political project. Otherwise, as a deed of isolated individuals, the result is neurosis. 'Libido can take the road of self-sublimation only as a *social* phenomenon: as an unrepressed force, it can promote the formation of culture only under conditions which relate associated individuals to each other in the cultivation of the environment for their developing needs and faculties' (ibid., p. 191). Expressed in this way, Narcissistic Eros goes beyond the prevailing conditions and allows us both to recall and to anticipate a world that is not to be mastered and administered but to be liberated – and, Marcuse thinks, here resides the political potential of narcissism.

Nine years later, Marcuse discovers that modern capitalism has the capacity to absorb and contain the revolutionary thrust of Eros. Technological advancement has both reduced the need for and limited the scope of sublimation. The result is a repressive desublimation which actively sponsors a 'sexual revolution' as the release of constrained sexuality within the established institutions. Satisfaction, in this context, generates submission. Desublimated sexuality 'is part and parcel of the society in which it happens, but nowhere its negation' (Marcuse, 1964, p. 77). Stripped from its sublimated form, sexuality neither resists integration into the existing patterns nor sustains the Great Refusal. Clearly, Marcuse's assessment of sexuality now applies to narcissism as well. Desublimation – replacing mediated gratification by unmediated, immediate gratification – occupies a central place in the phenomenon of narcissism. Desublimated narcissism does not struggle against the opposition of culture and nature, subject and object, it simply denies that such opposition is real; it aims not to humanize nature but to naturalize humans, and thus it is not culture-building, it is culture-destroying.

Marcuse observes in 1965 (p. 57) that 'the flattening out of the antagonism between culture and social reality ... takes place not through the denial and rejection of the "cultural values", but through their wholesale incorporation into the established order ...'. This situation has changed, for today the tension between culture and social reality is reduced for many by the very obliteration of culture itself. Encouraging direct sensory experience, desublimated experience free of symbolic meaning and mediation, the culture of narcissism is an anti-culture with no ideals, no sublimated strivings, that must be repelled.

Narcissistic freedom, in sum, entails submission to a rational and rationalizing but unreasonable reality. It is the freedom that comes from surrender to the facts of this reality and thus a freedom that conceals a weakened capacity to resist these facts. One key fact of the reality of advanced capitalism is the enormous difficulty in maintaining warm, close, committed, trustful, and enduring relations. Rather than struggle against this fact, more and more people simply submit to it and pursue the easy if ultimately unsatisfying pleasures of casual, impersonal experiences. In so doing, they leave untouched the forces which underlie the fact of truncated relationships. Narcissistic freedom is fraught with despair, for it is the freedom of domination in the context of administrative rationality, the innocuous search for pleasure in an unpleasurable reality. It is the freedom of a society with rationality but without reason, to recall C. Wright Mills, the freedom of the mutilated subject left by itself in the rubble of destroyed human relationships. Of course, as Jacoby (1975, pp. 112–13) reminds us, the 'concept of freedom lies elsewhere; it is anchored in the sustained relation between two individuals; it can transcend and go beyond this – and ultimately must – but cannot bypass it'.

Conclusion

The modernist claim that freedom is to be found away from reason, in the impulsive and spontaneous, is based on the acceptance of the view that reason and freedom are enemies. It thus accepts as it denies the instrumental concept of reason. On one level, Freud appears to concur with this claim, noting the indispensability of the renunciatory and repressive aspects of reason to the growth of civilization, never a friend of freedom. Yet, on another level, Freud sees the reason of the rational ego as the essential precondition of ego-freedom, the important and healthy freedom from instinctual compulsion. Although Freud defends instru- mental reason in this form as necessary for ego-freedom and civilized life, his work nevertheless contributes to the popularization of modernist themes and the emergence of a therapeutic culture which encourages the denial of reason in the name of individual emancipation.

Modernist ideas eventually evolve into a culture of narcissism where ego-rationality is weakened and freedom as narcissistic desublimation is spawned. While in fundamental respects an extension of modernism, narcissistic freedom is more of a complement to rather than an opponent of instrumental reason. The irony is that the freedom promoted by a cultural modernism antagonistic to instrumental rationality is the freedom most suited to that rationality. The narcissistic freedom anticipated by modernism is found not outside but within instrumental reason.

In developing the critique of modernism and its current narcissistic forms of expression, we should not commit the mistake made by Daniel Bell and Christopher Lasch. Bell's analysis, Habermas (1981, p. 7) notes, 'shifts onto cultural narcissism the uncomfortable burdens of a more or less successful capitalist modernization of the economy and society ... and thus blurs the relationship between the welcomed process of societal modernization on the one hand, and the lamented cultural development on the other'. With Bell and, ultimately, Lasch as well, the critique of modernism expands to become a critique of modernity and modernization, one which often implies a rejection of the important and truly progressive achievements of each. The ambiguity which should characterize our understanding of the dialectical character of modernity and modernization, the very ambiguity which marks Marcuse's treatment of these issues, is lost in what frequently becomes an attempt to vilify the accomplishments of modern society in the name of some romanticized image of the past. Recall that while Marcuse celebrates the disappearance of the bourgeois individual ('Freudian man') for the emancipatory potential it makes possible, at the same time he worries that the antagonistic content found in the unconscious and in the culture of the bourgeois individual, the image of the uncompromised ideals and needs of humanity sustained by each, will be flattened out, incorporated harmlessly in the logic of administrative rationality and instrumental domination. By actively fostering the demise of bourgeois individuality, does modernity bring us closer to a civilization guided by reasoned eros, or does it produce the 'cheerful robot' who, without inner resources, bereft of antagonistic content, implicates himself in his own unfreedom? Marcuse is unsure.

Recent assessments concur with Marcuse's claim that capitalist modernization has damaged severely and irreparably the bases of bourgeois individuality, but their interpretations of what this development portends are emptied of the dialectical ambiguity characteristic of Marcuse's analysis. One set of interpretations finds that modern capitalism, by exhausting the bases of ordinary competence, has manufactured helplessly dependent, internally empty persons for whom the pursuit of private gain has been replaced by the more desperate goal of psychic survival, a goal which prompts a search for momentary gratifications. In this view, the eclipse of bourgeois individuality converges with the expansion of the scope of rationalized domination. Occurring when and how it does, it is indeed a regressive development. A second set of interpretations, one influenced more by Nietszche than by Freud, discovers in this development an emancipatory potential, the possibility of the post-individual. As modernity banishes the repressive illusion of the individual, people are better able to abandon the restraining myth of a unitary, continuous, stable identity and thus begin to desire the satisfaction of desire instead of its repression.

Christopher Lasch, as seen above, forcefully presents the first type of interpretation, Gilles Deleuze and Felix Guattari (1977) the second. The two positions are remarkably similar in their assessments of the impact which modernity as the experience of advanced capitalism has had on bourgeois individuality. They break ranks quite substantially, however, both in their analyses of what this impact has made possible and in the strategies they propose in response to this possibility. The dispute, as it is raised on this level, is one of anti-modernism versus post-modernism. Lasch is committed to the post-bourgeois individual and defines his task in terms of combating those forces unleashed by modernity which destroy the continuity, the permanence, the sense of place, and the civility indispensable to any kind of individuality, not simply bourgeois individuality. Deleuze and Guattari give their commitment to the post-individual and envision their task as facilitating the move beyond modernity. Each position, for contending reasons, wants to abandon the project of modernity – Lasch because it goes too far in destroying the conditions of individuality, Deleuze and Guattari because it does not go far enough, that is, it blunts the realization of what it makes possible, the post-individual, the 'schizo', unrestrained by either social codes or a bounded, unitary concept of self and thus wholly committed to the immediate satisfaction of desire.

Marcuse's understanding of the emancipatory implications of narcissism enables us to avoid the extremes represented by Lasch on the one hand and Deleuze and Guattari on the other. Two central points are implied by Marcuse's analysis. First, as the location of desire in the self, narcissism is an essential aspect of all relationships. While it often takes the form of selfishness, self-centeredness, and self-absorption, narcissism is also expressed as self-worth, pride, and dignity. Expressed in these terms and placed in the service of reason (as distinct from the service of the rationalizing forces of corporation and state), narcissism advances the building of emancipatory culture. Secondly, if narcissism is to be developed positively and not simply be unleashed as raw, overcoming, infantile desire, it requires the presence of socially coherent human surroundings which are supportive of community, civility, and concern for the other. Against Lasch, then, Marcuse suggests that it is not our task to oppose narcissism in the name of post-bourgeois individuality, for the post-bourgeois individual will be defined in part at least by narcissistic tendencies – a refusal to participate without good reason in self-sacrifice, in impulse-control, and in the perpetuation of relations and practices which are personally dissatisfying. Commitment to painful or stultifying roles and obligations – a sign of virtue for the bourgeois individual – is rejected by the post-bourgeois individual. Not rejected, however, are culture and sublimation, civility and community. Here, Marcuse opposes Deleuze and Guattari in his insistence that the task is not to promote the post-individual, the schizo living beyond community and culture; it is, rather, to cultivate the collective action and social relations appropriate to a reasonable narcissism, the basis of the post-bourgeois individual.

Modernity, Marcuse suggests, is enormously more complex than either Lasch or Deleuze and Guattari would have us believe. Modernity does make possible repression without socialization (and with it the eclipse of the individual), but it simultaneously affords the basis for socialization without repression, the basis, that is, for realizing the Enlightenment promise of the autonomous and reasonable yet playful, expressive, and desire-seeking individual. Modernity, in short, intertwines the positive and the negative. Block and Hirschhorn (1979, pp. 380–1) put this matter well:

> The break-up of existing family patterns ... creates both dangers and possibilities. The danger is that as people find it increasingly difficult to stay together in families, the vast reaches of people's emotional lives find no structured outlet, no forum in the organization of social life. Instead, their needs find expression in the more anomic settings of swinging sex, the cult of pornography, and various forms of addiction. As the linear life course decays, emotional energies are let loose on a vast plane of disordered mass impulses. But possibilities also emerge for a much richer range of nondestructive forms of expression. Sexual minorities that had been directly oppressed by the tyranny of the linear life course have greater freedom, and men and women have the opportunity to rebuild family life on a more solid foundation than female subordination and male dominance.

The realization of the positive moment requires neither anti-modernism nor post-modernism, but an appreciation of the achievements of modernity and modernization. These achievements make possible a political imagination which, as Elshtain (1980, p. 111) describes it, works 'as a species of fantasy of a particular sort, tapping moral and aesthetic impulses, public and private identities: a dynamic concatenation of individual psychic states, wishes, fears, desires, reasonings, which, transformed into visions, may manifest themselves on the social level'. A precondition of this political imagination is civility, but one predicated on a respect for a fluid, flexible life course, one which encourages the greater self-awareness which emerges from the experience of fluidity. Civility is a prerequisite precisely to the extent that the positive moment requires for its articulation conscious, reasoned collective action.

Appropriate to this political imagination of modernity, then, is a new principle of social organization which ties together a public sphere in which people come together as individuals to discover through open, non-constrained communication the common interest, and a private sphere in which individual needs, yearnings, and desires are able to receive non-distorted expression, so that each sphere mutually reinforces the other. Essential to each is both a new mode of socialization, socialization without repression, and protection from the rationalizing and totalizing tendencies of state and market. Here, Lasch and Deleuze and Guattari are correct in pointing to the need to contain and reverse the spread of rationality without reason. However, this reversal is predicated on, as it anticipates the further development of, not Lasch's narcissistic personality bereft of ordinary competence or Deleuze and Guattari's overcoming schizo, but the real individual promised by, yet so far denied by, modernity. From different perspectives and with different intentions, the anti-modernists and the post-modernists share an opposition to completing the project of modernity spawned by the Enlightenment. 'There are', Thomas McCarthy (1984, pp. v–vi) writes,

> good reasons for being critical of the illusions of the Enlightenment. The retreat from 'dogmatism' and 'superstition' has been accompanied by fragmentation, discontinuity and loss of meaning. Critical distance from tradition has gone hand in hand with anomie and alienation, unstable identities and existential insecurities. Technical progress has by no means been an unmixed blessing; and the rationalization of administration has all too often meant the end of freedom and self-determination … [Yet] if we wish to avoid a precipitate abandonment of the achievements of modernity … [w]hat is called for … is an enlightened suspicion of enlightenment, a reasoned critique of Western rationalism, a careful reckoning of the profits and losses entailed by 'progress'. Today, once again, reason can be defended only by way of a critique of reason.

A key task of the day is to participate in the completion of the project of modernity, not its abandonment.

5

Capitalist Rationalization and Democracy

The purpose of this chapter is to bring together many of the arguments and points made previously in order to understand in terms of reason and freedom some of the central dilemmas of contemporary society, particularly the United States. This goal is pursued on the basis of an analysis of the spread of capitalist rationalization and its impact on the conceptualization and the practice of democracy. By focusing on democracy, our concern with freedom is both narrowed and broadened – narrowed because democracy refers to a particular kind of freedom, the freedom to participate in the determination of collective ends; broadened because the concept of democracy bears not simply on the question of freedom but also on those of equality and reason and the relation that obtains among the three.

The logic of capitalist rationalization refers both to the process of calculation, standardization, formalization, and administration (and reflects Weber's concern with efficiency) and to the process of appropriating and centralizing the bases of ordinary competence – for instance, the means of production and productive skill and knowledge (and expresses Marx's concern with capital accumulation). In the previous chapter implicit reference is made to the dynamics of capitalist rationalization in the account of the development of cultural modernism and narcissism. In Bell's discussion of the formalization and standardization of consumption, as in Lasch's assessment of the rationalization of the family, these dynamics are glimpsed, as are their effects on the whittling down of ego and personal responsibility. In this chapter, the analysis is extended to consider how the spread of capitalist rationality brings about a narrowing down of the democratic ethos and practice. If the analysis begins under the influence of Marx and Weber, it ends on a different note – the suggestion that the rationalization of democracy is starting to result in the kind of corporatist political arrangements long ago anticipated by Durkheim.

The Rationalization of Democracy

The marketplace rationality of industrializing capitalism gained full expression in the concept and institutions of nineteenth-century liberal democracy. Eventually, with the replacement of entrepreneurial by corporate capitalism, and the ensuing relocation of the center of rationality from the marketplace comprised of rational, self-interested individuals to the bureaucratic structures of the modern corporation and nation-state, liberal democracy gave way to various forms of democratic elitism. Associated with the rise of the elitist concept of democracy was the gradual but steady rationalization of large areas of social life at a severe cost to the bases of civic affection and public good. This is the source of what many take to be a crisis of democracy. In recent years, the effort to meet the problem of governability in the advanced capitalist democracies increasingly entails the substitution of a corporatist for the elitist conception of democracy. Reflected in this development is a move to rationalize further the political economy of capitalism.

The shift from the liberal to the elitist notion of democracy, the subsequent rise of a 'crisis of democracy', and the present effort to remedy this crisis with a corporatist definition of democracy gain clarity when viewed in terms of the expansion of capitalist rationalization. As capitalism has advanced, as it has been transformed in the face of economic crises, democracy has been redefined in accordance with ever more rationalized conditions and requirements. Invariably, this redefinition has meant a narrowing down of the concept of democracy and the scope of democratic freedoms.

Marketplace Rationality and Liberal Democracy

Liberal democracy is the political form most compatible with the marketplace of industrial capitalism. Constituted by the voluntary exchanges of individuals seeking to maximize their self-interest, the capitalist market is presented as a rational decision-maker of the first order. Without compassion or sentiment, unbound by ties of affection or blood, insensitive to human suffering and moral obligation, the 'free' market is said to be able to decide on matters of production, distribution, allocation, and consumption in a way that promotes both self-regulation and individual freedom of choice. Entailed by the capitalist market, Lindblom (1977, p. 250) observes, is 'the preference-guided or volition-guided society' which denies the presence of objective criteria of rightness and, in turn, makes rightness a function of the volitions or preferences of 'the people'. At bottom, the capitalist market is the arena where individuals exercise subjective rationality by engaging in activities which are no more or no less calculated means designed for the efficient accumulation of private property, the successful acquisition of which is the condition of maximized self-interest. Formal and impersonal, calculative and instrumental, essentially a means for the satisfaction of individual wants as distinct from needs, marketplace rationality set the terms by which liberal democracy was defined and established.

Early liberal thought held that capitalism and democracy are incompatible. Democracy represents class rule by the wrong class and thus poses a threat to established market relations. Resting on a defense of private property, pre-democratic liberal thought vigorously opposed democracy on the grounds that the majority rule it affirms would place governance in the hands of the poor and the propertyless, with the likely result being the abridgement of the right to private property on which individual liberty is secured. Early liberal thought is non-democratic, if not anti-democratic, in character.

Liberal democratic society was liberal long before it was democratic. Indeed, the democratic franchise was introduced, and with some great reluctance, only after the competitive market society and the liberal state had been firmly established. 'By the time the liberal state was democratized', Macpherson (1972, p. 47) notes, 'the old idea of democracy had been liberalized.' The old idea of democracy as rule by the majority was regarded as incompatible with the preservation of a class-based society where the majority was comprised of laborers and the poor. Democracy had to be liberalized, made consistent with the liberal defense of private property and capitalist social relations, and this was accomplished in several ways. For instance, the initial democratic franchise was highly restrictive, available only to those who could indicate, say, by virtue of their property holdings, a stake in the established arrangements. In addition, liberal democratic participation was confined to a public sphere prevented from interfering with the private activities of the market. In so far as considerable and major decision-making powers were housed in the private sphere – the market protected from unwarranted state intervention – the importance and possible impact of the participation afforded by liberalized democracy was minimal. Through such measures as these, democracy was emptied of those features potentially threatening to liberal industrial capitalism.

The liberal democratic state, then, was liberal in the sense of being limited and democratic in that it provided legal provisions for the periodic election of its governors. Its primary task was to protect and to foster an individual liberty whose basis is private property. Democratic participation was introduced to help assure that the state performed this task without abridging the prerogatives of the market. In short, the exercise of power by the liberal democratic state was virtually limited to the protection of the market mechanism, the creation of the material and immaterial preconditions of capitalist economic production, and the modification of civil law in accordance with changes in the process of capital accumulation. Liberal democracy quite clearly was suited to the logic of marketplace rationality during the entrepreneurial period of industrial capitalism. Equally evident, from Bentham to John Stuart Mill, was the central role of marketplace rationality in the formulation of liberal democratic thought.

As formulated by Jeremy Bentham and James Mill, the utilitarian case for democracy is both instrumental (democracy is a means for securing limited government) and subjectivized (the individual is the best judge of his wants). This conception of democracy is clearly drawn from the logic of marketplace rationality, the full impact of which appears in the exclusionary thrust of the utilitarian position, best indicated in the insistence that eligibility for the franchise rest on a certain property qualification. Embedded in the argument for a restrictive property qualification is the view that democratic participation in the form of the vote should be extended only to those who have proven themselves capable of rational judgement and action, such proof residing in one's success in the capitalist marketplace. The market is the one central arena where individuals exercise their rationality; it acts both as a school for the inculcation of rationality and as a kind of cleansing force which rids people of irrational and non-rational influences. Rational are those who meet the unremitting and impersonal demands of the market, and only the rational – on the grounds of utility – warrant the vote.

Utility becomes the overriding criterion for evaluating all institutions, policies, and activities in society. Liberty, based on private property, and, ultimately, democracy, shaped to be consistent with the right to unlimited private property, are justified in terms of individual protection of self-interest; only with the vote are individual citizens able to protect themselves from government and safeguard the private sphere against intrusions which threaten the property basis of liberty. 'A democracy', wrote Bentham (in Macpherson, 1977, p. 36), 'has for its characteristic object and effect, the securing its members against oppression and depredation at the hands of those functionaries which it employs for its defense.'

The protective case for liberal democracy made by utilitarianism is often contrasted to John Stuart Mill's much more forceful and positive embrace of democratic government. For him, democracy is a morally transformative force and democratic participation does more than merely safeguard self-interest, it makes people more informed, energetic, and virtuous. Democracy is justified more for the contributions it makes to the development of individual capabilities than for its instrumental utilities. While Mill's formulation of liberal democracy, as Macpherson (1967) has shown, rests on a conception of human essence (man as exerter and enjoyer of human capabilities) considerably different from that employed by utilitarianism (man as consumer of utilities, an infinite desirer and appropriator), it retains the overriding influence of marketplace rationality.

Convinced by 1848 that 'the poor have come out of leading-strings and cannot any longer be governed or treated like children', Mill (1966, p. 763) proceeded to observe that 'whatever advice, exhortation or guidance is held out to the laboring classes must henceforth be tendered to them as equals, and accepted by them with their eyes open. The prospect of the future depends on the degree in which they can be made rational beings.' In important respects, and here Mill concurred with utilitarianism, whether or not and to what extent a being is rational is determined by how well one fares in the marketplace, that testing ground of rationality.

In his argument for a broad extension of the suffrage, Mill (1910, pp. 281-2) identified among others the following exclusionary criteria: 'Those who pay no direct taxes, disposing by their votes other people's money, have every motive to be lavish and none to economize ... and, therefore, any power of voting possessed by them is a violation of the fundamental principle of free government.' Additionally, 'the receipt of parish relief should be a peremptory disqualification for the franchise ... To be an uncertified bankrupt, or to have taken the benefit of the Insolvent Act, should disqualify for the franchise ... Non-payment of taxes, when so long persisted in that it cannot have arisen by inadvertence, should disqualify while it lasts.' Even with these restrictions in place, Mill (ibid., p. 238) argued, the suffrage, 'with only slight abatement', would be universal, with the result that 'The greatest majority of voters ... would be manual laborers; and the twofold danger, that of too low a standard of political intelligence and that of class legislation, would still exist in a very perilous degree.'

To minimize these dangers, Mill proposed a system of plural voting. Finding objectionable any effort to define superiority of influence on the basis of property, since its allocation often has more to do with the accident of birth than with merit, Mill (ibid., p. 285) insisted that the 'only thing which can justify reckoning one person's opinion as equivalent to more than one is individual *mental* superiority'. In the absence of a credible system of general education, Mill turned to the market, in this case the labor market, to ascertain levels of mental superiority.

An employer of labour is on the average more intelligent than a labourer ... A foreman is generally more intelligent than an ordinary labourer, and a labourer in the skilled trades than in the unskilled. A banker, merchant, or manufacturer is likely to become more intelligent than a tradesman ... In all these cases it is not the having undertaken the superior function, but the successful performance of it, that tests the qualification ... Subject to some such condition, two or more votes might be allowed to every person who exercises any of these superior functions. (ibid., p. 285)

These criteria for restricting the franchise and for determining the weight of an individual's influence clearly express Mill's adherence to the logic of marketplace rationality. In the capitalist market, occupational status is taken as an imperfect but generally reliable indicator of ambition, diligence, ability, and capacity to act rationally. While the system of plural voting he proposed never was incorporated into the institutions of Western liberal democracy, it does make explicit the centrality of marketplace rationality to Mill's work, which itself was so immensely influential to the theory and practice of liberal democracy.

To summarize, liberal democracy is defined to be consistent with a marketplace expression of rationality. Here, the individual (the subjective locus of reason) rationally interacts with others with a calculated view toward maximizing self-interest. Predicated upon the logic of subjective and instrumental reason and possessing a real degree of autonomy in the sense of freedom from non-rational (that is, non-economic) pressures, the capitalist marketplace was capable of some degree of self-regulation and self-balance. Defined in its terms, democracy became liberalized, first, in its confinement to a public sphere limited in scope and responsibility and, secondly, in its exclusionary character, being restricted to those who had proven themselves rational by market standards. Gradually, of course, the democratic franchise was extended, and as it was the liberal conception of democracy began to give way to the elitist conception.

The Reification of Rationality and Democratic Elitism

Liberal democracy presupposes a public sphere which is depoliticized. In liberal democratic capitalism, major decision-making powers are located in the private sphere, the market protected from unwarranted state intervention. In so far as democratic political participation is confined to a public realm stripped of these powers, politics – which, after all, is about power – becomes depoliticized. Liberal democracy remains compatible with capitalism only to the extent that the autonomy and rational self-steering capability of the market is maintained. Once the market proves to be inherently unstable and in regular need of extensive state support, it becomes repoliticized, so that in Disco's (1979, p. 193) words, 'domination which is experienced in the market ... begins to assume a directly political form; that is, a form which is no longer anonymous and a function of abstract system requisites, but a form associated with human intentions and will'. As the state becomes increasingly indispensable to market stability, capital accumulation and economic growth, participation therein acquires the potential to influence and shape economic matters strongly. Economic contradictions are frequently deflected on to the public sphere where they are subject to political debate and action. In this context, a viable liberal democracy poses a threat to the *sine qua non* of capitalism – the power of the market to decide on fundamental questions of production, distribution, and allocation.

The repoliticization of the economic order that increases the potential effectiveness of liberal democracy occurs with the move from competitive to monopoly capitalism that takes place during the forty-year period that spans the end of the nineteenth and the beginning of the twentieth century. With the rise of monopoly capitalism, the corporation replaces the entrepreneur as the key capitalist, and formal organization replaces the individual as the locus of rationality. Rationality is reified, coming to rest in the impersonal procedures and regulations that comprise the bureaucratic structures of business, industry, and the state. It is in this context that the category of democratic elitism takes precedence over that of liberal democracy. In the name of scientific realism, the thesis of democratic elitism not only expresses the rationalization of social life that accompanies the development of monopoly capitalism, but also seeks to justify the reduction of political participation required by the extensive reliance of the emerging corporate economy on the state.

The dynamic of monopoly capitalism is one of increasing concentration and centralization, and entails the extension of capitalist rationality from the marketplace to the workplace and beyond to domains (for instance leisure and family) previously outside its grasp. Capitalist rationality enters the workplace as scientific management. Throughout the period of competitive capitalism, knowledge of the productive process resided by and large on the shop floor. Skilled workers exercised significant autonomy and discretion over most matters involving direct production. The emergence of large industrial corporations brought about an erosion of the limited but very real power over production held by craft workers. With 'huge financial resources, an ability to withstand long strikes, shift work from one plant to another, employ machinery which reduced their dependence on craft skills, and mobilize the forces of the state against workers', the corporations managed to clear the way for a reorganization of work along the lines advocated by scientific management principles (Brecher, 1978, p. 6).

The rationalization of the workplace sought by scientific management had two primary objectives: greater efficiency and greater managerial control over the productive process (the latter thought to be a precondition of the former). To achieve both, it was essential to appropriate from the workers the special knowledge and skills upon which their power over production rested and place them in the hands of management. Concern with such appropriation was forcefully expressed, as Braverman documents, in the underlying principles of scientific management. The 'first principle is the gathering and development of knowledge of labor processes, ... the second is the concentration of this knowledge as the exclusive province of management, ... the third is the use of this monopoly over knowledge to control each step of the labor process and its mode of execution' (Braverman, 1974, p. 119). Knowledge and skill, like capital itself, were to be monopolized.

With the implementation of scientific management principles, the labor process is made independent of the skills of workers, conception and execution are separated and arranged hierarchically with management responsible for the first and labor for the second, and more and more aspects of the labor process fall under the influence of pre-established and pre-calculated procedures. Labor is displaced as a subjective factor in the productive process and, writes Braverman (ibid., p. 171), 'the process is henceforth carried on by the management as the sole subjective element'. The subjective rationality of management, however, itself came to be displaced and depersonalized, finding a home in the bureaucratic structure of organization. Thus, in the workplace of monopoly capitalism, authority relations emerged not from the personal interaction of managers and workers but from the formal rules and regulations that comprised the corporate structure. Bureaucratic control, Edwards (1979, p. 131) observes, 'is embedded in the social and organizational structure of the firm and is built into job categories, work rules, promotion procedures, discipline, wage scales, definitions of responsibilities, and the like. Bureaucratic control establishes the impersonal force of "company rules" or "company policy" as the basis for control.' The corporation, whether viewed as a fictional individual legally accorded the rights of all other individuals or as an impersonal bureaucratic organization, becomes the locus of rationality.

The appropriation of ordinary competence and self-reliance was by no means confined to the workplace. By the 1920s, the effort to rationalize leisure was in high gear. Industrial recreation programs, 'designed to regulate employees' free time in the interests of higher productivity..., to reintegrate the new world of leisure into the new world of technified work ..., and to rationalize leisure for productive ends' (Goldman and Wilson, 1977, p. 158), were widely introduced. These programs were merely supplementary to the more extensive efforts to create a culture of consumerism, a way of life with consumption at its core. Resting on such innovations as mass advertising and credit purchasing, the development of consumerism not only offered some justification for the degradation of labor that resulted from the rationalization of work but also served as a means for bringing free time into line with the imperatives of the market.

The rationalization of reproduction that follows the rationalization of production is seen most clearly in the 'proleterianization of parenthood', the assumption of familial functions and the appropriation of parental authority by the large corporations and the bureaucratic state necessary for their survival (Lasch, 1977; Donzelot, 1979). In Lasch's (1979b, p. 157) words,

> As management extended its control over production, it appropriated the technical knowledge formerly controlled by the crafts and trades, centralized this knowledge, and then parcelled it out piecemeal in a confusing, selective fashion guaranteed to keep the worker in a state of dependence. Similarly the 'helping professions', by persuading the family to rely on scientific technology and the advice of scientific experts, undermined the family's capacity to provide for itself and thereby justified the continuing expansion of health, education and welfare services.

The parent, like the worker, became increasingly dependent on structures over which he or she had little control. The historical forces which underlay the transformation of the active producer into the passive consumer in the economic realm were the same which transformed the citizen into a client in the political sphere.

Indispensable to the corporate economy, indeed, actively involved in the creation of conditions for the realization of capital, the state in monopoly capitalism contributes to the rationalization of social life as it itself is rationalized, becoming less a public trust than an administrative apparatus where rational, efficient problem-solving takes precedence over democratic debate and dissent. The capacity to participate in the decision-making process is appropriated and centralized in the hands of political experts and political questions are recast as administrative technical problems. This is necessary, particularly as corporate capitalism advances, for, as Habermas (1973b, p. 648) argues, 'wide participation by citizens in the process of shaping political will – i.e., genuine democracy – would have to expose the contradiction between administratively socialized production and a still private form of acquiring the produced values. In order to keep the contradiction from being thematized ... the administrative system has to be sufficiently independent of the shaping of legitimating will.' Required by this situation is an elitist conception of democracy, one entirely consistent with the prevailing pluralist theory which regarded 'minimal participation', 'competiveness of leaders', and 'relatively small groups' as the essence of democracy (Ricci, 1971, pp. 152–3).

The category of democratic elitism is given distinctive shape in the early 1940s, a time when extensive reliance on political leaders becomes most obvious, and, within twenty years, is firmly established and widely accepted. In 1962, for instance, President Kennedy celebrated the 'end of ideology', a direct out-growth of democratic elitism, by noting that most problems now confronted

> are technical problems, are administrative problems. They are very sophisticated judgments which do not lend themselves to the great sort of 'passionate movements' which have stirred this country so often in the past. Now they deal with questions which are beyond the comprehension of most men ... The problems of ... the Sixties as opposed to the kinds of problems we faced in the Thirties demand subtle challenges for which technical answers – not political answers – must be provided. (Rousseas and Farganis, 1968, p. 320)

The rationalization of politics suggested by these comments, although, perhaps, much closer to the post-elitist notion of democracy presently being formulated, clearly was anticipated by Joseph Schumpeter's conceptualization of democratic elitism, one of the earliest and most influential efforts to bring democracy into line with the changed reality of capitalism.

Doubtful that 'the people' possessed the capacity for rational opinion and judgment and concerned with providing an efficient and realistic criterion of democratic government, Schumpeter (1942, p. 269) defined democracy as a method or 'institutional arrangement for arriving at political decisions in which individuals acquire power to decide by means of a competitive struggle for the people's vote'. The elitist implications of this understanding of democracy, later to be fully developed by others, were clearly recognized by Schumpeter. First, he argued, democracy as he defined it 'does not mean and cannot mean that the people actually rule in any obvious sense of the terms "people" and "rule". Democracy means only that the people have the opportunity of accepting or refusing the men who are to rule them' (ibid., pp. 284–5). This requires, secondly, that the citizens 'must understand that, once they have elected an individual, political action is his business and not theirs' (ibid., p. 295). In this light, the democratic process takes on much of the character of the labor process transformed by scientific management.

Like the social engineers of scientific management, the social scientists who advocated the acceptance of the elitist over the liberal conception of democracy equated extensive participation in and knowledge about the decision-making process with inefficiency. Rejecting the classical ideal of an active, informed citizenry as the indispensable precondition of democracy, they argued not simply that 'what we call "democracy" ... does seem to operate with a relatively low level of citizen participation' (Dahl, 1956, p. 87), but beyond this, wide participation, given the reality of citizen behavior, would be harmful to democracy, forcing emotional overtones and, in turn, polarization into the political process. Stability is the primary concern of democratic elitism and a stable democracy requires a citizenry that is in places apathetic and uninvolved. As long as the participation of the common man, a potential adherent of demagogic leaders and extreme movements, is reduced to the well-bounded act of voting in periodic elections, the stability of democracy is assured.

Just as, earlier, in the name of workplace and economic stability and efficiency active producers were transformed into passive consumers, so now active citizens were turned into political consumers. 'The people, even as they act', C. Wright Mills (1963a, pp. 583–4) observed at the time, 'are more like spectators than actors. The public ... acts, but only by acclamation, by plebiscite. It passively allows; it actively acclaims. Its activity does not spring from its autonomous decision and initiative; it is an implanted reaction to a controlled stimulus presented by centralized management.' The proletarianization of public discourse, like that of labor and parenthood, involves expropriation of opinion and centralization; in this case, the formulation of opinion is appropriated from people engaged in public discussion and placed in the hands of political managers. Democracy comes to rely on the knowledge and skill monopolized by the political leaders.

None of this is to say, and the democratic elitist position painstakingly emphasizes this, that political leaders are unresponsive or unaccountable. Democracy as an efficient method, a set of formal procedures, a rational system operates to encourage, if not guarantee, responsiveness and accountability. Like the managers who abide by the rules of the corporation, political elites act in a way consistent with the rules of the democratic system. While exercised by political leaders, the logic of rationality resides in and is expressed in terms of the democratic system itself. Despite the paucity of democratic attitudes and capacities in the citizenry, write the authors of the influential study, *Voting*, in 1954, 'the *system of democracy* does meet certain requirements for a going political organization ... This suggests that where the classic theory is defective is in its concentration on the *individual citizen*. What are undervalued are certain collective properties that reside in the electorate as a whole and in the political and social system in which it functions' (Berelson, Lazarsfeld and McPhee, 1954, p. 312). Where the rationality of the individual citizen falters, that inherent in the system takes over.

The replacement of the liberal with the elitist conception of democracy results from and reflects the spread of capitalist rationality, the penetration of the logic of appropriation and concentration into growing areas of social life, and the consequent movement of rationality from the individual to rational rules, procedure, and organizational forms. The reification of rationality furthers subordination to the immediately given. As its numerous critics have pointed out, democratic elitism, in its obsession with the facts of the established order, has transformed democracy from a set of ideals and moral ends to a method devoid of both. In the terms of this method, the concept of democracy is operationalized, and like all operational concepts (as discussed in Chapter 1) it expresses the logic of one-dimensional thought: the criteria it provides for judging a given state of affairs are drawn from that given state of affairs; democracy is defined with respect to what already exists and judgement is confined to the established facts. Democratic elitism asks us to submit not to what is right or even useful, it asks us to submit to what is.

Since the turn of the century, but most especially since the end of World War II, corporate capitalism needed a citizenry that simply acclaimed and did not initiate and participate. The category of democratic elitism expressed this need and, relying on scientific technique and terminology, gave justification to the political institutions and behavior which arose, as a consequence of the rationalization of production and reproduction, to meet this need.

Neo-Conservatism and the Crisis of Democracy

In the context of early liberalism, the initial advocates of capitalism argued that democracy and capitalism are wholly incompatible. From the nineteenth century on, later supporters of capitalism reversed this argument to insist that capitalism is a necessary condition of democracy. Present-day neo-conservatism offers a synthesis of the two views: democracy, unless checked, will undermine the stability of capitalism and, in turn, threaten its own viability since stable capitalism is a prerequisite of democracy. The crisis of democracy thesis as promulgated by neo-conservatism attributes many of the problems besetting advanced capitalist democratic societies to an overload of democracy. There is a democratic distemper, an excess of democracy, in the words of Samuel Huntington (1975, p. 104), and one result is that the 'public develops expectations which it is impossible for the government to meet'. Voters have lost both the incentive to inform themselves and an appreciation of budget constraint, notes Samuel Brittan (1975, p. 130), and, as a consequence, democracy has become a means for placing 'excessive burden ... on the "sharing out" function of government'. The crisis of democracy, the use or abuse of the democratic method to hasten an expansion in the scope of governmental responsibility, is rooted in the obsolescence of democratic elitism.

Democratic elitism gained ascendency as the state was transformed into an administrative system. The basic problem with the administrative state is that it is incapable of producing the cultural meaning and social morality necessary for bridging individual motives and public outcomes. The cultural and moral bases of *civitas* and public life, already weakened by the economic system, further deteriorate as the state takes on the character of administrative rationality.

A state unable to generate and sustain cultural meaning is compelled to ground its popular support in the provision of consumable values. The effort, according to Habermas (1973b, p. 661), is to engender a 'civil privatism' characterized by 'strong interests in the administrative system's output and weak interests in participation in the process of will-formation (high output orientation vs. low input orientation)'. As a strategy for eliciting mass loyalty while deflecting democratic participation, civil privatism requires the state to expand the services and goods it makes available to its citizens. Of course, with the overriding emphasis on instrumental output, meaning becomes an even scarcer resource and, in turn, a greater burden is placed on state output institutions. 'The rising level of aspirations is proportionate to the growing need for legitimation. The resource of value siphoned off by the tax office, has to make up for the scanty resource of "meaning"' (ibid., p. 659). As the administrative state secures mass loyalty through a civil privatism shaped by the provision of social welfare services, the justification of the state, like that of the economy, comes to rest upon its capacity for sustained growth. In this light, the so-called revolution of rising entitlements is an outgrowth of the state's effort to substitute consumable value for cultural meaning.

Civil privatism requires not the abandonment or legal restriction of the electoral process but a system of formal democracy which 'provides for the application of institutions and procedures that are democratic in form, while the citizenry, in the midst of an objectively political society, enjoy the status of passive citizens with only the right to withhold acclamation' (Habermas, 1975, p. 37). To secure political abstinence in this context, expectations of suitable reward must be promoted. The problem arises when the administrative state encounters limits that prevent it from meeting the expectations it has placed on itself. These limits – arising from the requirements of capital accumulation, the unwillingness of the population to bear further tax increases, and the natural and social barriers to continued economic growth – circumscribe the state's capacity to deliver goods, and this encourages a popular dissatisfaction which receives expression through formal democratic channels and which has the effect of inflating those demands which the state already has shown it is unable to satisfy. This lies at the bottom of the present crisis of democracy.

In fundamental respects, the crisis of democracy is a direct consequence of the spread of capitalist rationality. The deterioration of the moral foundation of society – or, more concretely, the unwillingness to sacrifice for the public good and the absence of 'budget constraint' among the voters, results from the strong emphasis on sustained growth found in both the economic and political spheres. No longer grounded in the 'people', collective identity is embedded in a 'political system', and, as Wolin (1978, p. 19) writes, the

> identity of the system ... is derived from the conception of rationality embodied in its structure. It is in that sense, a construct which is radically ahistorical, independent of time and place ... As a 'constitution' it represents the last vision of modernity, a constitution which, as it were, can only blink uncomprehendingly when it is asked, What does it mean to be a citizen of a system?

If the system finds it difficult to offer a response to this question, the typical citizen, according to Hirsch (1976, p. 134), does not: 'Why should I adopt moral standards helpful to the system if the outcome of the system for me cannot be validated on moral criteria? True, the system is said to work out for people as a whole ... But I am not people as a whole, I am me, and unless the system can be shown to give me a fair deal in the only currency it deals in – material advantage – it can't ask me moral favors.' This response is presently expressed in two forms, one, a basically middle-class phenomenon found most forcefully in the United States – what Lasch calls the 'culture of narcissism'; the other, what John Goldthorpe labels 'working-class maturity', found primarily in Western Europe.

A mature working class, the kind Goldthorpe finds today in Britain, is mature neither in the Marxist sense of being revolutionary nor in the accommodationist sense of being integrated into the established order. It is mature, rather, in that it takes seriously citizen rights, the scope of which has greatly expanded over the years, and rejects or, at least, refuses commitment to 'the basic principle of the system – namely, that the life-chances and welfare of individuals are most appropriately determined by the "free" working out of market forces' (Goldthorpe, 1978, p. 207). Characterized by a high degree of residential stability, internal recruitment and homogeneity, a strong sense of historical continuity, and continued adherence to labor movement traditions, the mature working class proves to be a more than even match for other social classes in the struggle over resources.

Indispensable to the development of working-class maturity has been the weakening of the status order and the decomposition of prestige – the depletion of the moral legacy from which legitimation for class inequality previously was drawn – wrought by capitalist rationalization. In the absence of such normative camouflage, the distributional processes of the market economy are increasingly viewed in political terms, with pressure being placed on the state to reduce class inequality or, at least, its effects. In the midst of worsening stagflation, the presence of a large and mature working class, willing on occasion 'to hold up the country to ransom', places considerable burden on the political system, threatens the legitimacy of the system, and, of course, invites the charge of excess democracy.

In the United States, where consciousness of class has never reached the level found in Western Europe, the spread of capitalist rationalization has produced not a mature working class but a narcissistic culture, distinguished by an impulsive self in constant flight from durability, continuity and sociability. Characterized by an indifference to the collective arena of politics and a search for instantaneously gratifying experiences, narcissism, in the words of William Connolly (1982, p. 20), represents a 'withdrawal of sentiment from the larger life', a repudiation of 'civic virtue and the common good as restraints on pleasure'. Like the rigidly moral fundamentalism of the New Right, narcissism involves a quest for private meaning and constitutes a defensive response to the loss of public meaning brought by rationalization. 'The retreat to pleasures of the self and to punitive moralism', Connolly (ibid., p. 21) observes, 'represent diverse responses to a common experience: the devaluation of the common good available in the social order.'

Captured in the apparently expanding culture and personality of narcissism are the disappearance of a meaningful public life, the erosion of *civitas*, and the lack of budget constraint. Although expressed as a subjective search for subjectivity and not as a collective effort to minimize market inequality, narcissism shares with working-class maturity a refusal to sacrifice or even postpone in the name of some public good. Accordingly, narcissism, whether described as a 'flight into subjectivity' or the 'new hedonism', is seen as potentially disruptive to democratic governance.

Fuelled by either a mature working-class or a culture of narcissism, the crisis of democracy serves to heighten dissatisfaction with democratic elitism. The strategy of civil privatism on which democratic elitism rests is effective only as long as state output is able to match popular expectations and demands. As the gap between the two widens, the state is compelled to replace civil privatism with more direct measures, ones designed both to lower expectations and to secure depoliticization on a firmer basis.

The strategy of civil privatism is the centerpiece of what Thomas Weisskopf (1981) calls the institutional order of security capitalism. Predicated upon American hegemony over the world capitalist system, and characterized by a state-sanctioned compromise between corporate capital and organized labor, a strong reliance on Keynesian techniques of economic stabilization, and a commitment by the state to protect business and citizens against the harsher consequences of the market, security capitalism arose in response to the economic collapse and social dislocation of the 1930s and was consolidated in the years after World War II. On virtually every dimension of assessment, this institutional order proved extraordinarily effective for over twenty-five years. Yet the complex of crises presently besetting American society originated in the very successes of security capitalism. The effective promotion of the means of capital accumulation throughout the world system, the reliance on Keynesian techniques of demand management, and the state's commitment to a social wage generated the conditions which led to the loss of privileged access to cheap foreign resources, to the discouragement of productive investment, and, in the form of a 'revolution of rising entitlements', to a substantially more costly method of legitimation.

Security capitalism and, with it, civil privatism and democratic elitism have grown obsolete. Security can no longer be provided and this increases the probability that formal democratic channels will be used to make demands which the state clearly cannot meet. Were this to happen in a significant way, the very legitimacy of the state would be seriously challenged. Required is a new institutional order, one which will allow the further rationalization of the political economy by reducing popular demands and increasing depoliticization. Further economic rationalization, in the view of the neo-conservatives, rests on the capacity to curb democratic excesses. Foremost among the many efforts to formulate a conception of democracy consistent with the requirements of further rationalization is the increasingly influential work of the neo-conservatives, whose assumptions are quite similar to those of Saint-Simon and Comte.

The constitutive assumptions of the neo-conservative treatment of democracy have been carefully identified by Peter Steinfels (1979, p. 268): First, 'democracy is not a way of constituting or realizing government; it is a *check* on government'. Secondly, 'government means *management*, the successful accomplishment of technical tasks posed by the economic and industrial order. A well-governed order is an efficiently managed one.' Finally, 'government is (and should be) a largely independent managing force, ... performing its work in a technically competent, professional manner'. Democracy, in this view, is a constraint on this independent, managerial governing body, and it retains positive value only so long as it does not interfere with the efficient operation of government. Given these assumptions, the immediate task in the present situation, in Huntington's words, is to move 'toward a democratic balance', to confront head on the 'excess of democracy' which is a decisive factor in the crisis of governability now besetting democratic states. Not only are there 'potentially desirable limits to economic growth', Huntington (1975, p. 115) has argued, 'there are also potentially desirable limits to the indefinite extension of political democracy.' Democracy is proper and valuable to the extent that it is moderated, and this requires both some degree of apathy on the part of some segments of the electorate and the recognition that in many situations democratic claims justifiably may be overridden by 'the claims of expertise, seniority, experience, and special talents' (ibid., p. 133). The neo-conservative conception of democracy suggested here currently acquires significance not so much in the area of policy formation as in its marked contributions to an expanding ideological context, within which sound economic management is of primary importance and that government is best whose economic intervention is designed to enhance not electoral popularity but capital accumulation.

On a superficial level, the neo-conservative conception of democracy has much in common with the notion of democratic elitism. Both, for instance, favor restricted participation in the making of key decisions and, beyond this, each entails the translation of political into technical questions with the ensuing withdrawal of these matters from the realm of public discourse. However, the differences between the two are substantial and important.

The elitist conception of democracy rests in part on the assumption that large segments of the citizenry are uninformed, intolerant, incapable of reasoned debate and compromise, and bereft of the attitudes necessary for democratic participation. In this form, the democratic system has a built-in susceptibility to demagogic extremes. Mobilized around emotional appeals, the participation of the presently apathetic would constitute a real danger to the democratic system. In contrast to this view, neo-conservatism fears not the participation of demagoguery-induced extremists, but that too many people will become informed, involved, and insistent that larger areas of policy formation and decision-making be made subject to popular influence. What worries the neo-conservatives is not that a Hitler or a George Wallace will be elected, but that people will use democratic institutions to try to improve the quality of their lives and, in doing so, make for unpredictability, disorder and system overload.

A more fundamental difference between the two is suggested by Habermas's distinction between decisionistic and technocratic models of the relation of technical knowledge to political practice. The elitist conception of democracy promotes a decisionistic model in the sense that while the politician relies on the knowledge of the expert in arriving at decisions, his exercise of power rests on a process of acclamation not justifiable in rational terms, since it involves matters of will, value and interests. 'In this way, power, untouched in its irrational substance, can be legitimated but not rationalized' (Habermas, 1970, p. 68). In the technocratic model anticipated by neo-conservatism, however, the rationalization of power, the transformation of political power into rational administration, and the hinging of decisions of political elites directly to the objective necessity disclosed by technical expertise is the goal. In this context, Habermas (ibid., pp. 63–4) writes,

> The dependence of the professional on the politician appears to have reversed itself. The latter becomes the mere agent of a scientific intelligentsia, which, in concrete circumstances, elaborates the objective implications and requirements of available techniques and resources as well as of optimal strategies and rules of control ... The politician would then be at best something of a stopgap in a still imperfect rationalization of power ... the state appears no longer an apparatus for the forcible realization of interests that have no foundation in principle and can only be answered for decisionistically. It becomes instead the organ of a thoroughly rational administration.

The rationalization of political power entailed by the technocratic model would deprive democracy of its object.

Sheldon Wolin (1980, p. 11) sees in recent developments the movement toward 'a political economy in which the state will seek to ground its claims of legitimacy in the authority of technical and scientific knowledge rather than in democratic consent ...'. Wolin, like Habermas, takes the technocratic implications of the neo-conservative conception of democracy to their extreme, and in this form they clearly are incompatible with even the narrowest view of democratic participation. In less extreme forms, however, the technocratic aspects of the neo-conservative category of democracy imply not the elimination of democracy but the establishment of corporatist democracy. Clearly anticipated by Saint-Simon, Comte and, most especially, Durkheim, corporatist democracy is much more narrowly defined than liberal democracy and elitist democracy, and is eminently compatible with the effort to rationalize further advanced capitalist society.

Corporatist Democracy

The corporatist solution to the crisis of democratic elitism requires the creation of an active and streamlined state apparatus responsible for coordinating national industrial policy and directing the reorganization necessary for the resolution of the crisis. Unlike the forms of intervention associated with civil privatism and democratic elitism, corporatist state intervention aims not 'merely to facilitate, regulate, ameliorate, augment, stimulate, stabilise or support private economic activity; the state [tries] to direct and control it – but without public appropriation' (Winkler, 1977, p. 82). Within corporatist political structures, public policy is formulated through a process of consultative interaction between public authorities and representatives of important interest groups or national interest associations. Scrupulously non-partisan and non-ideological, the process is designed to promote consensus, collaboration, and commitment to national goals.

Long influential in Western Europe, the corporatist strategy for political stability and economic growth only recently has gained ascendency in the United States. The expanding appeal of corporatism rests on the increasingly accepted neo-conservative premise that the resolution of the set of crises facing advanced capitalist society minimally requires the insulation of the policy-making and implementation process from popular pressures. In response to the 'democratic excess' and 'governmental overload' caused by the breakdown of the party system and the consequent vulnerability of policy-makers to extraordinary demands of a vast array of groups, the effort is to erect a state within which technical necessity takes precedence over popular will so that government does what is necessary, no matter how politically unpopular. The aim is to rationalize further – and thereby depoliticize further – government.

Corporatist Politics

Corporatist political structures center around a mode of interest group representation where the state coordinates the activities of the private sector in more or less institutionalized consultation with the representatives of a limited number of hierarchically organized, functionally differentiated, non-competitive, singular and compulsory interest associations unified about a common interest in social stability and economic prosperity (Schmitter, 1979, p. 13). Within these structures, '"citizens" participate through the exercise of voting rights in relation to a corporation which represents their interests in the formulation of state policy; the unit of representation is the corporation rather than the constituency organized on a territorial basis and citizens participate in their capacity as economic agents' (Jessop, 1978, p. 48). At the leadership level, the various interest groups are integrated on the basis of a system of representation and direct cooperative interaction so that the participation of functional groups in the creation of public policy occurs in such a way that the linkage of each group to the state emerges from the interaction it has with other groups. Participant groups do obtain greater say in the making of policy. However, in return for active and continuous involvement in the area of policy formation, the national representatives of interest associations are expected to provide the state with expert advice, internal information and, most importantly, agreement to abide by and contribute to the legitimacy of effected policies. In effect, these associations serve the state by controlling and mobilizing their members.

Schmitter distinguishes liberal or societal corporatism from authoritarian or state corporatism, regarding the former as 'the concomitant, if not ineluctable, component of the postliberal, advanced capitalist, organized democratic welfare state' and the latter as 'a defining element of, if not structural necessity for, the antiliberal, delayed capitalist, authoritarian, neomercantilist state' (Schmitter, 1979, p. 42). Authoritarian corporatism is imposed and maintained with the systematic use of state coercion. Liberal corporatism is a more or less voluntary response to evolving social developments, among the most important of which are: growing economic concentration and rising competition between national economies, which makes specific sectoral planning more appropriate than indicative planning or the simple manipulation of overall demand; the increasing need to establish social peace by inducing the cooperation of recalcitrant groups, particularly organized labor, in a national program of economic recovery; the decline of parliamentary and party systems and the consequent shift in decision-making to administrative agencies; and growing pressure to rationalize the process of policy formation by supplying the state with 'the professional expertise, specialized information, prior aggregation of opinion ... and deferred participatory legitimacy' which only consensually organized interest associations can provide (ibid., p. 47).

In contrast to the authoritarian corporatism which preceded the rise of fascist governments in Germany and Italy and which is found today in several Latin American countries, the liberal corporatism presently advanced as a solution to political and economic crises is said to be consistent with democratic principles and institutions. Liberal corporatist structures neither completely replace conventional legislative forms nor extrude from the political arena pluralist competition, particularly as it takes place among the unincorporated segments of society. These structures are partial in scope, designed to coexist with the established democratic agencies of policy formulation. Moreover, they promise to widen the process of policy making by involving the direct participation of relevant associations. Finally, liberal corporatist arrangements are said to enhance the capacity of participant groups to shape the interests of and the tactics employed by their members, so that greater moderation is brought to the practice of democracy and limits are placed on the demands made to the state. These arrangements, write Johansen and Kristensen (1982, p. 193), prevent 'zero-sum game situations from occurring. The participating interest groups ... do not run the risk of becoming "winners" or "losers": instead, they are "sharers" in compromises where all parties gain something, and for which they take common responsibility ... [This] makes it extremely difficult to "overload" corporatist political systems.' In this view, corporatist structures assist in restoring a democratic balance. In their actual operation, however, they do not so much balance as constrict the democratic process.

Corporatism and Democracy
Participation in corporatist structures is not predicated upon success in the political arena. Relative importance in the social division of labor, not capacity to mobilize the electorate, determines whether or not national interest associations will be allowed or persuaded to collaborate in the formulation of public policy. Corporatist participation, Kvavik (1974, p. 110) finds, 'is established within administrative decision-making procedures that acknowledge certain organization positions as requisite and legitimate voices of a collective interest'. In this context, functionally important groups are entitled to engage in the establishment of guidelines by which state intervention in the economy takes place only as long as they accept the legitimacy of the system within which they operate.

Consensus on these matters is facilitated by the strong tendency of corporatist decision-making to operate in accordance with technocratic criteria and in the absence of public surveillance. 'Functional rather than substantive accountability makes the decision-makers responsible only in terms of expert criteria, to experts, not to the public – which is thus shut out of the decision-making process' (Heisler and Kvavik, 1974, p. 79). In this setting, considerable pressure is exerted to avoid politicizing the issues. Interest participation in committees, Kvavik (1974, p. 113) observes,

> is characterized by an emphasis on technical argumentation realized by sending technocrats as representatives and by preparing statements in a well-researched technical format. How much technical information can be presented in a technical format by a well-known and respected specialist is the key to success. Accordingly, technical factors are the criteria for success ranked most highly by the organizations' representatives.

In short, corporatist structures mute the competitive orientation of dominant interest groups. With the incorporation of leaders or representatives into the process of policy formation, interest groups shed their private and protective character to become quasi-public agencies engaged in regular cooperative relations with government and responsible for enforcing and legitimating effected policy.

Corporatist democratic structures serve to depoliticize the decision-making process. The depoliticizing impact of corporatism is identified clearly by Claus Offe (1981, p. 145).

> First, the formal admission of corporate groups to the process of public policy formation favors the production of decisions that minimize the probability that social power will be used in order to obstruct or resist public policy ... Second, to the extent that interest organizations do control the attitudes and behavior of their members ..., this organizational discipline can be used to prevent opposition from groups within the organization's membership. In this way the authority of the group's leadership is, so to speak, added to that of the state ... Third, in case a policy meets or creates conflict and opposition, in spite of these safety mechanisms, the government alone is not to blame: All the actors that have participated in the process of making the decision in question would be held responsible. This makes such opposition less likely than otherwise, for any 'relevant' opposing group would have to attack not only the government but also its own leadership.

This last point is of considerable importance and warrants further comment, for it suggests how corporatism, by protecting the state from popular democratic opposition, contributes to the rationalization of the state.

Increased planning does not in itself, of course, signify the emergence of corporatist political structures. Required as well is regular and institutionalized collaboration of functional groups in the formulation of public policy, a collaboration which is premised upon and reinforces a framework of elite consensus, within which groups consent to enforce agreements on their members, and the state is permitted to restrict and channel market forces, devalorize capital and discriminate among particular firms. The state acts as the national coordinator of economic development and in this role is shielded from popular demands. Its capacity to act rationally is thereby enhanced.

While corporatist structures of decision-making give national interest associations greater say in the formulation of policy, they simultaneously enlarge the state's influence on if not control over these groups. National associations are recognized and licensed – they are accorded a representational monopoly – by the state. 'In return for the granting of representational privileges', Nordlinger (1981, pp. 170–1) observes,

> the state is able to maintain some control over the associations … Public officials are able to define demands that diverge overly far from their own preferences as unacceptable and attempts to bring overbearing pressures upon them as unallowable. It appears that the peak association leaders have generally abided by these limitations over time, while centralized organization has enabled them to mediate and control membership attempts to overstep the limits … [In addition] consultation and participation are guaranteed the association, but the allocation of seats, the overall and more precise formulation of the agenda, and the direction of the deliberations are far more influenced by public than private officials.

In this way, the state is in a position to constrict demands made and lessen pressures exerted by participant associations.

In this context, increased state control does not translate into increased accountability. Indeed, the active and continuous involvement in the area of policy formation by the national representatives of functional groups reduces pressure on the state to intervene in the economy with a constant eye toward electoral success. In the first place, as discussed above, the articulation and implementation of public policy in the corporatist framework occur in accordance with depoliticized technocratic-administrative criteria; rarely are deliberations made into a publicly partisan matter. Secondly, when the effected policy is found wanting, discontent is directed most forcefully at the national leaders or representatives, not the state. The government is virtually assured, Kvavik (1974, p. 11) finds, 'little adverse reaction to legislation once effected; that reaction, should it come, would be directed not toward the government, but at the participants – the interest groups and their representatives – who accept the legislation on behalf of the organization membership'. So sheltered from popular demands for accountability, the state, according to Schmitter, 'would be relieved of decisional and implementational responsibility over "nonessential" matters (welfare, health, etc.) and could then devote more attention and effort to such "essential" tasks as internal security, external defense, foreign affairs and economic growth (Schmitter, 1979, p. 35).

Corporatist democracy converges well with the neo-conservative effort to meet the crisis of governability in advanced capitalist society by restoring a 'democratic balance'. It has the capacity to mitigate the problem of democratic excess caused by the breakdown of democratic elitist political arrangements (by subordinating pluralist to corporatist modes of interest-intermediation), and to solve the related problem of governmental overload (by delegating some authority and responsibility to participant groups) in a way that partly insulates the state from popular pressures. Corporatism affords the state the opportunity to do what is technically necessary but politically unpopular.

Neo-conservatives insist that the revitalization of the infrastructure and capital goods base of the capitalist economy necessitates decreased expenditures in the areas of health, education, and welfare. Yet the paradox they face concerns how a program of reindustrialization premised on rapid and massive capital accumulation can be accomplished, given the precondition of a substantial reduction of social welfare provisions. A government without authority, neo-conservatives insist, is incapable of imposing necessary sacrifices. For a long time, however, governments in advanced capitalism have based their authority precisely on those measures which now must be reduced. Corporatist democracy appears capable of providing a way out of this paradox by reversing in effect the logic of civil privatism with its emphasis on delivering the goods in the form of a social wage. Conceiveably, corporatism could enable the substitution of greater participation in selected areas of policy formation for material concessions in the name of consensus and sacrifice for the national good. Since corporatist participation is confined to national leaders loyal to both pre-established goals and technical procedures of decision-making, and preoccupied with questions of means and the allocation of the burdens of sacrifice, it serves to depoliticize and rationalize the state further in the guise of expanded democracy.

To emphasize once again, the heavy weight of any popular displeasure directed at policy formulated in corporatist fashion is not borne by the state. Protected from such displeasure, the state is better able to create and implement policy which is rational but at odds with the preferences of significant segments of the electorate. More than anything else, it is this enhanced state capacity to act rationally that makes the corporatist strategy indispensable to the governability of advanced capitalist societies. The neo-conservative attack on democracy, note David Dickson and David Noble (1981, p. 276), is

> cast in terms of a need for a more efficient, competent, streamlined government to match the technologically sophisticated requirements of a changed political economy. Science and technology ... demand the abandonment of democratic norms. In [this] formulation, democracy [has] become not the hallmark of Enlightenment, but of popular reaction, not the highest expression of progress, but its major obstacle.

Shaped in corporatist terms, democracy becomes less of an obstacle and more of a handmaiden to expert knowledge and rational administration.

Saint-Simon, Comte and Durkheim

Several features of corporatism appear in the positivist strategy of societal reconstruction developed by Saint-Simon and Comte (and discussed in Chapter 2). In their conviction that the minimal requirement for the restoration of economic growth and social order is subordination to objective facticity – a government which does what is necessary, not what is politically expedient – Saint-Simon and Comte anticipated exactly the basic premise underlying the twentieth-century corporatist calls for sacrifice for and consensus around this or that conception of national cause or public good.

The corporatist spirit of consensus and collaboration advanced today is offered as a way of promoting the social harmony, restraint, and mutual responsibility its advocates regard as necessary for the economic development and prosperity on which a more enduring and meaningful consensus can be established. Despite its celebration of the public good, the corporatist spirit of consensus subordinates normative to pragmatic concerns. The consensus sought is non-ideological and non-partisan. Thus, Felix Rohatyn (1982, p. 28), a leading advocate of corporatist strategy in the United States, argues that the day is fast approaching

> when, on the national level, conservatives and liberals, Democrats and Republicans, will have to forget their ideologies, their theories, and their prejudices. They may have to join together ... and, with the cooperation of government, business, and labor, intervene vigorously where intervention may be required – to save our cities, to save our industrial and financial institutions, to save the regional balance of our country and the social balance of our society.

In order to be effective, intervention must be based on policies formulated in the absence of public surveillance, that is, policies established through a process shielded from popular pressure. Thus, consensus entails not simply the setting aside of ideological and partisan differences but also a decision-making structure which employs technocratic and administrative as opposed to democratic criteria. The consensus invoked by the corporatist spirit, in Offe's (1981, p. 132) words, requires agreement not on 'some normative conception of a good and just political order but [on pragmatic issues of] functional requirements, limits of tolerance, and economic mechanisms'. It is, in short, a consensus to defer to expertise, to place the objectively necessary before the politically popular.

Clearly, the corporatism proposed here is non-democratic, if not anti-democratic, in form and substance. For this reason especially, it runs directly counter to the corporatist solution offered by Emile Durkheim. While borrowing liberally from the strategy of societal reconstruction developed by Saint-Simon and Comte, Durkheim maintained a strong commitment to democracy, one he justified sociologically, and this commitment infused his model of corporatism.

Durkheim's defense of corporatism, examined in Chapter 2, rested on the claim that the corporatist-democratic state would foster the growth of autonomous individuals who, as active and reflective members of the citizenry, would become responsible participants in social and political life. Yet, as it has developed and probably will continue to develop in response to the political and economic crises of maturing capitalist societies, corporatist democracy displays little respect for Durkheim's active and responsible citizenry – despite the fact that corporatist democratic arrangements are structurally quite similar to Durkheim's position.

Durkheim valued democracy not so much as a way of determining collective goals or political objectives – for these have to do with scientifically knowable, societal-based requirements and imperatives – as for its capacity to enable the interaction and communication through which these goals or collective representations are able to receive general, lawful, and meaningful articulation. The view, derived in part from Saint-Simon and Comte, that the goals around which corporatist consensus is to be built and maintained are given in the form of the collective representations associated with modern complex society is inconsistent in the last analysis with any vibrant conception of democracy, for it deprives democracy of its very object – the active creation of collective ends and purposes. Durkheim's solution, in short, rested on two irreconcilable commitments: the one to corporatism, the other to a democracy respectful of active and informed individuals. Adherence to Durkheim's claim that strong corporatist politics make for strong democratic politics is no longer possible.

Socialism and Democracy

The 'first step in the revolution by the working class', Marx and Engels (1970b, p. 57) write, 'is to raise the proletariat to the position of ruling class, to win the battle of democracy'. Used in this way, democracy refers to a class state, and, of course, this usage is consistent with the classical image of democracy as class rule – rule by the poor and the propertyless, those who constitute the majority in society. Marx endorses this notion of democracy 'for exactly the same reasons that for 2000 years it had been condemned: A democracy would attack the institutions [and legal basis] of private property and dissolve the orders and classes of society' (Manicus, 1974, p. 173).

Lenin's understanding of democracy is similar to Marx's. Democracy, like all forms of the state, rests on the organized and systematic employment of force, but it is distinctive in that it accords formal equality of citizenship, the equal right of all citizens to influence the structure and administration of the state. While in its bourgeois form, democracy often does little more than provide the citizenry with opportunities to 'decide every few years which member of the ruling class is to repress and crush the people through parliament' (Lenin, 1949, p. 43), it nevertheless has proved of enormous importance to the working class in its struggle against the capitalists. Lenin argued that the defining attributes of the democratic state, representative institutions and the elective principle, stripped of their bourgeois restraints, would become even more important in the socialist transition from capitalism to communism.

Socialism, according to Lenin, must rely on the externally constraining powers afforded by a state apparatus if it is to contain counter-revolutionary tendencies while at the same time undertaking the leadership and mobilization required for the further development of material conditions and, in turn, human consciousness. The socialist state portrayed by Lenin is a proletarian democracy based on class rule. Like the capitalist democratic state, this socialist democratic state is a dictatorship, but, more in accord with the classical image of democracy, a dictatorship of the majority. As envisioned by Lenin (and discussed in Chapter 3), the proletarian democratic dictatorship of the proletariat has as its aim the disappearance of itself – that is, it seeks to guide the creation of a classless society, one whose achievement spells the termination of the era of class rule of any type. With the withering away of the state, communism emerges from socialism, and democracy is overcome. The 'abolition of the state means also the abolition of democracy; the withering away of the state means the withering away of democracy'. Lenin (ibid., p. 75) carefully explains this point:

> At first sight this assertion seems exceedingly strange and incomprehensible ... [Yet] in striving for socialism ... we are convinced that it will develop into communism and, therefore, that the need for violence against people in general, for the *subordination* of one man to another, and of one section of the population to another, will vanish altogether since people will *become accustomed* to observing the elementary conditions of social life *without violence* and *without subordination*.

In short, while recognizing the indispensability of democracy to the workers' struggle for emancipation in capitalism and in socialism, Lenin claims that once emancipation has been achieved democracy is made obsolete, for in communism there is neither state nor class rule.

All current communist societies display a well-developed, extraordinarily powerful and strongly fortified state apparatus, whose presence is justified by adherents with the argument that these societies remain in the socialist transitional stage of development and require, for the reasons enumerated by Lenin, a vigilant and forceful dictatorship of the proletariat. While the state is alive and, for the most part, well in these societies, the same cannot be said for democracy, proletarian or otherwise. Indeed, the very first socialist state, the Soviet state, began, under Lenin's direct guidance, not as a class democracy, but as a vanguard state under the command of 'professional revolutionaries' and 'scientific socialists'. To understand the entrenched opposition to democracy which has come to mark the Soviet state (and, by implication, most other socialist or communist states which, willingly or not, have been shaped in important respects by the Soviet experience), we would do well to examine the force of instrumental reason, the same primary source of resistance to democracy in capitalism.

In Lenin's conceptualization, the dictatorship of the proletariat would combine proletarian democracy, permitting the large mass of the population to assume an active, direct and independent role in the everyday administration of the state, with centralized control and direction. The anticipated balance between democracy and centralized control proved elusive in the aftermath of the Bolshevik victory in Russia. Faced with the urgent need to rebuild the country and working from the assumption 'that the level of the forces of production determines superstructural [including political] relations and that, *under the circumstances of Soviet power*, industrial development ranked more highly than democratic procedures', Lenin now proceeds to criticize 'the idea of "industrial democracy" as being "half-baked and theoretically false". "Industry is indispensable, democracy is not ..."' (Lane, 1981, p. 60). Lenin's focus here is on industrial organization and economic development, and his concern, given a labor force so long precluded from participation in the modern world by repressive traditions and autocratic czarist rule, is that the Soviet government take as one of its most immediate tasks the inculcation of modern work habits. Crucial to this task is the program of scientific management proposed by Frederick Taylor to facilitate capitalist control over the labor process. 'The Taylor system, the last word of capitalism in this respect, like all capitalist progress', Lenin (in Fleron and Fleron, 1972, p. 80) writes, 'is a combination of the refined brutality of bourgeois exploitation and a number of the greatest *scientific achievements in the field of analyzing mechanical motions during work*, the elimination of superfluous and awkward motions, the elaboration of correct methods of work, the introduction of the best methods of accounting and control.' The success of the Soviet effort to advance the level of productive forces depends in some large measure on the effectiveness with which all that is valuable in the scientific and technological achievements of capitalism are introduced and adapted to socialist ends.

Recall that it was through Taylor's scientific management system that instrumental rationality first systematically penetrated the workplace in capitalism, bringing with it the separation of conception from execution which underlay the establishment of strict hierarchical organization and a largely deskilled workforce stripped of productive knowledge and basic competencies. Lenin's argument, one which continues to be made today by Soviet theoreticians, is that the evils associated with scientific management (and the large-scale organization and high-volume standardized production it unites) are attributable to capitalism. Socialism eliminates the contradictions between property relations and the full development of productive forces, and, as a result, the advancement of science and technology occurs unimpeded and to the benefit of all. Again, the important assumption is that the scientific and technological development of the productive forces in socialist circumstances assures the creation of those material conditions which promote the human capacity for freedom and for democracy. Until such conditions are realized, however, democratic freedoms must be restricted by the imperatives of scientific and technological rationality.

Factory discipline is not to be confined to the factory. Rather, it 'will extend to the whole of society ... [as] a necessary *step* for thoroughly cleansing society of all the infamies and abominations of capitalist exploitation, and for further progress' (Lenin, 1949, p. 93). Accomplished by the actual generalization of factory domination to the larger society was the repressive fusion of technological and political rationality which initiated the complete transformation of the proletariat from the active subject to the passive object of the revolutionary process (Marcuse, 1958, p. 32). With this transformation the party, as the vanguard of professional revolutionaries and scientific socialists, becomes the social and political equivalent of scientific managers, leading and administering society in accordance with their scientific knowledge of the laws of socio-historical development. Compliance to the 'one correct way' is expected both inside and outside the factory. Justified at the start by the generally backward conditions faced by the leaders of the newly created Soviet Union, strongly centralized industrial and political organization soon came to reside as a more or less permanent fixture at the center of socialist strategy.

This strategy culminates in an administered society 'in which an entrenched and extraordinarily powerful ruling group lays claim to ultimate and exclusive scientific knowledge of social and historical laws and is impelled by a belief not only in the practical desirability, but the moral necessity, of planning, direction, and coordination from above in the name of human welfare and progress' (Kassof, 1964, p. 558). Within the administered society, political leaders do not merely rely on scientific and technical experts for assistance in formulating and executing a vast array of plans and programs; rather, as scientific socialists they themselves become technicians of a sort – political technicians issuing commands on the basis of their expert knowledge of the laws of socio-historical development. Since their commands are rooted in specialized knowledge which, like the knowledge of engineers, is not yet widely diffused, and, further, since they express what is necessary for socialist advancement, compliance with them is viewed as a matter of technically necessary subordination, to be undertaken with the strictest discipline and without challenge and criticism.

The administered society in socialism is an 'intellectually guided' society. Capitalism implies a 'preference-guided' model of society, one built on the assumption that society should be responsive to individual volitions, the individual being the best judge of his needs and wants. In contrast, the intellectually guided society, as Charles Lindblom (1977, p. 249) describes it, 'specifies that some people in society are wise and informed enough to ameliorate its problems and guide social change with a high degree of success'. Those who possess this wisdom and information are the intellectual leaders who have both the capacity and the responsibility for formulating the comprehensive theory by which society is organized, and its major institutions, plans and policies shaped. The test and, ultimately, the legitimacy of these institutions, plans and policies rest on their correctness, not on some public opinion comprised of aggregated individual preferences. The method for organizing society and, in turn, for determining institutional practice and policy direction is not chosen, it is discovered through rigorous analysis and scientific inquiry. 'The right method of social organization is not a matter of opinion or volition or of reconciliation of preferences or interests. It is a question of fact calling for diagnosis. There is a "single correct solution"' (ibid., p. 251). The criterion for correctness is straightforward enough: how well do the institutions, policies, and plans correspond to man's true and objectively knowable physical, psychological, and social needs? Objective knowledge of needs, not the subjective experience of wants which so often motivates individual preference, is to guide society. Accordingly, Lindblom (ibid., p. 251) notes, 'the intellectual elite is simultaneously a political elite. Hence, the political party has a special place ... In the U.S.S.R., "the Party leadership lays claim to a monopoly over the interpretation and application of the sole scientific theory of social development". In China, understanding society ... is the prerogative of a correct political leadership in the party.' Political elites as intellectual leaders often know better than the individuals involved what their needs are and how they are best satisfied. This enables the leadership to formulate correct policy, correct because it assures harmony between the planned management of society and the needs and interests of the people.

Lindblom suggests that his characterization of socialism as an intellectually guided society is ironic, for it reverses the common identification of reason with liberal democracy and of unreasoned authority with socialism.

> However greatly actual communist societies constrain discussion and inquiry, communist doctrine displays a faith in elite intellectual capacity that is in sharp contrast to the troubled concern about fallibility that is characteristic of liberal democratic society as represented by Mill. The liberal democrat's faith in reason is historically impressive only in contrast to earlier traditionalism and authoritarianism in science, religion, and politics. Compared to the Marxian and communist faith in reason, it is puny. Marx's scientific socialism was meant to be scientific; the term is not just a slogan. (ibid., p. 252)

What Lindblom should say – and had he said it the irony of his characterization would have been lost – is that socialism displays a faith in instrumental, scientific, technological reason, not a commitment to emancipatory reason, that ally of freedom, which compelled the Enlightenment project to struggle for democracy.

The idea of reason which animated the Enlightenment project centered on the autonomous individual whose independent and critical thinking discovered and implemented the emancipatory possibilities inherent in the existing order of things. The realization of these possibilities would mean a society which had transformed nature into a virtually inexhaustible source of material for the development of human needs and faculties, a society in which the subjective reason of the autonomous individual coincides with objective reason. In the Enlightenment view, the attainment of this state of affairs, Marcuse (1958, p. 72) reminds us, 'depended to a large extent on the autonomy of the individual, that is, on the distinction and tension between subjective and objective Reason, and on a solution to this tension in such a way that objective Reason (the social need and the social interest) preserved and developed subjective Reason (the individual need and the individual interest)'. Under the pressure of the development of industrial capitalism, as we have seen, the reality status of objective reason was denied, leaving a subjectivized and privatized reason which recognized only individual volitions and preferences, particularly as they received expression in and through the marketplace.

In socialism, reason also is instrumentalized, but in a fundamentally different way. Here objective reason is defended over subjective reason, and as a consequence the primary locus of reason is not the marketplace comprised of freely interacting rational individuals, but the planning elite whose superior rationality enables the discovery of objective needs on which objectively necessary and technically correct policy is predicated. As in capitalism, reason is reduced to a rational means for attaining economic growth and industrial development. The important difference is that in socialism the cognitive qualities of rationality are shifted from the individual to the prescriptions of the state. Justifying this shift, Marcuse (ibid., p. 73) observes, is the view that socialist revolutions create

> a 'conformity' between production relations and the 'character of the productive forces' which eliminates the conflict between the individual and society, between the particular and the common interest. Consequently, Reason ceases to be split into its subjective and objective manifestations; it is no longer antagonistic to and beyond reality, a mere 'idea' – but it is realized in the society itself. This society, defined as socialist in terms of Marxian theory, becomes the sole standard of truth and falsehood; there can be no transcendence in thought and action, no individual autonomy because the Nomos of the whole is the true Nomos.

Dissent in this context becomes a political crime. Further, given the primacy of instrumental reason to the underlying logic of intellectually guided socialist society, civil liberties are seen as carrying the potential for technical stupidity, and thus are politically illegitimate.

In these circumstances, the dictatorship of the proletariat becomes a dictatorship over needs within which people are prevented from expressing their needs for freedom. Demands for the opportunities to do so are regarded as incorrect and thus illegal, since they contravene the 'only correct social knowledge' embodied in the official plan. The regular suppression of opportunities to articulate needs for freedom and democracy can no longer after all these years be interpreted as an aberrant or distorted consequence of historically or culturally unique factors. Rather, it appears to be a precondition of the systematically rationalized practices of the planning elite; in Ferenc Feher's (1978, p. 35) words, a 'constitutive principle of the system of the dictatorship over needs: civil liberties, pluralism, contract, and representation are incompatible with the hyper-rationalistic determination of needs prior to their actual "empirical" appearance'. In practice, the political elite as intellectual leaders, under the banner of discovering the true, objective needs of the people, set out to replace certain of these needs, especially those associated with freedom and democracy, with prescriptions designed to accomplish a rational adjustment to the established arrangements. The proletarian democracy envisioned and celebrated by Lenin before the October Revolution has been actively combatted by the Soviet state almost from the start, a consequence in no small measure of democracy's incompatibility with the requirements of instrumental rationality.

In capitalism, the tendency is to rationalize democracy; in socialism, it is rationally to suppress democracy. As long as socialism is defined as a transitional society, an intellectually or scientifically guided dictatorial step to some communist utopia where, amid material abundance, the free association of highly developed individuals makes external constraint unnecessary, a handy justification remains for this suppression of democracy: 'the most methodical system of domination is to prepare the ground for freedom, ... the policy of suppression is justified as the policy of liberation' (Marcuse, 1958, p. 80). Some (Nove, 1983; Siriani, 1981) suggest that a minimal requirement for abolishing this justification is a conception of 'feasible socialism' which rests on recognizable human beings, similar to those who currently exist, not on the emergence of some utopian New Man. While feasible socialism would not represent the end of history, neither would it be merely a transitional stage to something outside itself. With some inequality, some alienated labor, some markets and considerable democracy for its still flawed human beings, it would be in many respects an imperfect society, but one whose shape and direction were determined in large part by the active and informed participation of its members. The image of feasible socialism appears in the recurrent attempts in places like Hungary, Czechoslovakia and Poland to replace the Soviet model with a more democratic socialism. Strong democracy, whether in socialism or in capitalism, depends on a vibrant public sphere protected from while standing in opposition to the rationalizing forces of market and state. This argument is pursued more vigorously in the next chapter.

Conclusion

As capitalist rationality spread from the marketplace to the workplace, the liberal conception of democracy gave way to the elitist. With the rationalization of culture and self, a direct result of the socialization of reproduction entailed by democratic elitist forms, public life further eroded. Expressed in the refusal to sacrifice immediate gain in the name of civic virtue, grounded in both working-class maturity and the culture of narcissism, is the eclipse of reason, the rise to prominence of instrumental rationality. This is at the core of what neo-conservatives label the crisis of democracy, a crisis that can be remedied, it is suggested, by reconceptualizing democracy along corporatist lines. Corporatist democracy promises to ameliorate the crisis of rationality, particularly as it relates to industrial decline and political delegitimation, while doing nothing to reverse the decline of reason and the disappearance of genuine public discourse. No longer primarily located in either the marketplace or bureaucratic organization, reason as rationality is found in the objective necessity disclosed by technical expertise, and corporatist democracy is appropriate to this fact. Socialist societies, particularly those predicated on the Soviet model, to date offer no alternative to this state of affairs. If democracy is rationalized in capitalism, it is rationally suppressed in socialism.

Rationality in the sense of transforming into objects of decision things which previously were not objects of decision bespeaks a democracy which rests on, in Habermas's (1970, p. 57) words, 'the institutionally secured forms of general and public communication that deal with the practical question of how men can want to live under the objective conditions of their ever-expanding power of control'. A viable public sphere is necessary for the convergence of reason and democracy, and for this reason C. Wright Mills assigned to contemporary social and political theorists the task of building new publics and strengthening those that have managed to persist. Almost from the very start of the process of capitalist rationalization, social and political theorists, with few exceptions, have failed to take this task seriously.

This failure is another reflection of the triumph of instrumental reason. In its instrumental form, reason is antagonistic to freedom and democracy. On this score, Saint-Simon, Comte, Durkheim, Weber, the modernists, Freud and the neo-conservatives are correct. Where they go wrong, however, is in equating reason with the instrumental reason of capitalist rationalization – the repressive reason of adjustment, adaptation, and technical advancement. They lose sight of the second and critical dimension of reason – the practical reason which emerges from the rationalization of consciousness and which is concerned with ends, values, and objectives. This reason is the friend, indeed, the predicate, of freedom and democracy.

In the quarter-century since Mills wrote *The Sociological Imagination*, rationality without reason has taken firmer root and the bases of freedom and democracy have become much weaker as a consequence. Nevertheless, the project he formulated for strengthening reason, freedom, and democracy remains appropriate today, at least as a starting point. Part 3 takes up Mills's project and its implications for public life and social theory.

PART 3

The purpose of this final section is to consider what should be done to combat the continuing growth of rationality without reason and to restore reason as an ally of freedom. In opposition to the rationalization of social life examined in Part 2, the task is to cultivate, broaden, and strengthen the public sphere. In opposition to the instrumentalization of sociological thought discussed in Part 1, the task is to formulate a critical social theory. The two tasks are intimately related, so much so, as is evidenced in the concluding two chapters, that it is impossible to separate entirely the discussion of one from that of the other.

Chapter 6 concentrates on the public sphere. Following Mills and Habermas, the discussion examines both what there is about the public sphere that makes it the essential ground of reason and freedom and how this ground has been scarred in the modern world. In turn the contribution sociology can and should make to the revitalization of the public sphere through liberal education and through a reaffirmation of its traditional defense of an autonomous civil society is taken up.

Chapter 7 concentrates on critical social theory and returns us to many of the theoretical issues addressed in Part 1. The assumptions, commitments, and character of critical social theory, particularly as they pertain to the relation between the sociological enterprise and the effort to rejuvenate the public sphere, are examined to highlight what can be done to avoid the instrumentalization of social thought. Of particular importance here is the way critical social theory draws its relation to political practice. While critical social theory has an avowed political and practical intention, it refuses to legitimate any particular political practice on the grounds that such practical questions are answerable only by those involved in and affected by that practice. Critical social theory addresses these people with the aim of initiating among them processes of self-reflection and practical discourse, so that their search for answers will be guided by the former and rooted in the latter. The conditions of each, self-reflective judgement and practical discourse, are those which go to constitute a vibrant public sphere. The intent of critical social theory is to discover intellectually and establish practically these conditions. Expressed by this intention is critical social theory's commitment to reason and freedom and to the public sphere which is their ground.

6

The Public Grounding of Reason, Freedom and Democracy

In this chapter our concern is with what can be done to oppose the instrumentalization of reason and to reverse the narrowing down of freedom and democracy that results from its continued expansion. This general question is addressed quite specifically to the responsibility of social theorists and to what C. Wright Mills calls the promise of sociology. For both Mills and Habermas, the responsibility and promise of social theory point to the cultivation of the public sphere. Each would agree with Gadamer that social theory is the equivalent of what the Greeks named *theoria*:

> to have been given away to something that in virtue of its overwhelming presence is accessible to all in common and that is distinguished in such a way that in contrast to all other goods it is not diminished by being shared and so is not an object of dispute like all other goods but actually gains through participation. In the end, this is the birth of the concept of reason: the more what is desirable is displayed for all in a way that is convincing to all, the more those involved discover themselves in this common reality; and to that extent human beings possess freedom in the positive sense, they have their true identity in that common reality. (Gadamer, 1981, p. 77)

The public sphere is the ground of the sociological imagination, the social basis of what Habermas calls the interest in emancipation, a safeguard against the rationalization of discourse and interaction. Accordingly, Mills and Habermas take the revitalization of the public sphere as the *sine qua non* of the effort to approximate the ideals of reason, freedom and democracy in contemporary society. For each, the commitment to these ideals is also a commitment to the public sphere. On this score, Mills and Habermas are influenced strongly by John Dewey, the American educational philosopher and mainstay of the Progressive movement in the early decades of the twentieth century. A brief consideration of Dewey's argument will serve as an introduction to the more developed positions of Mills and Habermas.

The social ideal Dewey employs to evaluate the worth of a given form of social life has two related parts: 'The extent in which the interests of a group are shared by all its members, and the fullness and freedom with which it interacts with other groups' (Dewey, 1916, p. 99). For a society to be assessed favorably in these terms, Dewey argues, it must be built around democratically organized publics which interact freely with one another, give full recognition to the mutual concerns of their members, and facilitate 'the participation of every mature human being in formation of the values that regulate the living of men together' (Dewey, 1939, p. 400).

Democratic publics rely on those conditions which foster debate, discussion and dialogue and which have as their end the agreeable formulation of common purposes and objectives. Necessary to a vital and vibrant public life are the following: freedom of social inquiry and freedom of expression, so that the results of social inquiry gain wide dissemination – that is, are given full publicity; frequent and active participation in the use of the freedoms of inquiry and expression; and, most significantly, 'free and systematic communication' – discourse not distorted by 'barriers of class, race, and national territory', communication free from the influence of both 'publicity agents', those 'hired promoters of opinion' and 'exploiters of sentiment', on the one hand, and 'emotional habituations and intellectual habitudes' on the other (ibid., pp. 391-4). Democratic publics encourage their members to assume responsibility for and to take direct participation in the formation of the ends which guide their activity. As a consequence, Dewey writes, 'their activity becomes free or voluntary and loses its externally enforced and servile quality' (Dewey, 1916, p. 260). Additionally, they promote that search for genuine agreement among individuals engaged in open, free, non-distorted communication which produces public opinion – those critical judgements about public affairs formed and entertained by those who constitute the publics.

Dewey's defense of public life, his argument in favor of maximizing autonomous public life and enlarging the range of social interaction and the opportunity for equable communication as the bases of movement toward a more desirable society, is taken up, in somewhat different ways, by Mills and Habermas. Each agrees with Dewey that the eclipse of public life seriously threatens the existence of democratic attitudes, capacities and institutions and severely obstructs the formation of *theoria*, whether in the form of public opinion or social theory. Moreover, each envisions a revitalized public life as the ground on which reason and freedom once again can become allies.

Publics

Mills's image of the public is influenced largely by his understanding of those public associations found in the small towns and urban communities of pre-World War II America. Habermas conceptualizes the public with reference to the bourgeois public sphere that existed in eighteenth- and nineteenth-century Europe. Ultimately, however, each is concerned primarily with the principles of publicness embodied in the concrete cases. As a result, their treatments of the public – their accounts of the decline of public life, their views on the indispensability of publics to reason and freedom, their arguments about the urgency of recovering a vital public life – are remarkably alike.

Mills on Publics

For Mills, as we saw in Chapter 1, the intellectual task of the sociologist is to clarify in order to reinvigorate the ideals of reason and freedom. If human reason is to assume a central role in the making of history – and it must if human freedom is to be achieved – sociologists must become one of its staunchest defenders and major carriers. Minimally, Mills argues, this requires that the values of reason and freedom appear prominently in the defining themes of sociological work, and that this work be addressed to two audiences in particular. For those with power and with awareness of it, work of this kind should be used to persuade them to take responsibility for the consequences of their decisions. For those who lack both power and awareness of their powerlessness, this work should reveal to them the structural sources and public character of their troubles and unease. In an effort to make human reason effective in the governance of human affairs, Mills (1959, p.181) writes, sociologists must 'direct this work *at* kings ... [and] *to* "publics"'. The intellectual task of the sociologist allied with the values of reason and freedom is at once educational and political both in substance and implication.

> The primary aim of the sociologist as political educator is continually to translate personal troubles into public issues, and public issues into the terms of their human meaning for a variety of individuals. It is his task to display in his work – and, as an educator, in his life as well – this kind of sociological imagination. And it is his purpose to cultivate such habits of mind among the men and women who are publicly exposed to him. To secure these ends is to secure reason and individuality, and to make these the predominant values of a democratic society. (ibid., pp. 187–8)

A democratic society, according to Mills, is one where people have an effective voice in the making of those decisions which vitally affect them, where the power to make such decisions is publicly legitimated, and where those who exercise this power are publicly accountable. A democratic society, like reason and individuality, requires the strong and extensive presence of publics and the stuff of publics, active and self-educating individuals.

Very much like Dewey, Mills defines the public as a space conducive to the free ebb and flow of discussion, a place where authority is grounded in discussion, a result of 'the hope that truth and justice will somehow come out of society as a great apparatus of free discussion' (Mills, 1956, p. 299). More specifically, Mills identifies what he takes to be the major characteristics of the public. First, in a public, those who express opinions are roughly equal in number to those who receive opinions. Discussion is open, personal, and moves back and forth easily among the discussants. Secondly, discussion proceeds so that there is an opportunity to respond quickly and effectively to any expressed opinion without fear of internal or external, informal or formal reprisals. The rules of discussion promote wide participation in the symmetrical formulation of opinion. Thirdly, such opinion is regularly expressed in collective forms of action (even at those times when the action is antagonistic toward established structures of power and authority) and such action is effective in influencing decisions of powerful consequence. Fourthly, the public is neither penetrated nor manipulated by formally instituted authority; it has genuine autonomy from the rational and rationalizing agents of formal authority and from the sources of bureaucratized discourse. Finally, the public exists in a community of publics, interacting fully and freely with its counterparts in an effort to shape a broad-based and effective public opinion (ibid., pp. 303–4).

Sociologists become and remain carriers of human reason only in the presence of strong and meaningful publics. In the first place, publics constitute the primary audience for sociological work thematized around the values of reason and freedom. In the second place, such sociological work is best conceived and carried out in a public setting. In many respects, the sociological imagination is formed as public opinion is, and it requires for its vitality both a place where ideas and alternatives are seriously discussed and genuinely debated and a real chance to influence decisions important to the commonwealth. But these conditions do not prevail today. As a result, the chances of sociologists successfully carrying and reinvigorating reason are slim. The established political structure is built around a decisive centralization of the means of history-making (means expropriated from the many and concentrated in the hands of the few), according to Mills, and as a consequence we witness the collapse of the Enlightenment hope that reason and freedom would come to be the decisive forces in the making of human history. Behind this collapse is the erosion of public life.

Mills attributes the erosion of the community of publics to four fundamental structural chances, each reflecting the growing rationalization of social life. Bureaucratic structures of decision-making have come to predominate in both the economy and the polity, blunting the effectiveness of publics as intermediary associations. The institutions of power have become more centralized and inaccessible, less political and more administrative, and, as a result, less accountable. In addition, the means of opinion-making have been rationalized, particularly with the growth of the media of mass communication. The mass media have promoted a technological illiteracy by obstructing small-scale discussion and the leisurely exchange of views, by distracting attention from the connections between public issues and personal troubles, and by discouraging the transcendence of the particular and the immediate. Furthermore, the old middle class of independent entrepreneurs and practitioners has been replaced by a new middle class of salaried white collar workers, who lack both an independent basis of power and the commitment to place which is necessary for strong civic spirit. Finally, the growth of the metropolis with its segregated and fractionalized division of labor has been accompanied by the decline of community structure. In sum, Mills (ibid., p. 305) writes,

> there is a movement from widely scattered little powers to concentrated powers and the attempt at monopoly control from powerful centers, which ... are centers of manipulation as well as authority. The small shop serving the neighborhood is replaced by the anonymity of the national corporation: mass advertisement replaces the personal influence of opinion between merchant and customer. The political leader hooks up his speech to a national network and speaks, with appropriate personal touches, to a million people he never saw and never will see. Entire brackets of professions and industries are in the 'opinion business', impersonally manipulating the public for hire.

In this setting, the genuine clash of viewpoints, the reflection, debate and organized action by which a community of publics comes to feel and to define itself and comes alive as an active influence in public affairs are difficult to achieve. Under these circumstances, the public gives way to the mass.

Mills defines the mass as the reverse of the public. In the mass, those who receive opinions far outnumber those who express them; the structure of communication makes it virtually impossible for the individual to respond to expressed opinions quickly and effectively; the translation of opinion into action is guided by external authorities in a position to shape the channels and patterns of such action; the mass is dependent on and is manipulated by formal institutions of authority and is penetrated by agents of rationalizing forces who or which lessen its autonomy in the formulation of opinion. Where people in publics acquire knowledge which enable them to translate personal troubles into public issues amenable to organized and collective action, those 'in masses are gripped by personal troubles, but they are not aware of their true meaning and source ... They lose their will for rationally considered decision and action because they do not possess the instruments for such decision and action; they lose their sense for political belonging because they do not belong; they lose their political will because they see no way to realize it' (ibid., p.324).

The erosion of public life and the rise of mass society are the culmination of those developments which have served to invalidate the assumption that an increased rationality brings increased freedom. Despite the enormous difficulty these circumstances entail for retaining commitment to the alternative view which sees human reason as the predicate of freedom, Mills implores the sociological community to sustain this commitment and, through liberal education, to help others make it as well. His view on this matter, also influenced by Dewey, is taken up after our examination of Habermas's treatment of the public sphere.

Habermas on the Public Sphere

In the public sphere, Habermas (1974, p. 9) writes, individuals 'confer in an unrestricted fashion – that is, with the guarantee of freedom of assembly and association and the freedom to express and publish their opinions – about matters of general interest'. The public sphere is an autonomous and protected arena for rational public discourse where people are assured the opportunity to assemble and discuss matters of common concern; where discourse is critical, that is, views are challenged, debated, contradicted, and, if need be, rejected; where no social differences or privileges are recognized; where discourse takes place in accordance with the standards of reason, not those of emotion, dogma, or established authority. In the public sphere, public opinion – critical judgements about public life formed on the basis of reflective, constraint-free communication (as opposed to that opinion produced by an unreflected acceptance of ingrained custom, prejudice, or cultural taste) – is formed. When mobilized into a political force, public opinion of this kind is capable of making political authority more reasonable and social life less oppressive. Habermas derives this image from the bourgeois public sphere which clearly emerged in eighteenth-century Europe.

The public sphere, according to Habermas, originated in several particular features of seventeenth- and eighteenth-century bourgeois society. Most significantly, its development was the result of a movement of the then rising bourgeoisie against those provisions of the absolute state which precluded their participation in political life. Growing out of an array of voluntary associations – salons, café, literary clubs with their own intellectual newspapers and journals – the bourgeois public sphere was situated between the state and the private domain (and was distinguished clearly from the two), and offered a place for discussion free from the distorting influence of market and state, social ranking and privilege. The image of the bourgeois model of public sphere, Habermas claims, is reflected perfectly in the first modern constitutions:

> they guaranteed the society as a sphere of private autonomy and the restriction of public authority to a few functions. Between these two spheres, the constitutions further insured the existence of a realm of private individuals assembled into a public body who as citizens transmit the needs of bourgeois society to the state, in order, ideally, to transform political into 'rational' authority within the medium of this public sphere. The general interest, which was the measure of such rationality, was then guaranteed ... when the activities of private individuals in the marketplace were freed from social compulsion and from political pressure in the public sphere. (ibid., pp. 52–3)

In this context, the bourgeois public became an autonomous base from which the public authority of the state and the political norms of absolute structures of power were debated and critically assessed by private persons assembled into a public body for the purpose of public discourse. Ultimately, the state was compelled to justify its laws and policies, its actions and decisions, before this forum wherein the standard of legitimate judgement was taken to be the principle of reason created or discovered in the open discussion of enlightened individuals. 'To the principle of the existing power', Habermas (ibid., p. 52) writes, 'the bourgeois public opposed the principle of supervision – that very principle which demands that proceedings be made public' and thus accountable to reasonable standards of legitimacy.

The bourgeois public was regarded by those who participated in it as serving the general interest. Actually, it represented the specific interests of the participants, drawn by and large from the bourgeoisie. Nevertheless, the bourgeois public sphere was of great historical importance, for it was the source of public autonomy, public freedom and enlightened public opinion as universal ideals. As a consequence, it was able to induce movement toward the greater democratization of political life. The demise of the bourgeois public sphere constituted the loss of one of the more important social bases of democracy (Cohen, 1979; Hohendahl, 1979; Held, 1980).

Like Mills, Habermas attributes the decline of the public sphere to the spread of rationalization and the subsequent tendencies toward depoliticization and the privatization of needs and interests (tendencies which culminated in the civil privatism discussed in the previous chapter).

> The transformation of the family with the loss of its socializing and economic functions, the massification of culture and the substitution of passive consumers for the literary public of enlightened participants, the bureaucratization of parties and the transformation of the press from the genuine expression of public opinion to the instrument of organized particular interests moulding 'public opinion' through advertizing techniques (Cohen, 1979, p. 81)

are some of the major factors which contribute to the public sphere's demise.

With the rationalization of society, Habermas argues, public life was brought under the wing of bureaucratic administration and the public sphere became less hospitable to unrestricted and unconstrained discussion of practical questions and common goals. In the official public sphere, rational discussion as a basis of self-determination and political emancipation gave way to a search for technical solutions to complex administrative problems. Moreover, the official public sphere became an arena for the expression of particularistic interests and thus an obstacle to the pursuit of universal themes and general interests.

As a consequence of these developments, the classical aims of public opinion – to express and to advocate the general interest and to oppose in its name irresponsible and unreasonable exercises of power – was undercut. Using the techniques of advertising and market and consumer research, 'public relations work' and 'public opinion research' replaced public discussion as the source of public opinion. Friedrich Pollock (1976, p. 227) describes the process as follows:

> A number of questions are put by the interviewers of the institutes for public opinion to a statistically representative cross-section of the population. The answers received are grouped according to content and in the process of interpretation are related to a series of objective qualities of the interviewees. The results are then presented in tabulated

form, the tables are interpreted and the product regarded as public opinion.

The problems with the operationalized concept of public opinion are obvious enough. Public opinion in this form is subjectivized, taking no account of the relation of consciousness or judgement to objective reality. More troublesome, public opinion of this sort is simply the sum of individual opinions, the aggregation of private concerns, and thus is not really public at all – or, at best, is merely public opinion in the absence of publics, produced not by discoursing persons assembled as a public body but by tabulating the personal responses given privately and anonymously to a public opinion poll.

The bourgeois public sphere has been effectively undermined by the rationalizing forces of capitalism. While the institution is now obsolete, the principles behind it remain indispensable to the effort to re-establish conditions hospitable to the commitment to reason and freedom. Habermas examines and develops these principles in some detail.

According to Habermas, the bourgeois public sphere embodied three major normative principles: accessibility in the dual sense of requiring that information be available to the public and assuring, in turn, that the public be open to all; elimination of all privileges so that people engage in public discussion as equal speakers; and search for general norms and rational standards of legitimacy. In delineating these principles, Habermas's concern is to discover how the ends of political and economic activity can be brought under the influence of rational discussion and ethical reflection. His position, as summarized by Cohen (1979, p. 71), is that 'the clarification of what is practically necessary and objectively possible, of how to interpret norms and values, interests and needs in relation to technological possibilities, can be achieved only within institutionally secured public spaces that allow for the articulation of all needs, interests, and values ... [that is, within] a reactivated public able to freely form its political will'. By incorporating the three normative principles, the reactivated public sphere would institutionalize the individual autonomy, democratic interaction and non-constrained communication necessary for achieving intersubjective consensus on values, norms, and criteria which can be used to assess and to resolve the practical questions concerned with how we are to live our lives given what is desirable and what is presently possible.

For Habermas, non-distorted communication would be the most important aspect of the reactivated public sphere. Non-distorted communication is not constrained by social divisions, formal authorities, bureaucratic imperatives, technological requirements, or internalized controls. It enables people to locate themselves in history and in society, to move back and forth between the concrete and the abstract, the particular and the general, to arrive at intersubjective agreements, to make themselves understood and to understand others, to find themselves in while distinguishing themselves from the intersubjective, and to reflect upon and give reasons for doing what they do. Non-distorted communication is indispensable to reasoning publics.

Non-distorted communication, John Keane (1982, pp. 26–8) notes, is secured on the fulfillment of three necessary conditions. The first is 'development of symmetrical, reciprocal relations between speaking actors ... [so] that no one speaker (or group of speakers) could rightly monopolise the powers and means of assertation, disputation and persuasion'. The second is the creation of intersubjective communities of speaking actors whose norms and values promote the autonomy of individuals and groups and thus maximize individuation and group diversity within a community setting. The third and most obvious condition is the unfettering of critical discussion.

> Liberated from any form of official evaluation from above, discussions ... would be unrestricted. No dogmatically fixed or majority opinion could permanently avoid being made the object of public debate and criticism. Political 'space' would be created, wherein the hitherto 'minority' position of a fraction of the public could become, through sustained, unrestricted, and compelling argument, acceptable to broader sections of the political community.

The satisfaction of these three conditions – conditions which foster critical and uncompelled argumentation between individuated, equal and communicatively competent citizens – secures the possibility of both non-distorted communication and autonomous and authentic public life.

Only with the realization of these conditions will the enlightenment of political will and the formulation of authentic public opinion proceed. Commitment to them is commitment to democracy, and it requires practice aimed at the rationalization of politics – rationalization not as the extension of technical control but as the extension of emancipation, individuation, and communication free of domination. Rationalization of this type, a rationality with reason, is the predicate of human freedom and it takes the form of reactivating and revitalizing the public sphere.

Both Mills and Habermas agree that the fundamental task of social theory is to assist in the rebuilding of democratically organized public life. The constitutive features of this life – individuality, autonomy, equality, rational discourse and non-distorted communication – form the ground out of which reason and freedom grow and sustain the impulse toward reason and freedom which animates the sociological imagination and critical theory. Given the continued presence of those forces which have vitiated the public sphere, the problems each confronts has to do with how this task is best accomplished. Mills's strategy focuses on liberal education and urges sociologists to make the recovery of public life the most important of their academic responsibilities. Habermas has little to say about this strategy, but others whose work is congenial to his, most notably Alvin Gouldner, follow Mills in making the connection between reactivated publics and liberal education. The nature of this connection and its significance for the rescue of reason and freedom from the distorting pressures of instrumental rationality are taken up below.

Liberal Education and Publics

The relation of liberal education to democracy was of foremost interest to John Dewey. Liberal education, Dewey argued, was the major contributor to the 'civic efficiency' necessary for democratic society. Through liberal education, individuals develop the traits and capacities that make them active and knowledgeable citizens. They learn 'to judge men and measure wisely and to take a determining part in making as well as obeying laws'; they acquire 'a cultivated imagination for what men have in common and [an antipathy toward] whatever unnecessarily divides them'; they obtain 'the power to join freely and fully in shared or common activities' (Dewey, 1916, pp. 120–3). By involving people in the deepest problems of common humanity, liberal education affords them the opportunity to develop the distinctive capacities of citizenship. In return, it expects the liberally educated to give to others the same opportunity for acquiring the wisdom and developing the abilities that make for reasoned participation in democratically organized publics.

In Alvin Gouldner's terms, liberal education is concerned primarily with knowledge as awareness, as distinct from knowledge as information. Knowing in the sense of being informed consists of the lessons of experience and the facts, skills, and training acquired through this experience or from technicians or experts who have codified the lessons. Knowing in the sense of being aware consists of rational understanding and insight, the ability to discover that hidden by the facts, and the capacity to implicate the self, the knower, in the known. While the first type of knowledge expands a body of information, the second cultivates a certain quality of mind. The function of knowledge as awareness is not 'simply awareness for its own sake, in the sense of mere apprehension of truth; it is also concerned with changing behavior; it is a practically effective knowledge, a knowledge manifested in everyday behavior and choice' (Gouldner, 1965, p. 108). Acquired through discussion with those who are committed to rational discourse and who feel free to say what they believe without fear of community sanctions or political reprisals, this practically effective knowledge depends upon as it promotes the extension of the conditions of public life.

Dewey's and Gouldner's view of the strong affinity between liberal education and democratic politics is consistent with the democratic theory of culture which evolved concurrently with the bourgeois public sphere. Constituted as that place where free and equal individuals rationally discuss and debate public issues, the public sphere required participants with access not merely to information but also to an education which induced a quality of mind congenial to 'civic efficiency' and rational understanding. The liberal arts were grounded in this conception of citizenship and public wisdom. 'For men such as Paine, Jefferson, Franklin, Rousseau, Robespierre, and Kant reason was not only a universal human capacity but the political obligation of citizenship. Cultivation was considered to be the duty of all free men, whether merchants, farmers, or mechanics' (Oestereicher, 1982, p. 1006). To the extent that such cultivation was its central responsibility, liberal arts education was highly politicized, its aim being to prepare people to participate in the public sphere's striving for self-determination and opposition to traditional authority. The study of history, art, the classics, moral philosophy and the natural sciences was regarded as essential to active participation in the public life. Thus, the notion of liberal education, Emil Oestereicher (ibid., p. 1012) writes, 'was tied to the vision of a public sphere, to the concept of the citizen whose civic duty was to practice his wisdom in everyday life'.

The decline of the public sphere that results from the rationalization and, in turn, depoliticization of society no doubt makes the contributions to citizenship offered by liberal education seem irrelevant. Equally certain, as rationalization penetrates education in the form of a vocationalism which prizes marketable skills and information over awareness as a quality of mind, the capacity of the liberal arts to advance the traits and abilities required for meaningful public life is placed in jeopardy. Nevertheless, the university remains one of the few places hospitable to public discourse and the liberal arts. With the erosion of the community as the authentic site of public discourse, Gouldner (1976, p. 189) observes, came 'the *transfer* of ... public space, its *movement* from the larger community into the smaller and more limited public space of the university'. Similarly, Oestereicher (1982, p. 1011) notes, the 'liberal arts were more and more restricted to the universities. Thus it was no longer the citizen but rather the university professor who became the upholder of what came to be known as civilizational values.' Under the pressure of rationalization, scientism, and vocationalism, the university professor, as Mills argues, often became an abstracted empiricist, disavowing any and all claims of upholding civilizational values. Despite this, Mills recognizes that the vast majority of sociologists work within the university, that the university continues to sustain both public space and the liberal arts, and that here is where the effort must be made to rebuild the public grounding of reason and freedom.

For Mills, the central and continuing task of liberal education is to assist people in developing the disciplined and informed mind which is the prerequisite for the self-educating and self-cultivating individual who resists being overwhelmed by the burdens of modern society. In this sense, liberal education is a liberating education which fosters the growth of the free and rational individual, the basis of genuine publics and democratic society. Given these objectives, the key responsibilities of the sociologist as liberal educator are two:

> What he ought to do for the individual is to turn personal troubles and concerns into social issues and problems open to reason – his aim is to help the individual become a self-educating man, who only then would be reasonable and free. What he ought to do for the society is to combat all those forces which are destroying genuine publics and creating a mass society – or put as a positive goal, his aim is to help build and strengthen self-cultivating publics. Only then might society be reasonable and free. (Mills, 1959, p. 186)

To meet these responsibilities, the sociologist must engage the range of liberal education from the training of people in the basic skills of reading, writing, and oral expression to educating them in values, debating with them ways of living and encouraging them to move toward a vision of the way people should live. Liberal education is concerned with sensibility which includes skill and value and, as well, the cultivation of the art of controversy, an art which sharpens thinking when practiced with oneself and which enables debate when carried on with others (ibid., p. 187). The acquisition of sensibility rests on as it promotes 'the capacity to hear and respond to the initiatives of others, to participate in the kind of discursive interaction that permits generation of shared norms on a basis of moral autonomy and mutual respect' (Simonds, 1982, p. 598). It is this sensibility that Mills calls the sociological imagination, and its acquisition, he argues, permits people to become genuine participants in authentic publics.

Sympathetic to Mills's position and generally influenced by the work of Habermas, Alvin Gouldner argues that the sociological effort to build and strengthen self-cultivating publics should be focused initially on sociologists themselves. He calls for the creation of theoretical communities or theoretical publics conducive to both non-distorted communication and the pursuit of liberal arts sensibility. These communities or publics would serve two related purposes. First, they would promote the formulation of the kind of social thought Mills describes as the sociological imagination and Habermas calls critical theory. Secondly, they would function as testing grounds for figuring out the best way for reactivating publics and restoring to the broader society a meaningful public life.

Gouldner on Theoretical Publics

In his controversial *The Coming Crisis of Western Sociology* (1970), Gouldner followed the direction taken by Mills a decade earlier by launching a blistering attack against established sociology and, in turn, offering an alternative vision of the sociological enterprise. Gouldner calls for a 'reflexive sociology' which requires its practitioners to look at themselves, to deepen their self-awareness, and, in so doing, to clarify and strengthen the linkages between sociology and society. Reflexive sociology is a moral sociology, embodying and advancing the values of reason and freedom, and its aim is 'to *transform* the sociologist, to penetrate deeply into his daily life and work, enriching them with new sensitivities, and to raise the sociologist's self-awareness to a new historical level' (Gouldner, 1970, p. 489). In this sense, reflexive sociology embraces the sociological imagination, for it requires sociologists to cultivate in themselves those skills, values and sensibilities that enable them to recognize themselves in society and in others and thus to overcome the separation of knower and known. Reflexive sociology, then, includes much more than a 'bundle of skills'; it also includes a conception of how to live and how to think and learn about society (and therefore ourselves); it is responsible not merely for gathering reliable tidbits of information, but also for helping people 'in their struggle to take possession of what *is* theirs – society and culture – and [for] aiding them to know who they are and what they may want' (ibid., p. 509).

Given this goal, reflexive sociology seeks to formulate an emancipatory social theory which would 'liberate man's reason from any force, in or out of himself, symbolic or not, in the psyche and in the society, that cripples and confuses reason' (Gouldner, 1973, p. 102). Crucial to this endeavor is the reflexivity which enables the social theorist to search the immediate environment of his or her work and the larger society for those conditions which either oppose or facilitate rational discussion. On this point, Gouldner (ibid., pp. 100–1) writes,

> I concur largely with [critical theory] in general and Jürgen Habermas in particular. In short, what is sought is truth as *practical* reason; practical because relevant to the understanding and transformation of our daily

lives and the historically shaped society in which we live. We want to understand our social world and ourselves and others in it, so that we may change it in ways that enable us to understand it still better, to have fuller rational discourse in it, so that we may be better able to change it, and so on.

Following Habermas, Gouldner grounds emancipatory social theory in the culture of critical discourse, in reasonable dialogue, careful speech, and the grammar of rationality. In this view, the creators of social theory do not merely create knowledge, they also create language and culture. In attempting to understand the whole, to see the totality, theory and theorists order and conceptualize society and in the process create extraordinary languages, languages able to mediate between the world and the human quest for meaning, between deficient and incomplete understandings of reality and the reason and reflexivity offered by critical discourse. With this capacity, social theory is able to provide a language and a culture appropriate to authentic public life. While anticipating the recovery of public life in the larger society, emancipatory social theory presupposes public space within the domain of sociology itself. The initial step, then, is for social theorists to create and maintain their own publics, or what Gouldner calls 'theoretical communities'.

The first task, according to Gouldner, is the creation of communities which sustain the social and human conditions for rational discourse by social theorists. The primary source of reflexive sociology and emancipatory social theory, rational discourse is predicted on a community of theorists who speak a common language and share common norms and commitments. As a liberated social space, free of force and violence and open to 'true-speaking', as a community of equals where barriers to open communication have been broken down, as a place and an occasion where theorists can both receive help in coping with their anxieties and uneasiness and affirm their commitment to the values of reason and freedom, the theoretical community is the theorist's equivalent of the public sphere. In it, the emphasis, similar to that found in liberal education, is on acquiring a quality of mind, on pursuing knowledge as awareness.

Unlike the public sphere and liberal education, the theoretical community is always concerned with its structure and with the conditions that make it possible. With this concern social theory becomes fully reflexive. Social theory, Gouldner (ibid., p. 97) insists,

must determine, evaluate, critique the conditions that enable it to organize itself; in enacting these conditions it tests and appraises the worth of the theory it has established. In establishing and testing these conditions for itself social theory also acts universalistically, on behalf of the rest of the world. For the quest for rational discourse is not a sectarian need for social theorist's alone but a world need. The theorist's collective then becomes a strategic, theory-generating, theory-consolidating, theory-critiquing social matrix.

By reflecting on its own practice, the theoretical community might be able to suggest the direction needed for the recovery of public life in the larger society. In this way, the theoretical community seeks to reach beyond the university and the sociological enterprise to influence progressively the broader society. Should theoretical communities fail in this larger objective, their establishment would still prove valuable for they could sustain the spirit of public discussion and nourish the commitment to reason and freedom, keep them alive for what may be more propitious future times.

As Gouldner envisions it, the theoretical community is guided by what Habermas calls the interest in human emancipation and thus seeks knowledge in the form of critical analyses which free consciousness from dependence on seemingly natural and immutable forces and, in turn, restores to people a recognition of themselves as active human subjects (see Chapter 1). The basic assumption here is that by changing people's understanding of themselves and their world, the critical analyses offered by emancipatory social theory enable them to decide to change those conditions they find repressive and, as well, to alter their attitudes and behavior so as not to implicate themselves further in the reproduction of these repressive conditions. In contrast to the instrumentalist model which pursues knowledge as information that extends our power of technical control, the educative model implied by the theoretical community is reflexive in that it aims to move people into reflecting on the way they live and interact with others in order that they might arrive at a new understanding of themselves, of the sources of their unhappiness, and of their ability to transform existing practices. 'Both the instrumentalist and the educative models promise freedom', Brian Fay (1977, p. 207) notes,

but in the former it is the freedom that results from knowing how to achieve what one wants, whereas in the latter it is the freedom to be self-determining in the sense of being able to decide for oneself, on the basis of a lucid, critical self-awareness, the manner in which one wishes to live. In the educative model, the practical result of social theory is not the means for greater manipulative power but rather the self-understanding that allows one's own rational thinking to be the cause of one's actions; i.e., social theory is a means toward increased *autonomy*.

The freedom promised by the instrumentalist model is contingent on our ability to manipulate the causal and seemingly natural relations among reified powers so that they work in our favor; that anticipated by the educative model depends on a new way of looking at ourselves and our world, a way that makes the unintelligible intelligible and enables us to bring those forces which presently use us as an object under the rational control of reflective human subjects.

Fay reiterates Gouldner's very important point that the educative model associated with theoretical communities entails not simply changing ideas and self-understandings, but also transforming the organizational structures and behavioral forms which set the context of ideas and understandings. Crucial to this view is how people come to hold new self-understandings and ideas and how social theorists come to formulate them as emancipatory social theory. Rational discourse is the only legitimate basis for new self-understandings and emancipatory social theory. When brought about by techniques of manipulation, propaganda, and mind control, new self-conceptions simply represent the substitution of one dogma for another. When, however, the result of reasoned argumentation, independent reflection, and rational persuasion which take place in a context where reasons for change are given and can be rejected without fear of punishment, new self-conceptions promote autonomy and emancipation. Rational enlightenment, then, requires a particular institutional setting. 'These settings', writes Fay (1977, p. 230) in a way reminiscent of Dewey, Mills, Habermas and Gouldner, 'are groups that are relatively egalitarian ..., relatively free of recrimination between members, relatively committed to rationally discussing its members' situations and experiences, and relatively insistent that its members take responsibility for whatever claims, decisions, or actions they undertake to make'. These are the features of the theoretical community and, more importantly, the features of a vigorously ongoing public sphere. In the form of the theoretical community, they permit the formulation of emancipatory social theory; in the form of the public sphere, they encourage the formulation of enlightened public opinion. In both cases, they bespeak a commitment to reason and freedom. In terms of this commitment, Gouldner calls on social theorists to establish and maintain the theoretical communities which serve as models of the genuine public sphere that is the very ground of reason and freedom.

Public Sphere and Civil Society

Concern with the public sphere as the ground of reason and freedom brings us back to the early roots of sociology. These roots are fundamentally conservative in character, and their conservatism is expressed most clearly in a full and animated appreciation for civil society. Sociology emerges, as we saw in Chapter 2, as a defense of society – of the moral supports of social solidarity and the non-rational institutions and associations which more or less spontaneously promote order and progress. Society, in this view, is capable of self-management and ought to be protected from the atomizing influences of the marketplace on the one hand and the totalizing tendencies of the state on the other. Civil society, sociology's primary object, should not be allowed to be absorbed by either economy or state.

The civil society defended by early sociology was the central basis of the bourgeois public sphere. Shielded from traditional authority and the imperatives of the absolutist state, the civil society which began to flourish in the eighteenth century permitted the creation of new values and practices and new attitudes which encouraged people to participate in shaping the ends to which political power was put. Possessing an important degree of autonomy from the absolutist state and comprised of groups and associations built around occupation, religion, intellectual interest, literary taste, ethnicity, and numerous other bases of social difference, the new civil society fostered a spirit of independence, reflected initially in entrepreneurial activities and literary and scientific pursuits and, later, in concern over matters of public affairs and civic virtue. The bourgeois public realm was a consequence of this independence, constituted as it was by individual members of civil society who transcended their private, particularistic concerns to form a public body opposed to the impositions of the absolutist state. As members of a reasoning public, these private persons sought to generate in the form of a critically established and widely held public opinion the capacity to control the state (Poggi, 1978, pp. 81–4). The opinion openly and rationally established in the public sphere had as one of its central aims the safeguarding of civil society from the intrusions of the state. In the relation of civil society and public sphere, the public and the private mutually reinforced one another, as private individuals from particularistic groups became a public body committed to the common good. As a public body, private individuals exercised reason to arrive at the general interest, an important aspect of which was the freedom of civil society.

In the mid nineteenth century, Tocqueville found in this relation of civil society and public sphere the basis of America's vital democracy. To understand the bases of democratic life in America, Tocqueville argued, nothing deserves more attention than the country's civil associations, and they come in a 'thousand different types – religious, moral, serious, futile, very general and very limited, immensely large and very minute' (Tocqueville, 1969, p. 513). In these associations, people acquire the habit of acting together and learn to work toward agreement on common aims.

The free institutions of the United States and the political rights enjoyed there provide a thousand continual reminders to every citizen that he lives in society ... Through them large numbers see, speak, listen, and stimulate each other to carry out all sorts of undertakings in common. Then they carry these conceptions with them into the affairs of civil life and put them to a thousand uses. (Tocqueville, 1969, pp. 512, 524)

Thus Tocqueville argued, civil associations, arising from and reflecting the social differences that make up civil society, simultaneously sustain these differences by warding off efforts by the state to undermine the autonomy of civil society and, in the area of public affairs, seek to overcome these differences and the particularistic concerns they promote by enabling people to act as a public body interested in the general interest.

Tocqueville's argument that a vibrant civil society is the key precondition of democratic society is taken up by Durkheim, through whose influence civil society became sociology's central problematic. Given Durkheim's overriding concern with the erosion of the social bases of solidarity, moral belief and group structure, it comes as no surprise that he links sociology so directly to the defense of civil society. Civil society, for Durkheim, is made up of those institutions, groups, and patterns of interaction that provide the moral supports for order and stability. Accordingly, civil society is not only distinct from the market and the state, it is also capable of developing and maintaining itself without being subordinated to either. Indeed, Durkheim is convinced that the strategy for reconstructing society must focus on civil society – both the source of the moral individualism that will counter the egoistic selfishness produced by the market and the basis of democratic corporatist groups which will serve as intermediaries between the individual and the state and check the ever-present tendency toward state-dominated existence. Durkheim, thus, is seeking an alternative to the atomizing, anomic independence provided by the market and the totalizing dependence on domination offered by the state. He sees civil society, as Gouldner (1980, p. 370) writes, 'as a haven and support for individual persons, i.e., as de-atomizing; as a medium through which they can pursue their own projects in the course of their everyday lives; and as ways of avoiding dependence on the domination by the state'. For moral individualism and democracy to prevail, Durkheim argued, civil society must have some autonomy in the management of its own affairs. Were civil society to be dissolved into competitive economic relations or subsumed by the state, individualism, democracy, and, although Durkheim never explicitly mentioned it, the public sphere would be seriously threatened.

If civil society is the central focus of Durkheim's sociology, it is devalued in Marx's. Marx sees civil society basically as an arena where economic developments take place; he thus denies civil society a life of its own. In Marx's view, Gouldner (ibid., p. 358) notes

> only the economic had its own natural and spontaneous development; *it* was the source of initiative and action, the other spheres were sites of *re*-action. The sphere of human connectedness, of society and the social, shared by both the economic [substructure] and the political [superstructure], was shunted aside by the imperative need to *distinguish* the two and demonstrate the hegemony of the economic.

By treating civil society as a residual category, Marx envisages a socialism without safeguards against the centralization of power, a socialism where civil society is absorbed by the state.

In the light of the commitment to the recovery of the public sphere, and giving the dependence of the public sphere on civil society, the most important question for both socialism and capitalism concerns how civil society can be strengthened in order to resist better encroachments of the state. More specifically, the question is, writes Gouldner (ibid., p. 371),

> how may civil society be fortified so that Marxism's own liberative aspirations can be realized? Essentially, sociology's traditions – precisely because they have been *conservative* – have centered on the problems connected with developing a self-maintaining civil society. Deepened knowledge of this is certainly indispensable for any social movement, such as Marxism, which ... hopes to develop persons capable of mutual aid and independence, and to retain a viable 'public' sphere.

Without a strong civil society that can sustain the public sphere, in part by shielding it from the rationalizing forces of both state or economy, no emancipation is possible in modern society. Recognition of this has been central to sociology at least since Durkheim.

More importantly, this recognition guided the bourgeois struggles for an autonomous civil society and public sphere in the seventeenth century and, more recently, the Solidarity led movement in Poland in the early 1980s. The Solidarity movement arose from the fusion of three sets of demands: the first called for enterprise self-management and independent trade unions; the second for a reaffirmation of national identity as a way of symbolizing the desire for national independence; the third for an easing of censorship to allow for more democratic forms of expression. Made with full awareness of the major economic difficulties facing the Polish economy at the time, these demands incorporated a willingness on the part of the people to undertake necessary sacrifices. Underlying each of these demands, however, was the conviction that people should participate in deciding the scope and character of sacrifice and that such participation should be guided by self-realized needs (Goldfarb, 1982, p. 87; Touraine *et al.*, 1983a, p. 51). Focusing on self-realized needs, these demands amounted to both a call for greater individual and collective autonomy and a rejection of the state as a dictatorship over needs. Begun in the summer of 1980, Solidarity over the next sixteen months attracted almost ten million members and the active support of the vast majority of the Polish people, making it the most extensive and most enduring popular uprising ever to test Communist rule.

From the very start, this movement took as its primary goal the achievement of some freedom from and some influence over state power. Deliberately avoided was any effort to acquire state power itself. In this way, Solidarity distinguished itself from previous social movements in societies controlled by one-party systems, and, ultimately, by the Soviet Union: the 1956 Hungarian effort to overthrow the party through revolutionary means and the 1968 Czechoslovakian movement to reform the party from within met with Soviet invasions and quick failure. In this context, the Polish movement sought a third way and expressed this search in the form of demands for the end of censorship and secrecy and the start of public openness on the part of the state, and demands for the freedoms of assembly, collective action, association, press and speech. Unlike the revolutionary movements in Hungary and Czechoslovakia, Solidarity presented itself as a 'self-limiting' movement which eschewed violent confrontation with the state, which refused to challenge Poland's international alliances (fully aware that the international situation virtually prohibits the overthrow of Communist control in the Eastern bloc), and which moderated trade union demands in light of the economic crisis (ibid., 1983, p. 179)

If Solidarity did not set out to destroy the party or undermine the foundations of the regime, it did seek to liberate society from the totalitarian domination of the party, to attain 'areas of democratic life, rights, and sectors of autonomous social life' (Dubet, Touraine and Wieviovka, 1982, p. 130). Clearly, the movement was guided by the idea of reconstructing civil society against the state, building away from state power and outside the omnipotent party apparatus, structures of social solidarity and independent social institutions which would shelter autonomously different forms of collective activity (Arato, 1981, p. 24; Wojcicki, 1981, p. 103). Accordingly, Zygmunt Bauman (1981, pp. 52–3) writes, Solidarity 'can be interpreted as an attempt to regain the lost autonomy for civil society ..., a manifestation of a consistent and ongoing struggle for the redefinition and relocation of the whole sphere of public debate and public opinion as separate from the state'.

The legal guarantee of civil rights, the provision for publicity, and the acceptance of plurality sought by the Polish movement were prefigured in its organizational principles, the most important of which were the following:

> The means of pressure from below are organized as open and public, un-conspiratorial, and non-avant garde social movements – each representing one constellation of interest. Pressure from below can force the existing system to adhere to its own legality as well as to *de facto* toleration of the plurality constituted by social movements. The organization of plurality, in particular of an alternative, critical public sphere, can bypass the state altogether by setting up parallel institutions. (Arato, 1981, p. 32)

The movement achieved its greatest success with the August 1980 Gdansk Agreement, which permitted the creation of independent unions with the right to strike, reduced the range of permissible censorship, opened access to the media, and guaranteed the freedom of expression in public life. Before the year was out, the party, under enormous Soviet pressure, broke the Gdansk Agreement, imprisoned many of the movement's leaders, and regularly resorted to violence in its effort to block continuation of progress toward the reconstruction of civil society. This repressive response not only destroyed Solidarity as a social movement, it also signified 'the disappearance of the Communist model, the definitive failure of the totalitarian goal of the party-state stamping its ideological and political categories onto social life. From now on, authorities can no longer claim to express or represent society; it is but a system of domination, restraints, and repression' (Dubet, Touraine and Wieviovka, 1982 p. 136). Solidarity did not succeed in establishing an autonomous civil society and a strong public sphere, but the Soviet-backed military regime which arose in response to it finds it impossible to reconquer society, to legitimate its role, and to dictate to people their needs. The spirit of Solidarity, the very spirit which animates the aspiration for civil society and public life, remains alive amid these bleak and hostile circumstances.

Two aspects of the Polish situation are especially significant given the purpose at hand. First, it more forcefully makes the point that without civil society a reasonable and emancipated public sphere is not possible. Secondly, the Polish movement, typified by Solidarity, shows that Mills's call for the cultivation of strong, self-sustaining publics transcends mere academic interest. It is a call capable of mobilizing people in resistance against the enemies of reason and freedom. The problem of recovering civil society and public life is not confined to socialism. Indeed, throughout this book we have concentrated on the erosion of civil society and the public sphere in capitalist society. The spread of capitalist rationalization, while giving rise to a technically administrative, corporatist democracy which disavows the value of democracy, has moved people to withdraw to private, selfish, narcissistic concerns. Indifference and confusion now mark both private and public life, and indifference and confusion are as much obstacles to a genuine public sphere as is the repressive, paranoic, bureaucratic socialist state. If sociology is to assist people in freeing themselves from these various traps, it must, as a first step, retain that part of its tradition which affirms civil society and, in turn, add to it an equally strong affirmation of the public sphere. This requires a vigilant opposition to rationality without reason – whether it appears in the form of a socialist state which meets opposition by sending in tanks, or takes the form of a capitalist corporation which responds to opponents by taking out jobs and investment capital. Affirmation of a vibrant civil society and a vital public sphere, steadfast opposition to rationality without reason in whatever form it takes – these are the aims of a social theory committed to reason and freedom.

Conclusion

The promise of sociology requires, according to Mills, that sociological work focus on the relation of reason and freedom, that sociologists seek to preserve the ideals of reason and freedom in their time of peril, and that sociologists as liberal educators assist in the cultivation of both the reasonable and free individual and the self-maintaining public, the ground of reason and freedom. In this way, Mills renews the central Enlightenment theme, one which preoccupied the classical social theorists, especially Marx, Durkheim and Weber. By and large, the social theory formulated throughout much of this century has neglected this theme, and there is little doubt that this neglect is largely a consequence of the instrumentalization of reason, freedom, and the public sphere – and, beyond this, the instrumentalization of social theory itself. Critical social theory, wary of the dangers of instrumentalization and prepared to resist its force, is the topic of the next and final chapter.

7

Critical Social Theory

This chapter, like the preceding one, is concerned with the interaction of the public sphere and critical social theory, each defined ultimately by a commitment to reason and freedom. Where the previous chapter concentrates on the public sphere, this one focuses on critical social theory. If a vibrant public sphere is the foundation of any effort to reverse the instrumentalization of social life, critical social theory, with the goal of cultivating the public sphere, provides a way of overcoming the instrumentalization of social thought found in the positivistically rendered social sciences.

To draw the link between the scientization of social thought and the scientization of politics, consider Robert Beiner's argument, reminiscent of our earlier discussion, that in

> a political world that is everywhere dominated by technological imperatives, where the intrusion of technology and technological ways of thinking into every sphere of life, even the most private and intimate, continues to gather pace ... the simple exercise of reflexive judgement comes increasingly to be regarded as outmoded. There seems to be neither places nor status for the power of ordinary judgement, that is, for a capacity for making sense of the things around us that is unaccountable in, and cannot be submitted to, the terms of technical rationality. (Beiner, 1983, p. xv)

In this world, ordinary political reasoning is debased as experts, administrators, and political technicians acquire a monopoly over political intelligence, a monopoly which usually 'goes unquestioned because the exercise of political rationality is assumed to be beyond the competence of the ordinary individual, whose proper sphere of competence is the choice of his own moral and social "values"' (ibid., p. 1). Implied here is the distinction between facts and values, the former a matter of methodical rule, rational procedures, and technical expertise, the latter derived from an arbitrary subjectivism, incapable of validation. In the modern world, politics must be as distanced from reflective judgement as facts are from values in the realm of science.

In the world of scientific sociology, as in the world of politics dominated by technological imperatives, reflective judgement is associated with values seen as the expression of personal preference or subjective taste, private concerns removed from the procedures of scientific inquiry and political decision-making alike. In both worlds, reflective judgement is disavowed. Against this disavowal, critical social theory seeks to restore theoretical judgement to the sociological enterprise, and, through it, practical political judgement to the world of politics. The restoration of each has the same minimal requirement: active and informed people capable of both reflection and civil dialogue about the substance of their common life. At this level, the critical social theorist is to sociology what the citizen is to the public sphere.

Critical Social Theory: Tasks, Aims, Limitations

Critical social theory rejects the orthodox claim that the social sciences and the natural sciences share the same aim. According to this orthodoxy, the scientific ideal is to describe and explain accurately empirical phenomena and, on this basis, produce a scientific – a testable and in places already confirmed – theory. For sociology and physics alike, the successful pursuit of this ideal requires the methodical collection of data, the careful search for causal connections, the logical formulation of hypotheses and empirical generalizations, and, equally important, value-neutrality, since advocacy of a normative position irreparably damages the effort to arrive at empirical explanatory theory. In Randall Collins's (1975, p. 24) view 'the task in scientific-sociology-building is to free ourselves from the dead weight of ideological commitments ... A sociology that is politically relevant is constantly in danger of adding these distortions at any time'. Within the confines of scientific sociology, the critical and negative functions of theory are lost; moral seriousness as a concern with judging whether an outcome is good or bad, independent of the criteria afforded by the given empirical arrangements, is reduced to a distorting political relevancy; and self-reflection as the implication of oneself in the process of knowing is deemed an illegitimate violation of the value-neutrality necessary for objective description and explanation.

Sociology as empirical science, Robert Bellah (1983, p. 380) charges, exists in a moral vacuum, and the generalizations it offers are 'worthless, if not pernicious because to the degree that they are rhetorically persuasive, they act as self-fulfilling prophecies. They help to create the moral cretinism they describe.' In contemporary society it is often enough true that people resemble molecules in their moral timidity and failure to exercise reflective judgement. Sociology, no doubt, is obliged to describe and explain this resemblence, but not to justify it with the assumption that its subject-matter is sufficiently akin to that of physics so that knowledge of each is constituted in the same fashion. In this regard, sociologists should adopt as one of their defining intentions the self-understanding of society, interpreting society to itself while simultaneously interpreting themselves as part of society (Shils, 1980, p. 39). Guided by this ideal, sociologists would engage their subject-matter in dialogue about the common life we call society; they would include ends as well as means in that category of objects deserving of rational reflection in order to encourage people to distinguish themselves from molecules, to defy the presuppositions of the natural science model by exercising their capacity for self-reflective judgement.

This is the primary aim of critical social theory. Accordingly, critical social theory does not confine itself to the established empirical reality, seeking merely to determine how closely hypotheses correspond to the facts of that reality. Nor does it present itself as a disinterested, neutral form of inquiry. Rather, critical social theory 'aspires to bring the subjects themselves to full self-consciousness of the contradictions implicit in their material existence, to penetrate the ideological mystifications and forms of false consciousness that distort the meaning of existing social conditions' (Bernstein, 1976, p. 182). In contrast to a scientific social theory which, by equating the conventional with the natural, justifies the established arrangements, critical social theory pursues a theoretical understanding which, when accepted by those oppressed by the existing facts, facilitates their activity to alter the institutions and beliefs which sustain those facts. Critical social theory carries out this pursuit by means of critique.

Critique
As a critical enterprise, critique abandons the orthodox claim that sociology is a science limited to accurate description and explanation, as it incorporates the philosophical, historical, and critical sensibilities of the sociological imagination. With respect to the first point, the rejection of scientific orthodoxy, critique addresses itself not to an indifferent world of inert objects but to human beings who, while they are natural creatures inhabiting the natural world of causality, nevertheless are capable of self-reflection and self-transformation, capable, within certain limits, of making their own history. Critique refuses to take the world as it is given. Accordingly, and with regard to the second point, the incorporation of the sensibilities of the sociological imagination, critique eliminates the artificial boundary between philosophy and sociology by addressing questions of ends, purposes, and values, by asking 'What is a good

society?' and 'How is it best achieved?'. Critique is simultaneously historical, not simply in its appreciation of the past, the changes which have occurred over time, but also in the more profound sense of historicity – a recognition that many of these changes have been made by the human participants in the historical process who, in light of reflection, decided to transform what once seemed to be immutable patterns of social life.

Taking into account the human capacity for reflective self-transformation, critique understands the tenuous status of behavioral laws and empirical generalizations as they pertain to human practices. There is, writes Terence Ball (1983, p. 35), 'a sense in which behavioral "laws" hold true only as long as people *believe* them to be true (or rather, more precisely, *don't question* their truth)'. The aim of critique is to enable people to decide on the feasibility and the desirability of invalidating these 'causal laws' by altering the established patterns, the man-made facts, they express. Toward this end, critique assumes a particular form,

> one that isolates in the life of a group of people those causal conditions that depend for their power on the ignorance of those people as to the nature of their collective existence, and that are frustrating them. The intention here is to enlighten that group of people about these causal conditions and the ways in which they are oppressive, so that, *being enlightened, these people might change these conditions and so transform their lives*. (Fay, 1983, p. 127)

It is in this sense, finally, that critique is critical and negative. In the process of demystifying constraints on human action, critique moves to clarify historically possible emancipatory goals, and it reveals the alternative futures potentially available to us, offering them as the basis for critically reflecting on the existing forms of society (Giddens, 1982, p. 26).

The idea of critique as negative thought, a debunking activity concerned with unveiling false appearances which distort or hide the real, is a legacy of the Enlightenment project of political education whose affirmation of the public sphere incorporated the claim that critique is the essential activity of reason. During the Enlightenment period, Paul Connerton (1976, p. 16) notes, 'in salons, clubs, lodges and coffee-houses a new moral authority, the public, found its earliest institutions. Critique became one of its slogans and an endless stream of books and essays included the words "critique" or "critical" in their title.' Critique had two different meanings in this setting. The first, associated with Kant, regarded critique as reconstruction; the second, found in Hegel's writings, saw critique as criticism. Where the former meaning 'denotes reflection on the *conditions* of possible knowledge: on the potential abilities of human beings possessing the faculties of knowing, speaking, and acting', the latter 'denotes reflection on a system of *constraints* which are humanly produced: distorting pressures to which individuals, or a group of individuals, or the human race as a whole, succumb in their process of self-formation' (ibid., pp. 17–18). Critique as reconstruction identifies the criteria of correct knowledge and aims at extending the range and sophistication of theoretical knowledge. Critique as criticism, by revealing what has been concealed, sets off the process of self-reflection necessary if people are to free themselves from past constraints.

Critical social theory, particularly as it has been influenced by Habermas, joins both forms of critique in an effort to accomplish related methodological and political aims. The methodological objective is to distinguish the various categories of knowledge and to explain the rules and conditions appropriate to their acquisition in order not simply to separate the social world from the natural world as objects of possible knowledge, but also to have the pursuers of knowledge of the social world reflect on the rules and conditions of that knowledge. Such self-reflection is much more than a methodological requirement of the critical social theorist, for, as discussed earlier, when critique results in successful enlightenment, similar processes of self-reflection are set off among those to whom critique is addressed, serving to demystify prevailing relations of dependence. When this happens, the methodological intention of reconstruction converges with the political aim of criticism.

Habermas understands critique as a distinctive form of knowledge, one guided by an emancipatory interest. Critique is distinguished from the positivist or natural science approach to sociology which, guided by a technical interest, seeks knowledge as information which extends control and facilitates manipulation, and from the interpretative or hermeneutic approach which, guided by a practical interest, seeks knowledge as interpretation which enhances mutual understanding (see Chapter 1). In contrast to each, critique exhibits a moral commitment, a willingness to answer the question 'Knowledge for what?'. Yet, the answer to this question requires not the abandonment of the naturalist and interpretative approaches, but their exercise in a way consistent with the aims of critique.

Social life obviously displays empirical regularities and correlations (it does not exist after all outside the realm of cause and effect), and these must be carefully investigated. This investigation, however, should not cease once description and explanation have been made. Beyond this, we must also inquire as to whether these recurring patterns and correlations express invariant regularities of social action or, instead, exhibit ideologically frozen relations of dependence and determination –

particular conventions that falsely appear as nature-like necessities. Similarly, we are obliged to discover what it means to people to act or believe as they do in certain circumstances, to learn how they understand themselves and interpret their experiences. However, it is a mistake merely to interpret a complex of meaning in its own terms, assuming, as is so often the case in interpretative sociology, that there are no standards of evaluation other than those given by the categories internal to a particular meaning system. Along with interpretation we must ask whether people's self-understandings accurately reflect the structure, the patterns and regularities of social life or, instead, are ideologically distorted. Empirical information and symbolic interpretations are indispensable to the movement toward human emancipation, but only when they are placed in the reflective context of critique, where theory has had restored to itself its critical and negative function, do they come to serve the emancipatory interest. In the last analysis, as Bernstein (1976, p. 235) argues, 'we are not confronted with exclusive choices: *either* empirical theory *or* interpretative theory *or* critical theory. Rather, there is an internal dialectic in the restructuring of social and political theory: when we work through any one of these moments, we discover how the others are implicated. An adequate social and political theory must be *empirical, interpretative, and critical.*' All three come together in critique.

We are able to glimpse the potentially practical importance of these three dimensions of critique by drawing out more explicitly the parallels between political competence as defined from the standpoint of citizenship and the public sphere and theoretical competence as defined in terms of the aims of critique. A. P. Simonds discusses the first, Wolf-Dieter Narr the second.

'Political competence', writes Simonds (1982, p. 597), 'entails three different sorts of judgment ... : judgments about what *is*, judgments about what is *good or desirable*, and judgments about what is *possible*'. The first sort of judgement rests on an empirical competence, a familiarity with established facts, institutions and practices. The second requires a moral (or interpretative) competence, a capacity to evaluate autonomously what exists in terms of normative standards acquired in interaction with others. The last of these is grounded in historical-practical competence, an historical awareness that avoids both an underestimation of limits (anything is possible), and their overestimation (nothing is possible), by permitting judicious assessment of potential and opportunity. These dimensions of political competence are related sequentially. Empirical competence informs the development of moral autonomy and the capacity for independent, self-reflective judgement which both fosters a historical sensibility and sparks an optimism of the public will. Similarly, constraints on the acquisition of political competence are sequential in effect: 'a person kept in ignorance and isolation from the rest of the world is unable to participate in the discourse that establishes standards; a person whose norms are undeveloped, unreflectively affirmed, or entirely dependent on the directives of some external authority suffers on that account a diminished measure of historical freedom' (ibid., p. 598). Under the pressure of these constraints political competence is lost to ignorance, moral subordination, cynicism, withdrawal, and the erosion of civic virtue. This makes for a highly rationalized social and political life, one which generates a whole host of stable empirical generalizations, the very stuff of a positivistically rendered scientific sociology which critique seeks to defeat.

The concept of theoretical competence embodied in critique, according to Narr, obliges critical sociology to serve at least three related functions, information, orientation, and imagination. The function of information can be implemented only if sociology is 'theoretically and empirically able to isolate gaps in given information and correctly reinterpret that information. In a way, [sociology] has to institutionalize counterinformation to counter the conventional and dominant policies of information' (Narr, 1983, p. 285). Orientation involves making people understand what is going on, not merely in the Weberian sense of weighing the probable outcomes and human costs of this or that measure, but also in the more comprehensive sense of evaluating ends along with means. Finally, imagination entails proposing alternative futures as a way of yielding feasible solutions to existing problems. A disciplined, historically sensitive imagination is guided by the question of possibility, 'How can a "good" society be realized with the resources, and the limits on those resources, of today ... taken together and synthesized with the knowledge gained by analysis?' (ibid., p. 287). A proper or competent theoretical understanding satisfies each of these functions, and thus is capable of sustaining or stimulating the acquisition of empirical competence (with its information), moral competence (with its orientation), and historical-practical competence (with its imagination). Suggested here is the relation of theory and practice demanded by critique.

Theory and Practice

Like Marxist sociology, critical social theory, distinguishes itself from empirical and interpretative sociology by admitting to be in possession of guiding values and moral commitments. However, with its insistence that theory is never able to legitimate political practice, critical social theory draws the relation between theory and practice differently than does Marxism. 'Critique', Habermas (1973a, p. 2) writes, 'understands that its claims to validity can be verified only in the successful process of enlightenment, and that means: in the practical discourse of those concerned.' In this view, theoretical inquiry is able to enlighten us about our historical situation and the political state of affairs therein, it is able to instruct us about the requirements of political practice and thus contribute to the formulation of political consensus, but it does not have the capacity to justify what is to be done.

There are three levels to this argument as Habermas develops it: theoretical inquiry, the process of enlightenment and political practice. Theoretical inquiry, whose aim is true statements, involves the formation and elaboration of critical theorems which must pass the requirements of scientific argumentation or discursive examination for their claims to validity to receive tentative confirmation. A theory valid in these terms is realized only in successful processes of enlightenment, the aim of which is authentic insight. These processes are successful to the extent that the critical theorems are accepted freely and are used as the basis of self-understanding and interpretation by those toward whom these processes were directed. Theory, then, justifies and guides the process of enlightenment, but not political practice, whose aim is prudent decisions about the choice of appropriate strategy, the resolution of tactical questions, and the conduct of political struggle. Habermas (ibid., p. 33) distinguishes theory's relation to the process of enlightenment from its relation to political practice in the following way.

> While the theory legitimizes the work of the enlightenment, as well as providing its own refutation when communication fails, and can, in any case be corrected, it can by no means legitimize *a fortiori* the risky decisions of strategic action. Decisions for the political struggle cannot at the outset be justified theoretically and then be carried out organizationally. The sole possible justification at this level is consensus, aimed at in practical discourse, among the participants, who, in the consciousness of their common interests and their knowledge of the circumstances, of the predictable consequences and the secondary consequences, are the only ones who can know what risks they are willing to undergo, and with what expectations. There can be no theory which at the outset can assure a world-historical mission in return for the potential sacrifices.

No theory is capable of providing authoritative procedures for deciding strategic action or answers for what it to be done. The search for such a theory is, in the final analysis, an effort to transform politics and political action into matters of technical control and manipulation. While, as Habermas (ibid., p. 40) notes, 'the vindicating superiority of those who do the enlightening over those who are to be enlightened is theoretically unavoidable, ... at the same time it is fictive and requires self-correction:

in a process of enlightenment there can only be participants'. Critique seeks to combat the reduction of politics to manipulation through a process of enlightenment that fosters a reflective political judgement which is inconsistent with theory-predetermined answers to how the practical conduct of political affairs is to be carried out.

For this argument to have any chance of being successfully defended, Habermas (1984a, p. 19) tells us, 'we shall have to avoid rashly assimilating practical discourse, which is characterized by an internal relation to the interpreted needs and wants of *those affected* in a given instance, to theoretical discourse, with its relation to the interpreted experiences of *observers*'. As suggested above, theoretical discourse intends to confirm claims to theoretical or propositional truth, while practical discourse – individuals engaged in argumentation directed toward the rational formation of will, consciousness and consensus – seeks to redeem claims to the truthfulness of intentional expression and the rightness of norms. As the essential dynamic of critique, theoretical discourse rests on as it anticipates communication free of distortion and domination. It is from this point that theoretical discourse tries to inform and instruct practical discourse, and it does this by opposing 'all those intellectual and material tendencies that undermine or suppress practical discourse, and [by working] toward the achievement of those objective institutions in which such practical discourse can be concretely realized' (Bernstein, 1976, p. 219). Theoretical discourse, then, tries to make possible, without for one moment pretending to be able to legitimate, practical discourse. How does this serve the interest of reflective political judgement?

Were theory capable of authoritatively legitimating practice, political judgement would be displaced and the appreciation for the other and for the common interest embodied therein would be devalued. 'If theory alone could answer the question', Beiner (1983, p. 144) maintains, 'judgment would be rendered superfluous, and political man deprived of that quality of responsibility which we have argued is inalienable.' In the presence of belief in the existence of such theory, political judgement and the responsibility which accompanies it are lost to calculation, technique, expertise, and 'correct' procedure. As this occurs, the ideological vision replaces the tragic vision. The responsibility to deliver judgement carries a tragic burden in the sense that 'the one who judges can never escape the awareness that no judgment upon human affairs can master all possibilities and thus render a definitive resolution. But the burden can be borne as long as one does not relinquish hope, for hope without optimism and lack of optimism without despair are what ultimately sustain human judgment' (ibid., p. 118). As part of the process of critique, theoretical discourse displays an abiding respect for the alertness to limits emphasized by the tragic vision, an alertness diminished by the ideological vision with its claim that practice in conformity with proper and decisive (that is, ideologically correct) knowledge will solve all problems. Embracing this vision, the ideologue comes to have two primary tasks, to spread the word in a way to convince others of its unassailable truthfulness, and to construct a practice appropriate to, and justifiable in terms of, this word. For the ideologue, Gouldner (1976, p. 47) notes, what is needed 'is an effective rhetoric, organization, or practice and also vigilant counter-measures to defend this knowledge from those who mean to discredit it. But what is not needed is more "research" or more "critical thinking".'

In contrast to the ideologue, the critical social theorist recognizes the fallibility of theoretical discourse and understands that no theory possesses unquestionable authority or certainty. But more than this, the critical theorist remains committed to the view that people must freely and reasonably arrive at their own self-understandings, that in the absence of reflective political judgement no substantial human betterment is possible. Here resides the hope harbored by the tragic vision. Theory can inform and instruct, and it should, but it cannot legitimate and justify. Once it tries to do so, theory becomes still another ideology promoting a false and unreflected optimism that smothers not simply the despair but also the hope and the sense of responsibility which come together in reflective political judgement.

Given the way it draws the relation of theory and practice, critical theory has been characterized by many on the left as a political theory bereft of any serious concern with politics, an exercise in self-reflective 'navel-gazing', a sort of merry-go-round of continual enlightenment, which is and only can be politically unproductive. Those who make these charges tend to work with a narrowly conceived, potentially pernicious understanding of what political practice is and might be. Often, their understanding is informed by 'a fading, unreflective Leninism that views politics as a kind of career; as the sublimation and routinization of heroism. For them, politics is "made" by "professional revolutionaries", banded together in a self-transcending vanguard, applying the steel forceps to history to extract the reluctant revolution' (ibid., pp. 151–2). While wholly supportive of critical social theory's refusal to join the heroic vanguard, Gouldner raises a different concern, namely, that in its critique of ideologically anchored morality, authority and limits, it may promote a repudiation of all morality, authority and limits, and in this way lead to 'the development of lawlessness or anomie; or to a naked egoism and a cynically unashamed pursuit of private interest, whatever their consequences for the commonweal' (ibid., p. 284). The danger he sees is that critique may focalize the despair and silence the hope that are bound up with political judgement.

Yet critique is not simply negative – a debunking, unmasking, revealing enterprise – it is also positive in its anticipation of alternative futures which require for their realization a process of enlightenment in which all affected are active participants. In this sense, critical social theory, to return to the first criticism, takes politics very seriously, for its goals are to assist in restoring to people their political competence and to enlarge that public sphere where political competence, in the form of debate, discussion and reflective judgement, can be practiced. To the extent this goal is achieved, people acquire a sharper understanding of themselves, others and society – a prerequisite for successfully engaging in the mobilizations, struggles, and movements that, in opposition to the structures of the technocratic domination and the logic of instrumental rationality, aspire to create the autonomous space of civil society. The practical thrust of critical social theory is expressed in these efforts.

What this means for a concrete research strategy has yet to be carefully worked out. However, the recent work of Alain Touraine suggests a useful beginning. Touraine and his colleagues do research whose purpose is to contribute to the development of social movements committed to freeing 'society's capacity for action on itself from the technocratic domination which seeks to identify itself with that capacity and to reduce it to its own interests' (Touraine *et al.*, 1983b, p. 158). Toward this end, they have formulated a research strategy – sociological intervention – which they bring to such movements as the anti-nuclear protest in France and the Solidarity struggle in Poland. Using the method of sociological intervention, the researcher is neither neutral observer nor movement ideologue.

> On the one hand, if he adopts the attitude of a remote and objective observer, he cannot reach the very thing which he seeks to understand: the coldness of objectivity will hold him back from the heat of the social movement. Conversely, if he identifies with the actors' struggle, he ceases to be an analyst and becomes nothing more than a doctrinaire ideologist; in this case, his role becomes entirely negative. (Touraine *et al.*, 1983a, p. 7).

To avoid this difficulty, the method obliges the researcher to identify not with the struggle itself but with the meaning of that struggle, particularly as that meaning merges with the intention of critique. The researcher, then, is neither external to the group nor identified with it. Rather, the researcher tries to have the group focus on and clarify those meanings of its action which challenge the constraints on practical discourse and the active formation of political will.

The method of sociological intervention consists of four general stages which Touraine and his colleagues summarize as follows:

1. Two *intervention groups*, each composed of a dozen participants in the ... struggle, hold discussions with *interlocutors* chosen by themselves: allies, opponents, experts, politicians, ... and so on.
2. the researchers, called the *agitator* [responsible for provoking movement toward self-analysis by incitement or hypothesis] and the *secretary* [responsible for recording and summarizing the ensuing discussion], encourage the group to analyse the conditions and the meaning of their action.
3. The researchers formulate their hypotheses and tell the groups what seems, in their opinion, to be the *highest possible meaning* of their action and help them to understand that action from such a vantage point. This central phase is called the *conversion*.
4. After drafting initial conclusions, the researchers discuss them with the intervention groups and other interested parties and study the ability of the actors to transform this analysis into a programme of action. This phase is called *permanent sociology*. (Touraine *et al.*, 1983b, pp. 10–11)

The first two stages amount to direct intervention where the researchers enter into a relationship with the social movement, establish the intervention groups, and encourage the kind of discussion and confrontation that may lead to enhanced self-analysis and reflection. While the researchers remain alert to the task of mediating between theoretical discourse and the practical discourse of the participants, they assume at these stages only minimal involvement in the latter. The primary aims of this phase of the research are to constitute the conditions of practical discourse for the intervention groups and to introduce as initial topics of discourse 'hypotheses' or critical theorems which either increase understanding (and are therefore taken as satisfactory) or produce noise, disorder, or inconsistent responses (and are therefore falsified). To the extent they are satisfactory, conversion results.

With conversion, the intervention groups become analyst groups, interpreters of their own movement, examining the movement's struggle and the previous discussions and confrontations from the vantage point established in the earlier stages of the research. As self-analysts, the groups gain a certain distance from the concrete level of action and the previous debates. At this point, the researchers become responsible for helping to assure that this distance, indispensable to analysis, is maintained. Part of what is involved here is suggested by the conversion process undertaken by the Solidarity groups with which the Touraine team worked.

This 'conversion' was all the easier to attain in that it corresponded to the expectations of the militants: just as Solidarity expected its intellectuals to operate as advisers and not as ideologists or a kind of political avant-garde, so our groups wanted the sociologists to place them in a situation of analysis, rather than behaving like group leaders, distributing the Word, and collecting opinions and reactions in return. The researchers put forth and defended their analyses with the help of diagrams and tables; the militants reacted, drew other diagrams, added to or modified the tables. The groups were thus engaged in a joint enterprise in which the actual and potential meanings of the movement were gradually brought to the surface. (Touraine *et al.*, 1983a, pp. 103–4)

Analyst groups do not remain centered on themselves. At some point they are expected to return to the action, bringing with them of course the understandings acquired through sociological intervention, understandings which clarify the movement's goal and orient its practices. If these understandings are not to be smothered by the immediate pressures of political practice, that is, for the exchange between analysis and action to endure, a permanent sociology must be established. Permanent sociology prolongs the relation between the actors' self-understanding and the sociologists' intervention so that as the analysis is brought into the field of political action, the researcher participates more directly in the group's analytical work, deepening his sociological interpretation of the movement while at the same time contributing to the continued viability of the group's recently obtained self-analysis. This analytical work must never be confused with the work of sociological interpretation, Touraine (1981, pp. 143–4) insists,

and the sociologist cannot become a member of the group on the same footing as the other members, because the group does not cease to be militant: the group's categories of analysis remain linked to those of action, while the sociologist transcribes his observations into the categories of this theory of social action. The fact, however, that the researcher is an 'outsider' does not preclude his [permanent] involvement in the movement: he is not a militant, but his independence is itself of service

in maintaining the distance indispensable to the group's self-reflective analysis.

With this last point, Touraine comes very close to endorsing a partisanship which violates the limits of the theory–practice relationship described earlier. These limits suggest that theorists as theorists commit themselves to the intellectual discovery and the practical creation of the conditions requisite for rational discourse and human liberation. In the name of this commitment, Gouldner (1973, p. 121) writes, theorists 'should positively seek out involvements with and on behalf of specific social strata and contribute to them and to social movements representing them in practical political ways ... [But, their relations with movements or parties] should be governed by the principle that each is *autonomous* of the other organizationally, but collaborate on the basis of their common commitment to human emancipation.' For Gouldner, Touraine's permanent sociology carries the danger of subordinating theory to the pressing requirements of movement activism, reducing it to merely another means to improved practice. Lose the distance between theorists and movement or party activists, and you lose the distinction between theory and ideology.

For the most part, however, Touraine's sociological intervention appears well suited to the emancipatory aims of critical social theory. In the first place, it is a method which incorporates reflection as its central principle. Its strong opposition to indifferent quietude, technocratic certitude, and mindless activism is matched by its equally powerful commitment to practical discourse. In the second place, its focus on 'new' social movements – the anti-nuclear movement, the ecology movement, the women's movement, Solidarity, and the like – which are defined both by their opposition to the 'programmed' society and by their support for an enlarged public sphere, links it directly with the concerns of critique.

Primarily social and only indirectly political in character, the new social movements seek not the seizure of power but the mobilization of civil society in the name of reactivating the public sphere (Feher and Heller, 1984, p. 37). Indeed, they might be labelled citizenship movements since they pursue 'the revival of public discussion on the meaning of democracy, ... the contesting of quasi-official definitions, ... [and] public debate of issues that were formerly the province of technocrats' (Cohen and Arato, 1984, p. 330). Yet there is an anti-modernist, even regressive, strain within these social movements, one often in conflict with the outwardly democratic thrust they display. Cohen and Arato (ibid., pp. 328–9) describe this conflict as it exists in the West German 'Green' or ecology movement: The anti-modernists are 'hostile to complexity, economic growth, industrialism, and the state, defining "life" as the highest value ... [Their] ideal community is small-scale, autonomous, and technologically primitive.' In contrast are those who

> believe that a sane approach to the ecological problem entails not a rejection of modernity but a realization of its potential – that is, control by society as a whole over its own development ... Scientific

assessments of interventions in the environment would inform public discussion of alternatives. The use of counterexpertise ... implies a shift of emphasis from exclusive concern with 'life' itself to considerations of the 'good life' – the kind of society we need and want.

The modernists combine freedom and life as the ultimate values, regarding the sense of life as just as important as its mere living. In their commitment to freedom and life resides the source of what is progressive about the new social movements (Feher and Heller, 1984, p. 44). Critical social theory could assume no more important task for itself than to advance the progressive tendencies of these movements by clarifying their meaning with regard to

the historical project of a post-capitalist institutionalization of freedom ... above all the institutionalization of public spaces for political participation and communal action, which would not only provide a basis for a democratic control of economic and administrative processes, but which also would provide the social basis for a viable identity of individuals who are increasingly threatened by anomie and alienation. (Wellmer, 1983, p. 107)

Were it to do this, critical social theory would reaffirm its commitment to the completion of the project of modernity.

Critical social theory, Habermas argues, must remain aware of the dark side of the project of modernity as it searches for ways to indicate the emancipatory aspirations it has embodied since the Enlightenment. Modernity as the spread of instrumental rationality leads to 'the impoverishment of expressive and communicative possibilities ... that enable individuals to find themselves, to deal with their personal conflicts, and to solve their common problems communally by means of collective will-formation'. (Habermas, 1984b, p. 20). Rather than respond to this development with vapid traditionalism or a narcissistic celebration of intimacy, 'we must again bring to consciousness the dignity of modernity, the dimension of a nontruncated rationality' (ibid., p. 15). The autonomy of this non-truncated practical rationality, Habermas claims, is established sociologically in Durkheim's 'moral individualism', in Weber's 'inner logic of differentiated value spheres', and in Marx's acceptance of the Enlightenment's call for a freedom that extends to all humanity. More significantly, elements of practical rationality have been established and continue to be preserved 'in the universalist principles of modern constitutions, in democratic forms of political organization, in forms of scientific, political, or aesthetic discourse, or in the self-interpretations and goals of social movements which fight for the rights of the individual, the integrity of the life world, or the democratic organization of collective will formation' (Wellmer, 1983, p. 100).

These emancipatory strains are present today, a legacy of the project of modernity. But this project has a second legacy as well – a technical rationality that constantly threatens the fragile autonomy of practical rationality. This very tension suggests the value of retaining together Durkheim's defense of civil society as the institutionalization of democratic forms of discourse, Weber's understanding of the instrumentally rationalizing tendencies of modern society, and Marx's vision of an emancipated society. This tension further suggests the difficulties facing any effort to complete the project of modernity. In pursuit of reason and freedom, despair mingles with hope, and, in this regard, critical social theory has much in common with political judgement.

Conclusion

The classical tradition of sociology is losing its hold on the discipline. The obligatory course in social theory remains in place at most institutions but it does little to deter either the retreat to the alleged neutrality of sheer fact or the ever-increasing tendency to subordinate liberal education to strictly vocational pursuits. This tradition, as Mills (1960, p. 9) notes, is in some cases 'suppressed by political authority'; in others, it is 'diverted by those institutions and academic trends that form the climate of cultural work'; in still others, and more commonly, it is 'suppressed by the default of those who ought to be practicing it'.

Critical social theory challenges these sources of suppression and diversion, and seeks to rejuvenate those aspects of the classical tradition which have theory confront urgent public issues and which assign to theory the task of enlightenment in the form of advancing the self-understanding of society. Yet critical social theory distinguishes itself from, as it shows its appreciation for, the classical tradition. Unlike Durkheim and Weber, critical social theory explicitly holds the emancipatory values of reason and freedom. Unlike them and Marx, it is explicitly reflexive in the relation it has toward these value commitments. This reflection is important, for at times, particularly in the midst of despair, it is easy for critical social theory to assume a defensive arrogance, regarding itself as the locus of the conscience of humanity. However, when it is at its best, as Gouldner (1976, pp. 293-4) writes, critical social theory

eschews all temptations to claims of moral elitism and superiority, as well as all posturings of innocence. It never imagines – when it is at its best – that its own self-understanding can be taken at face value, or that its commitments are lacking in ambiguities or even contradictions ... Affirming human emancipation as a goal, it never allows itself to intimate – when it is at its best – that it itself has already achieved that emancipation and never allows itself to forget that it, too, possesses a repressive potential ... Knowing it will win no easy victories, relying upon its continual work and struggle, ... critical theory seeks to understand itself as well as the world, and it suspects – as self-serving and sycophantic – all offered conceptions of itself that bring it no painful surprises. When it is at its best.

A critical social theory which is at its best most of the time is capable of reversing the growth of rationality without reason within sociology, and, further, of contributing to a revitalized and broadened public sphere that is effectively able to combat the rationalization of social life itself. Critical social theory, then, proposes a new project of enlightenment, this one directed not against aristocracy, nobility, traditional authority, and simple-minded superstitions, but against the contemporary enemy of freedom, rationality without reason. Mills and, more recently, Habermas and Gouldner ask for our participation in this project. This book is a modest effort to extend their invitation to a wider audience.

Bibliography

Anderson, P. (1984), 'Modernity and revolution', New Left Review, no. 144, 96–113.

Antonio, R. (1979), 'The contradiction of domination and production in bureaucracy', American Sociological Review, vol. 44, no. 6, pp. 895–912.

Arato, A. (1981), 'Civil society against the state: Poland, 1980–1981', Telos, no. 47, pp. 23–47.

Ashton, T. S. (1955), An Economic History of England (London: Methuen).

Ball, T. (1983), 'The ontological presuppositions and political consequences of a social science', in D. Sabia and J. Wallulis (eds), Changing Social Science (Albany, NY: SUNY Press), pp. 31–51.

Barrett, W. (1962), Irrational Man (New York: Doubleday).

Bauman, Z. (1981), 'On the maturation of socialism', Telos, no. 47, pp. 48–54.

Beiner, R. (1983), Political Judgment (Chicago: University of Chicago Press).

Bell, D. (1980), The Winding Passage (Cambridge, Mass.: Abt Books).

Bell, D. (1976), The Cultural Contradictions of Capitalism (New York: Basic Books).

Bellah, R. (1983), 'The ethical aims of social inquiry', in R. Bellah, N. Haan, P. Rabinow, and W. Sullivan (eds), Social Science as Moral Inquiry (Berkeley, Calif.: University of California Press), pp. 360–81.

Bendix, R. (1956), Work and Authority in Industry (New York: Harper & Row).

Berelson, B., Lazarsfeld, P., and McPhee, W. (1954), Voting (Chicago: University of Chicago Press).

Berger, P. (1969), The Sacred Canopy (New York: Doubleday).

Berman, M. (1982), All That is Solid Melts Into Air (New York: Simon & Schuster).

Bernstein, R. (1976), The Restructuring of Social and Political Theory (New York: Harcourt, Brace, Jovanovich).

Birnbaum, N. (1969), The Crisis of Industrial Society (New York: Oxford University Press).

Block, F. and Hirschhorn, L. (1979), 'New productive forces and the contradictions of contemporary capitalism', Theory and Society, vol. 7, no. 3, pp. 363–95.

Bradbury, M. and McFarlane, J. (1976), 'The name and nature of modernism', in M. Bradbury and J. McFarlane (eds), Modernism (New York: Penguin), pp. 19–56.

Braverman, H. (1974), Labor and Monopoly Capital (New York: Monthly Review Press).

Brecher, J. (1978), 'Uncovering the hidden history of the American workplace', Review of Radical Political Economics, vol. 10, no. 4, pp. 1–22.

Brittan, S. (1975), 'The economic contradictions of democracy', British Journal of Political Science, vol. 5, no. 2, pp. 129–59.

Brown, N. (1959), Life Against Death (New York: Vintage Books).

Bullock, A. (1976), 'The double image', in M. Bradbury and J. McFarlane (eds), Modernism (New York: Penguin), pp. 58–70.

Clawson, D. (1980), *Bureaucracy and the Labor Process* (New York: Monthly Review Press).

Cohen, G. A. (1979), 'Capitalism, freedom, and the proletariat', in A. Ryan (ed.), *The Idea of Freedom* (New York: Oxford University Press), pp. 9–25.

Cohen, J. (1979), 'Why more political theory?', *Telos*, no. 40, pp. 70–94.

Cohen, J. and Arato, A. (1984), 'The German green party', *Dissent*, vol. 31, no. 3, pp. 327–32.

Coles, R. (1980), 'Civility and psychology', *Daedalus*, vol. 109, no. 4, pp. 133–41.

Collins, R. (1980), 'Weber's last theory of capitalism: a systematization', *American Sociological Review*, vol. 45, no. 6, pp. 925–42.

Collins, R. (1975), *Conflict Sociology* (New York: Academic Press).

Comte, A. 'Dependence of science upon society', in G. Simpson (ed.), *Auguste Comte: Sire of Sociology* (New York: Crowell), pp. 126–31.

Connerton, p. (1976), 'Introduction', in P. Connerton (ed.), *Critical Sociology* (New York: Penguin), pp. 11–39.

Connolly, W. (1982), 'Civic disaffection and the democratic party', *Democracy*, vol. 2, no. 3, pp. 18–27.

Dahl, R. (1956), 'Hierarchy, democracy, and bargaining in politics and economics', in H. Eulau (ed.), *Political Behavior* (Glencoe, Ill.: Free Press), pp. 82–92.

Dahrendorf, R. (1968), *Essays in the Theory of Society* (Stanford, Calif.: Stanford University Press).

Deleuze, G. and Guattari, F. (1977), *Anti-Oedipus*, trans. M. Seem, H. Lane, R. Hurley (New York: Viking).

Dewey, J. (1939), 'The modes of societal life', in J. Ratner (ed.), *Intelligence in the Modern World* (New York: Random House), pp. 365–404.

Dewey, J. (1916), *Democracy and Education* (New York: Macmillan).

Dickson, D., and Noble, D. (1981), 'By force of reason: the politics of science and technology policy', in T. Ferguson and J. Rogers (eds), *The Hidden Election* (New York: Pantheon), pp. 260–312.

Disco, C. (1979), 'Critical theory as ideology of the new class', *Theory and Society*, vol. 8, no. 2, pp. 159–214.

Donzelot, J. (1979), *The Policing of Families* (New York: Pantheon).

Draenos, S. (1982a), *Freud's Odyssey* (New Haven: Yale University Press).

Draenos, S. (1982b), 'The totalitarian theme in Horkheimer and Arendt', *Salmaqundi*, no. 56, pp. 155–69.

Dubet, F., Touraine, A., and Wieviovka, M. (1982), 'A social movement: Solidarity', *Telos*, no. 53, pp. 128–36.

Durkheim, E. (1974), *Sociology and Philosophy*, trans. D. F. Pocock (New York: Free Press).

Durkheim, E. (1972), *Selected Writings*, ed. and trans. A. Giddens (Cambridge: Cambridge University Press).

Durkheim, E. (1965), *The Elementary Forms of the Religious Life*, trans. J. W. Swain (New York: Free Press).

Durkheim, E. (1962), *Socialism*, trans. C. Sattler (New York: Collier Books).

Durkheim, E. (1958), *Professional Ethics and Civic Morals*, trans. C. Brookfield (New York: Free Press).

Durkheim, E. (1938), *The Rules of Sociological Method*, trans. S. Solovay and J. Mueller (New York: Free Press).

Durkheim, E. (1933), *The Division of Labor in Society*, trans, G. Simpson (New York: Macmillan).

Edwards, R. (1979), *Contested Terrain* (New York: Basic Books).

Elshtain, J. B. (1980), 'The self: reborn, undone, transformed', *Telos*, no. 44, pp. 101–11.

Engels, F. (1981), 'Communism as abundance', in J. Elliott (ed.), *Marx and Engels on Economics, Politics, and Society* (Santa Monica, Calif.: Goodyear, pp. 456–60.

Ewen, S. (1976), *Captains of Consciousness* (New York: McGraw-Hill).

Fay, B. (1983), 'General laws and explaining human behavior', in D. Sabia and J. Wallulis (eds.), *Changing Social Science* (Albany, NY: SUNY Press), pp. 103–28.

Fay, B. (1977), 'How people change themselves: the relationship between critical theory and its audience', in T. Ball (ed.), *Political Theory and Praxis* (Minneapolis, Minn.: University of Minnesota Press), pp. 200–69.

Fay, B. (1975), *Social Theory and Political Practice* (London: Allen & Unwin).

Feher, F. (1978), 'The dictatorship over needs', *Telos*, no. 35, pp. 31–42.

Feher, F. and Heller, A. (1984), 'From red to green', *Telos*, no. 59, pp. 35–44.

Fleron, F. and Fleron, L. J. (1972), 'Administrative theory as repressive political theory: the communist experience', *Telos*, no. 12, pp. 63–92.

Freud, S. (1971), 'Dostoevsky and parricide', in R. Smith (ed.), *Guilt* (New York: Doubleday), pp. 63–84.

Freud, S. (1965), *New Introductory Lectures on Psychoanalysis*, trans. J. Strachey (New York: Norton).

Freud, S. (1964), *The Future of an Illusion*, trans. W. D. Robson-Scott (New York: Doubleday).

Freud, S. (1962), *Totem and Taboo*, trans. J. Strachey (New York: Norton).

Freud, S. (1961), *Civilization and Its Discontents*, trans. J. Strachey (New York: Norton).

Freud, S. (1960), *The Ego and the Id*, trans. J. Strachey (New York: Norton).

Freud, S. (1948), 'Formulations on the two principles of mental functioning' in J. Strachey (ed.), *The Standard Edition of the Complete Psychological Works of Sigmund Freud* (London: Hogarth Press).

Friedland, W. (1969), 'For a sociological concept of charisma', in B. McLaughlin (ed.), *Studies in Social Movements* (New York: Free Press, pp. 243–57.

Fromm, E. (1941), *Escape From Freedom* (New York: Avon).

Gadamer, H.-G. (1981), *Reason in the Age of Science* (Cambridge, Mass.: MIT Press).

Gay, P. (1979), 'Freud and freedom', in A. Ryan (ed.), *The Idea of Freedom* (New York: Oxford University Press), pp. 41–60.

Giddens, A. (1982), *Sociology* (New York: Harcourt, Brace, Jovanovich).

Giddens, A. (1978), *Emile Durkheim* (New York: Penguin).

Giddens, A. (1973), *The Class Structure of the Advanced Societies* (New York: Harper & Row).

Giddens, A. (1972), 'Durkheim's writings in sociology and social philosophy', in A. Giddens (ed.), *Emile Durkheim: Selected Writings* (Cambridge: Cambridge University Press), pp. 1–50.

Giddens, A. (1971a), *Capitalism and Modern Social Theory* (Cambridge: Cambridge University Press).

Giddens, A. (1971b), 'Durkheim's political sociology', *Sociological Review*, vol. 19, no. 4, pp. 477–519.

Goldfarb, J. (1982), *On Cultural Freedom* (Chicago: University of Chicago Press).

Goldman, R. and Wilson, J. (1977), 'The rationalization of leisure', *Politics and Society*, vol. 7, no. 2, pp. 152–70.

Goldthorpe, J. (1978), 'The current inflation: towards a sociological account', in F. Hirsch and J. Goldthorpe (eds), *The Political Economy of Inflation* (Cambridge, Mass.: Harvard University Press), pp. 186–215.

Gouldner, A. (1980), *The Two Marxisms* (New York: Seabury).

Gouldner, A. (1976), *The Dialectic of Ideology and Technology* (New York: Seabury).

Gouldner, A. (1973), *For Sociology* (New York: Basic Books).

Gouldner, A. (1970), *The Coming Crisis of Western Sociology* (New York: Basic Books).

Gouldner, A. (1965), *Enter Plato* (New York: Harper & Row).

Greisman, H. C. (1976), 'Disenchantment of the world', *British Journal of Sociology*, vol. 27, no. 4, pp. 495–507.

Habermas, J. (1984a), *The Theory of Communicative Action*, Vol. 1, trans. T. McCarthy (Boston, Mass.: Beacon Press).

Habermas, J. (1984b), 'Introduction', in J. Habermas (ed.), *Observations on 'The Spiritual Situation of the Age'*, trans. A. Buchwalter (Cambridge, Mass.: MIT Press), pp. 1–28.

Habermas, J. (1981), 'Modernity versus postmodernity', *New German Critique*, no. 22, pp. 3–14.

Habermas, J. (1975), *Legitimation Crisis*, trans. T. McCarthy (Boston, Mass.: Beacon Press).

Habermas, J. (1974), 'The public sphere', trans. S. Lennox and F. Lennox, *New German Critique*, no. 3, pp. 49–55.

Habermas, J. (1973a), *Theory and Practice*, trans. J. Viertel (Boston, Mass.: Beacon Press).

Habermas, J. (1973b), 'What does a crisis mean today?', *Social Research*, vol. 40, no. 4, pp. 643–67.

Habermas, J. (1971), *Knowledge and Human Interests*, trans. J. Shapiro (Boston, Mass.: Beacon Press).

Habermas, J. (1970), *Toward a Rational Society*, trans. J. Shapiro (Boston, Mass.: Beacon Press).

Hammond, J. L. and Hammond, B. (1936), *The Skilled Labourer* (London: Longmans).

Hawthorn, G. (1976), *Enlightenment and Despair* (Cambridge: Cambridge University Press).

Hearn, F. (1978), *Domination, Legitimation, and Resistance* (Westport, Conn.: Greenwood Press).

Heisler, M. and Kvavik, R. (1974), 'Patterns of European politics', in M. Heisler (ed.), *Political Europe* (New York: McKay), pp. 27–89.

Held, D. (1980), *Introduction to Critical Theory* (Cambridge, Mass.: MIT Press).

Hendin, H. (1975), *The Age of Sensation* (New York: McGraw-Hill).

Herf, J. (1981), 'Reactionary modernism', *Theory and Society*, vol. 10, no. 6, pp. 805–32.

Hirsch, F. (1976), *Social Limits to Growth* (Cambridge, Mass.: Harvard University Press).

Hobsbawm, E. J. (1962), *The Age of Revolution* (London: Weidenfeld & Nicolson).

Hohendahl, P. U. (1979), 'Critical theory, public sphere, and culture', *New German Critique*, no. 16, pp. 89–118.

Horkheimer, M. (1974), *Eclipse of Reason* (New York: Seabury Press).

Horkheimer, M. and Adorno, T. (1977), *Dialectic of Enlightenment*, trans. J. Cumming (New York: Herder and Herder).

Horowitz, G. (1977), *Repression* (Toronto: University of Toronto Press).

Hughes, H. S. (1958), *Consciousness and Society* (New York: Vintage Books).

Huntington, S. (1975), 'The United States', in M. Crozier, S. Huntington, and J. Watanuki (eds), *The Crisis of Democracy* (New York: New York University Press), pp. 59–118.

Israel, J. (1971), *Alienation* (Boston, Mass.: Allyn & Bacon).

Jacoby, R. (1975), *Social Amnesia* (Boston, Mass.: Beacon Press).

Jessop, B. (1978), 'Capitalism and democracy: the best possible shell?', in G. Littlejohn (ed.), *Power and the State* (New York: St Martin's Press), pp. 10–51.

Johansen, L. and Kristensen, O. (1982), 'Corporatist traits in Denmark, 1946–1976', in G. Lembruch and P. Schmitter (eds), *Trends in Corporatist Policy-Making* (Beverly Hills, Calif.: Sage), pp. 189–218.

Kant, I. (1959), *What is Englightenment?*, trans. L. Smith (Indianapolis, Ind.: Bobbs-Merrill).

Kaplan, A. (1968), *The Conduct of Inquiry* (San Francisco: Chandler).

Kassof, A. (1964), 'The administered society: totalitarianism without terror', *World Politics*, vol. 16, no. 4, pp. 558–75.

Keane, J. (1982), 'Elements of a radical theory of public life: from Toinnes to Habermas and beyond', *Canadian Journal of Political and Social Theory*, vol. 5, no. 3, pp. 11–49.

Kolakowski, L. (1968), *The Alienation of Reason*, trans. N. Buterman (New York: Doubleday).

Kumar, K. (1978), *Prophecy and Progress* (New York: Penguin).

Kvavik, R. (1974), 'Interest groups in a cooptive political system: the case of Norway', in M. Heisler (ed.), *Political Europe* (New York: McKay), pp. 93–116.

LaCapra, D. (1972), *Emile Durkheim* (Ithaca, NY: Cornell University Press).

Lane, D. (1981), *Leninism: A Sociological Interpretation* (Cambridge: Cambridge University Press).

Lasch, C. (1979a), 'Politics and social theory: a reply to the critics', *Salmagundi*, vol. 46, pp. 192–8.

Lasch, C. (1979b) 'The siege of the family', in *Sociology 79/80* (Guilford, Conn.: Dushkin), pp. 154–7.

Lasch, C. (1978), *The Culture of Narcissism* (New York: Norton).

Lasch, C. (1977), *Haven in a Heartless World* (New York: Basic Books).

Lemert, C. (1974), 'Sociological theory and the relativistic paradigm', *Sociological Inquiry*, vol. 44, no. 2, pp. 93–104.

Lenin, V. L. (1969), *Selected Works* (London: Lawrence and Wishart).

Lenin, V. L. (1949), *The State and Revolution* (Moscow: Progress Publishers).

Lenzer, G. (1979), 'Mind-forged manacles: Auguste Comte and the future', *Marxist Perspectives*, vol. 2, no. 3, pp. 62–88.

Levine, D. (1981), 'Rationality and freedom: Weber and beyond', *Sociological Inquiry*, vol. 51, no. 1, pp. 5–25.

Lindblom, C. (1977), *Politics and Markets* (New York: Basic Books).

Lipset, S. M. (1960), *Political Man* (New York: Doubleday).

Lukes, S. (1977), *Essays in Social Theory* (New York: Columbia University Press).

McCarthy, T. (1984), 'Introduction', in J. Habermas, *The Theory of Communicative Action*, Vol. 1 (Boston, Mass.: Beacon Press), pp. v–xxxvii.

McFarlane, J. (1976), 'The mind of modernism', in M. Bradbury and J. McFarlane (eds), *Modernism* (New York: Penguin), pp. 71–94.

Macpherson, C. B. (1977), *The Life and Times of Liberal Democracy* (New York: Oxford University Press).

Macpherson, C. B. (1972), *The Real World of Democracy* (New York: Oxford University Press).

Macpherson, C. B. (1967), 'Democratic theory: ontology and technology', in D. Spitz (ed.), *Political Theory and Social Change* (New York: Atherton Press), 203–20.

Manicus, P. (1974), *The Death of the State* (New York: Putnam).

Mann, M. (1970), 'The social cohesion of liberal democracy', *American Sociological Review*, vol. 35, no. 3, pp. 423–39.

Manuel, F. (1956), *The New World of Henri Saint-Simon* (Cambridge: Harvard University Press).

Marcuse, H. (1970), *Five Lectures* (Boston, Mass.: Beacon Press).

Marcuse, H. (1968), *Negations* (Boston, Mass.: Beacon Press).

Marcuse, H. (1965), 'Remarks on a redefinition of culture', *Daedalus*, vol. 94, no. 1, pp. 190–207.

Marcuse, H. (1964), *One-Dimensional Man* (Boston, Mass.: Beacon Press).

Marcuse, H. (1958), *Soviet Marxism* (New York: Penguin).

Marcuse, H. (1955), *Eros and Civilization* (New York: Random House).

Marcuse, H. (1941), *Reason and Revolution* (Boston, Mass.: Beacon Press).

Marks, S. (1974), 'Durkheim's theory of anomie', *American Journal of Sociology*, vol. 80, no. 2, pp. 329–63.

Marshall, G. (1982), *In Search of the Spirit of Capitalism* (New York: Columbia University Press).

Marx, K. (1981a), 'Communism as the suppression of alienation', in J. Elliott (ed.), *Marx and Engels on Economics, Politics, and Society* (Santa Monica, Calif.: Goodyear), pp. 433–40.

Marx, K. (1981b), 'Realm of necessity and realm of freedom', in J. Elliott (ed.), *Marx and Engels on Economics, Politics, and Society* (Santa Monica, Calif.: Goodyear), pp. 463–5.

Marx, K. (1970), *A Contribution to the Critique of Political Economy*, trans. S. W. Ryazankaya (New York: International Publishers).

Marx, K. (1966a), *The Civil War in France* (Peking: Foreign Languages Press).

Marx, K. (1966b), *Critique of the Gotha Programme* (New York: International Publishers).

Marx, K. (1964), *The Economic and Philosophic Manuscripts of 1844*, trans. M. Milligan (New York: International Publishers).

Marx, K. (1963), *The 18th Brumaire of Louis Bonaparte* (New York: International Publishers).

Marx, K. and Engels, F. (1970a), *The German Ideology* (New York: International Publishers).

Marx, K. and Engels, F. (1970b), *Manifesto of the Communist Party* (Peking: Foreign Languages Press).

Meszaros, I. (1970), *Marx's Theory of Alienation* (New York: Harper & Row).

Mill, J. S. (1966), *Principles of Political Economy in Collected Works*, J. M. Robson (ed.) (Toronto: University of Toronto Press).

Mill, J. S. (1910), *Representative Government* (London: J. M. Dent).

Mill, J. S. (1895), *Principles of Political Economy* (New York: Appleton).

Mills, C. W. (1963a), 'Mass media and public opinion', in I. L. Horowitz (ed.), *Power, Politics, and People* (New York: Oxford University Press), pp. 577–98.

Mills, C. W. (1963b), 'Mass society and liberal education', in I. L. Horowitz (ed.), *Power, Politics and People* (New York: Oxford University Press), pp. 353–73.

Mills, C. W. (1960), *Images of Man* (New York: George Braziller).

Mills, C. W. (1959), *The Sociological Imagination* (New York: Oxford University Press).

Mills, C. W. (1956), *The Power Elite* (New York: Oxford University Press).

Mitzman, A. (1973), *Sociology and Estrangement* (New York: Knopf).

Mitzman, A. (1970), *The Iron Cage* (New York: Knopf).

Morgenthau, H. and Person, E. (1978), 'The roots of narcissism', *Partisan Review*, no. 45, pp. 337–47.

Nachman, L. (1981), 'Psychoanalysis and social theory: the origin of society and guilt', *Salmagundi*, nos. 52–3, pp. 65–106.

Narr, W. D. (1983), 'Reflections on the form and content of social science: toward a consciously political and moral social science', in R. Bellah, N. Haan, P. Rabinow, and W. Sullivan (eds), *Social Science as Moral Inquiry* (Berkeley, Calif.: University of California Press), pp. 273–96.

Nietzsche, F. (1971), 'The origin of guilt', in R. Smith (ed.), *Guilt* (New York: Doubleday), pp. 27–62.

Nietzsche, F. (1966), *Beyond Good and Evil*, trans. W. Kaufman (New York: Random House).

Nisbet, R. (1978), 'Conservatism', in T. Bottomore and R. Nisbet (eds), *A History of Sociological Analysis* (New York: Basic Books), pp. 80–117.

Nisbet, R. (1969), *Social Change and History* (New York: Oxford University Press).

Nisbet, R. (1968), *Tradition and Revolt* (New York: Random House).

Nisbet, R. (1966), *The Sociological Tradition* (New York: Basic Books).

Nordlinger, E. (1981), *On the Autonomy of the Democratic State* (Cambridge, Mass.: Harvard University Press).

Nove, A. (1983), *The Economics of Feasible Socialism* (London: Allen & Unwin).

Oestereicher, E. (1982), 'The depoliticization of the liberal arts', *Social Research*, vol. 49, no. 4, pp. 1004–12.

Offe, C. (1981), 'The attribution of public status to interest groups', in S. Berger (ed.), *Organizing Interests in Western Europe* (Cambridge: Cambridge University Press), pp. 123–58.

Ollman, B. (1977), 'Marx's vision of communism: A reconstruction', in S. Bialer and S. Sluzar (eds), *Radicalism in the Contemporary Age*, vol. II (Boulder, Colo.: Westview Press), pp. 35–84.

Ollman, B. (1971), *Alienation: Marx's Concept of Man in Capitalist Society* (Cambridge: Cambridge University Press).

Palmer, R. R. (1959), *The Age of the Democratic Revolution* (Princeton, NJ: Princeton University Press).

Peckham, M. (1962), *Beyond the Tragic Vision* (New York: George Braziller).

Poggi, G. (1978), *The Development of the Modern State* (Stanford, Calif.: Stanford University Press).

Pollard, S. (1965), *The Genesis of Modern Management* (Baltimore, Md: Penguin).
Pollock, F. (1976), 'Empirical research into public opinion', in P. Connerton (ed.), *Critical Sociology* (New York: Penguin), pp. 225–36.
Prager, J. (1981), 'Moral integration and political inclusion: a comparison of Durkheim's and Weber's theories of democracy', *Social Forces*, vol. 59, no. 4, pp. 935–46.
Rieff, P. (1959), *Freud: The Mind of a Moralist* (New York: Doubleday).
Ricci, D. (1971), *Community Power and Democratic Theory* (New York: Random House).
Rohatyn, F. (1982), 'New York and the nation', *New York Review of Books*, 21 January, pp. 26–9.
Rossides, D. (1978), *The History and Nature of Sociological Theory* (Boston, Mass.: Houghton Mifflin).
Rousseas, S. and Farganis, J. (1968), 'American politics, the end of ideology', in C. Waxman (ed.), *The End of Ideology Debate* (New York: Simon & Schuster), pp. 206–28.
Rousseau, J.-J. (1959), 'A dissertation of the origin and foundation of the inequality of mankind', trans. G. D. H. Cole, in R. Hutchins (ed.), *Great Books of the Western World*, Vol. 38 (Chicago: Encyclopedia Britannica), pp. 323–66.
Saint-Simon, H. (1964), *Social Organization, The Science of Man, and Other Writings* (New York: Harper & Row).
Schaar, J. (1974), 'Legitimacy in the modern state', in R. Quinney (ed.), *Criminal Justice in America* (Boston, Mass.: Little, Brown).
Schlucter, W. (1981), *The Rise of Western Rationalism* (Berkeley, Calif.: University of California Press).
Schmitter, P. (1979), 'Still the century of corporatism?', in P. Schmitter and G. Lembruch (eds), *Trends Toward Corporatist Intermediation* (Beverly Hills, Calif.: Sage), pp. 7–52.
Schroyer, T. (1972), 'The dialectical foundations of critical theory', *Telos*, no. 12, pp. 73–114.
Schumpeter, J. (1942), *Capitalism, Socialism, and Democracy* (New York: Harper & Row).
Schwartz, B. (1973), 'Thoughts on Mao Tse-tung', *New York Review of Books*, vol. 20, no. 1, pp. 27–30.
Sennett, R. (1977), 'Destructive Gemeinschaft', in N. Birnbaum (ed.), *Beyond the Crisis* (New York: Oxford University Press), pp. 171–200.
Sennett, R. (1974), *The Fall of Public Man* (New York: Random House).
Sennett, R. and Cobb, J. (1973), *The Hidden Injuries of Class* (New York: Knopf).
Sherman, H. and Wood J. (1979), *Sociology: Traditional and Radical Perspectives* (New York: Harper & Row).
Shils, E. (1980), *The Calling of Sociology* (Chicago: University of Chicago Press).
Simonds, A. P. (1982), 'On being informed', *Theory and Society* vol. 11, no. 5, pp. 587–616.
Siriani, C. (1981), 'Production and power in a classless society', *Socialist Review*, vol. 11, no. 5, pp. 33–82.
Smelser, N. (1959), *Social Change in the Industrial Revolution* (Chicago: University of Chicago Press).
Steinfels, P. (1979), *The Neoconservatives* (New York: Simon & Schuster).
Stern, J. P. (1978), *Friedrich Nietzsche* (New York: Penguin).
Sztompka, P. (1979), *Sociological Dilemmas* (New York: Academic Press).

Tiryakian, E. (1978), 'Emile Durkheim', in T. Bottomore and R. Nisbet (eds), *A History of Sociological Analysis* (New York: Basic Books), pp. 187-236.

Tocqueville, A. de (1969), *Democracy in America*, trans. G. Laurence (Garden City, NY: Doubleday).

Touraine, A. (1981), *The Voice and the Eye*, trans. A. Duff (Cambridge: Cambridge University Press).

Touraine, A., Dubet, F., Wieviovka, M., and Strzelecki, J. (1983a), *Solidarity*, trans. D. Denby (Cambridge: Cambridge University Press).

Touraine, A., Hegedus, Z., Dubet, F. and Wieviovka, M. (1983b), *Anti-Nuclear Protest*, trans. P. Fawcett (Cambridge: Cambridge University Press).

Trigg, R. (1973), *Reason and Commitment* (Cambridge: Cambridge University Press).

Turner, J. and Beeghly, L. (1981), *The Emergence of Sociological Theory* (Homewood: Dorsey Press).

Turner, R. (1976), 'The real self: From institution to impulse', *American Journal of Sociology*, vol. 81, no. 4, pp. 989-1016.

Voegelin, E. (1975), *From Enlightenment to Revolution* (Durham, NC: Duke University Press).

Wallwork, E. (1972), *Durkheim: Morality and Milieux* (Cambridge, Mass.: Harvard University Press).

Weber, M. (1968), *Economy and Society*, trans. G. Roth and C. Wittich (New York: Bedminster Press).

Weber, M. (1958), *The Protestant Ethic and the Spirit of Capitalism*, trans. T. Parsons (New York: Scribner's).

Weber, M. (1949), *The Methodology of the Social Sciences*, ed. and trans. E. Shils and H. Finch (New York: Free Press).

Weber, M. (1947), *The Theory of Social and Economic Organization*, trans. A. M. Henderson and T. Parsons (New York: Free Press).

Weber, M. (1946), *From Max Weber*, ed. and trans. H. Gerth and C. W. Mills (New York: Oxford University Press).

Weber, M. (1927), *General Economic History* (New York: Greenberg).

Weisskopf, T. (1981), 'The current economic crisis in historical perspective', *Socialist Review*, vol. 11, no. 3, pp. 9-53.

Wellmer, A. (1983), 'Reason, utopia, and the dialectic of enlightenment', *Praxis International*, vol. 3, no. 2, pp. 83-107.

Williams, R. (1958), *Culture and Society* (New York: Harper & Row).

Wilson, C. (1965), *England's Apprenticeship* (London: Longman).

Winkler, J. P. (1977), 'The coming corporatism', in R. Skidelsky (ed.), *The End of the Keynesian Era* (New York: Holmes & Meier), pp. 78-87.

Wojcicki, K. (1981), 'The reconstruction of society', *Telos*, no. 47, pp. 98-104.

Wolff, R. P. (1968), *The Poverty of Liberalism* (Boston, Mass.: Beacon Press).

Wolin, S. (1980), 'Reagan country', *New York Review of Books*, vol. 27, no. 20, pp. 9-12.

Wolin, S. (1978), 'Carter and the new constitution', *New York Review of Books*, vol. 25, no. 9, pp. 16-19.

Wright, E. O. (1974), 'To control or to smash bureaucracy', *Berkeley Journal of Sociology*, no. 19, pp. 69-108.

Zeitlin, I. (1968), *Ideology and the Development of Sociological Theory* (Englewood Cliffs, NJ: Prentice-Hall).

Index

Index

48,321

DATE DUE
DATE DE RETOUR

NOV 4 1987			
NOV 1 6 1987			
NOV 2 8 1991			
APR 1 0 1993			
DEC 2 2 1996			
DEC 2 2 1995			
OCT 1 8 1999			
NOV 1 4 1999			
OCT 2 3 2001			
OCT 3 2001			